# War and Rape

Wartime rape has been virulent in wars of sovereignty, territory, conquest, religion, ideology and liberation, yet attention to this crime has been sporadic throughout history. Rape remains 'unspeakable', particularly within law. Rape has not featured prominently in post-conflict collective memory, and even when rape is 'remembered', it is often the subject of political controversy and heated debate.

In this book, Henry asks some critical questions about the relationship between mass rape, politics and law. In what ways does law contribute to the collective memory of wartime rape? How do 'counter-memories' of victims compete with the denialism of wartime rape? The text specifically analyzes the historical silencing of rape throughout international legal history and the potential of law to restore these silenced histories; it also examines the violence of law and the obstacles to individual and collective redemption. Tracing the prosecution of rape crimes within contemporary courts, Henry seeks to argue that politics underscores the way rape is dealt with by the international community in the aftermath of armed conflict.

Providing a comprehensive overview of the politics of wartime rape and the politics of prosecuting such crimes within international humanitarian law, this text will be of great interest to scholars of gender and security, war crimes and law and society.

**Nicola Henry** is a lecturer in the School of Social Sciences at La Trobe University in Melbourne. Her central research interest is the relationship between politics and law and how this can be understood in relation to violence against women, trauma, collective memory and human rights.

**Interventions**
Edited by: Jenny Edkins,
*Aberystwyth University*
and Nick Vaughan-Williams,
*University of Warwick*

'As Michel Foucault has famously stated, 'knowledge is not made for understanding; it is made for cutting'. In this spirit The Edkins Vaughan-Williams Interventions series solicits cutting edge, critical works that challenge mainstream understandings in international relations. It is the best place to contribute post disciplinary works that think rather than merely recognize and affirm the world recycled in IR's traditional geopolitical imaginary'.

Michael J. Shapiro, University of Hawai'i at Mānoa, USA.

The series aims to advance understanding of the key areas in which scholars working within broad critical post-structural and post-colonial traditions have chosen to make their interventions, and to present innovative analyzes of important topics.

Titles in the series engage with critical thinkers in philosophy, sociology, politics and other disciplines and provide situated historical, empirical and textual studies in international politics.

**Critical Theorists and International Relations**
*Edited by Jenny Edkins and Nick Vaughan-Williams*

**Ethics as Foreign Policy**
Britain, the EU and the other
*Dan Bulley*

**Universality, Ethics and International Relations**
A grammatical reading
*Véronique Pin-Fat*

**The Time of the City**
Politics, philosophy, and genre
*Michael J. Shapiro*

**Governing Sustainable Development**
Partnership, protest and power at the world summit
*Carl Death*

# War and Rape

Law, memory and justice

## Nicola Henry

Routledge
Taylor & Francis Group

LONDON AND NEW YORK

First published 2011
by Routledge
2 Park Square, Milton Park, Abingdon, Oxon, OX14 4RN

Simultaneously published in the USA and Canada
by Routledge
270 Madison Avenue, New York, NY 10016

*Routledge is an imprint of the Taylor & Francis Group, an informa business*

Typeset in Times New Roman by Glyph International Ltd
Printed and bound in Great Britain by T. J. International Ltd, Padstow,
Cornwall

*British Library Cataloguing in Publication Data*
A catalogue record for this book is available from the British Library

*Library of Congress Cataloging in Publication Data*
Henry, Nicola.
War and rape: law, memory, and justice / Nicola Henry.
  p. cm. – (Interventions)
Includes bibliographical references and index. 1. Rape as a weapon of war.
I. Title.
K5304.5.H46 2010
345'.02532–dc22     2010022753

ISBN 13: 978-0-415-56472-4 (hbk)
ISBN 13: 978-0-415-56473-1 (pbk)
ISBN 13: 978-0-203-83619-4 (ebk)

*... the 'perfect crime' does not consist in killing the victim or the witnesses ... but rather in obtaining the silence of the witnesses, the deafness of the judges, and the inconsistency (insanity) of the testimony.*

(Lyotard 1988: 8)

*... few legal issues have been the focus of such intense political, social, and scholarly debate as the crime of rape.*

(Conley and O'Barr 1998: 15)

# Contents

# Acknowledgments

My deep gratitude extends to many kind people who supported me throughout the writing of this book. I am very grateful to the Institute for Human Security at La Trobe University for the Teaching Relief Fellowship, which enabled me to get writing done during teaching-intensive time. Thanks also to the Faculty of Humanities and Social Sciences at La Trobe University for a generous early career research grant that facilitated research assistance and a trip to Europe. Thank you to Emma Colvin for your excellent research assistance.

I am grateful to Simon Clews and the University of Melbourne Writing Centre, and my mentor Martin Krygier, for helping me to get started on this book back in 2006. Thanks to Jennifer Balint and Fiona Haines for earlier support and inspiration. And thanks to the friendly people at the International Criminal Tribunal for the Former Yugoslavia and various women's NGOs when I visited Europe some years ago: Michelle Jarvis, Wendy Lobwein, Monika Naslund, Patricia Viseur-Sellers, Florence Mumba, Judith Armatta, Beate Ziegler, Gabi Mischowski, Monika Hauser, Karin Griese, Marcia Jacobs, Ajli Bajramović, Mirha Pojskić and Nurka Babović. A very special thanks to Jan Ruff-O'Herne for her grace and generosity. And to Craig Fowlie, Nicola Parkin, Emma Hart and Mary Dalton from Routledge, I am grateful to your guidance throughout the publication process.

Many thanks to the wonderful support of my colleagues and students at La Trobe University, in particular to Judy Brett, Sue Davies, Anastasia Powell and Bronwyn Bardsley. Thanks to the Green Pen Reading Group for helpful comments on earlier chapters: Raelene Wilding, Karl Smith, Anne-Maree Sawyer, Anastasia Powell, Nesam McMillan, Wendy Bowler and Claudia Slegers. I am indebted to Nesam McMillan for reading through various draft chapters and offering me excellent support, advice and feedback, and overall for her generosity and friendship. Heart-felt thanks also to David Yencken for putting me on a new path of writing that helped immeasurably with this book.

I wish I could thank all of my wonderful friends and family individually for their love and support. In particular, thank you to Harriet for your unwavering and loyal life-long, treasured friendship, which means the world to me.

And to my family: Dad, Mum, Justine, James, Esther, Emma, Mike, Isabel, Maya, Matt, Emily and Owen – thank you for your love, encouragement and endless support that has taught me so much about the sanctity of family.

And to my sweet Brent: there may be no such things as magic wands, but you always managed to have one up your sleeve to help me through all my worries and fears. Your generosity, support, humour and love has filled me to the brim with great happiness and much needed grounding, and I can't imagine life without you. I dedicate this book to you and our little Frederick.

Some chapters of this book are based on three previous publications of mine, although in substantially altered forms. Chapter 3 draws and expands upon a chapter I wrote about the Tokyo Tribunal ('Silence as Collective Memory: sexual violence and the Tokyo Trial', in Y. Tanaka, T. McCormack and G. Simpson (eds) *Beyond Victors' Justice? The Tokyo War Crimes Trial Revisited*, Leiden: Martinus Nijhoff Publishers, forthcoming 2010). A very small section of Chapter 4 appeared in an article about rape and war crimes courts ('Witness to Rape: the limits and potential of international war crimes trials for victims of wartime sexual violence', *International Journal of Transitional Justice*, 3: 114–34, 2009). And parts of Chapter 5 appeared in an article about trauma and rape ('The Impossibility of Bearing Witness: wartime rape and the promise of justice', *Violence Against Women*, 16(1), forthcoming 2010).

# 1 Introduction

## How the past is made to matter

To understand how collective memory works, we cannot restrict our inquiries to tracing the vicissitudes of historical knowledge or narratives. We must also, and I believe foremost, attend to the construction of our emotional and moral engagement with the past. When looking at public discourse, this translates into questions about how the past is made to matter.

(Irwin-Zarecka 2009: 7)

On 22 February 2001, the Trial Chamber at the International Criminal Tribunal for the Former Yugoslavia rendered its judgment for one of the biggest rape trials in international history. It sentenced Dragan Kunarac, also known as 'Zaga', to 28 years' imprisonment; Radmir Kovač, also known as 'Klafa', to 20 years' imprisonment; and Zoran Vuković to 12 years' imprisonment. The three defendants had no previous criminal convictions, all three were married, and at least two had young children. The crimes of which the three defendants were found guilty included crimes against humanity and war crimes for the enslavement, rape and torture of Muslim girls and women in the Foča region of Bosnia-Herzegovina.

The Chamber found that in July 1992 Kunarac had taken two girls to a house where they were raped by several soldiers and where he personally raped one of them, and aided and abetted the gang-rape of the other. In August 1992, Kunarac again took four girls to a house and personally raped one of them and aided and abetted the rapes of the others. In addition to this, on at least two other occasions, the accused took another girl to an apartment where she was raped by him and three other soldiers.

The Chamber found that four girls were taken to the accused Kovač's apartment in October 1992 and were 'constantly raped, humiliated and degraded' (*Foča* Judgment, 2001: para. 749). One girl, who was just 12 years old, was eventually sold off by the accused and was never seen again. The accused also handed two other girls over to Serb soldiers who kept them in another apartment where they were continually raped. Over the proceeding months, Kovač continued to sell off other Muslim girls and women to willing soldiers.

For the charges against the defendant Vuković, the Trial Chamber could only prove one incident beyond reasonable doubt involving a 15-year-old girl.

The Chamber found that the accused had threatened the girl's mother with death if she did not tell him where her daughter was hiding, and that in July 1992, the girl was taken to an apartment by the accused and another solider and was raped.

The judgment authoritatively declared:

> What the sum of the evidence manifestly demonstrates, is the effect a criminal personality will have in times of war on helpless members of the civilian population ... The women and girls were either lent or 'rented out' to other soldiers for the sole purpose of being ravaged and abused. Some of the women and girls were kept in servitude for months on end ... it is opportune to state that, in time of peace as much as in time of war, men of substance do not abuse women.
>
> (ICTY Press Release, Judgment of Trial Chamber II)

The judgment makes an important contribution to the collective memory of wartime sexual violence. The law shapes, selects and institutionalizes the way the past is remembered (Markovits 2001) through authoritatively declaring which crimes are deserving of international recognition and justice, and which crimes are to be relegated to the forgotten abyss of history. The law is thus both a potent source and site of memory, but also a powerful arbiter of memory. At the very least, trials provide an important avenue for public debate and international courts represent 'monumental spectacles' or 'moments of truth' because they provide, incite and encourage historical interpretation and moral pedagogy (Osiel 2000: 2–3). War crimes trials create a space for the airing of personal and collective memories of wartime terror and trauma. Ideally, these trials capture the public imagination by giving a voice to both victims and perpetrators, judging guilt, attributing responsibility and vindicating victimhood (Karstedt 2009). Moreover, war crimes courts represent a means to prevent social amnesia and forge a collective memory of the past.

Despite the obvious relationship between collective memory and the law, little socio-legal inquiry has been undertaken to explore the connection between the two (some exceptions include: Bloxham 2001; Campbell 2002; Douglas 2001; Fournet 2007; Karstedt 2009; Osiel 2000; Simpson 2007).[1] The law by its very design, however, is fixated on memory, constructing a narrative of the past, and shaping collective memory indirectly through dictating and selecting the events that are to be remembered (Savelsberg and King 2007). This has important ramifications as far as wartime sexual violence is concerned, particularly since in the past international courts were largely silent on this matter.

Although silence has traditionally shrouded wartime sexual violence both inside and outside law, rape has nonetheless existed as a lasting legacy of violent conflict throughout the centuries. During the First and Second World Wars, countless numbers of women were raped in concentration camps, military brothels and in occupied areas. In the latter part of the twentieth century, rape was no less ubiquitous: the rape of Bengali women during the nine-month conflict in Bangladesh in 1971 created a national crisis when thousands of women became pregnant and husbands rejected their wives (Brownmiller 1976). Sexual violence also forms a well-remembered part of the Vietnam War due to the rapes committed by American soldiers against civilian Vietnamese women, and the fact that few perpetrators have ever been brought to justice (see Weaver 2010). Likewise, during the 1980s conflict in Uganda, women once again suffered the effects of impunity and silence due to widespread forms of wartime sexual violence.

*war & rape consistantly go together*

While rape has been both central or peripheral to the history of warfare, it was not until the spate of mass rapes and the systematic sexual enslavement of women during the 1990s conflict in Bosnia-Herzegovina that international legal attention finally turned to war crimes against women. During the Bosnian conflict, rape was an integral component of an 'ethnic cleansing' campaign designed to render regions ethnically homogenous through force and intimidation. The consolidation of rape as an appalling crime of war thus emerged dramatically into historical consciousness during this period. This occurred also in the context of the mass rapes against Rwandan women during the 1994 genocide, where 'thousands of women were individually raped, gang-raped, raped with objects such as sharpened sticks or gun barrels, held in sexual slavery (either collectively or through forced "marriage") or sexually mutilated' (Human Rights Watch 1996: 1).

Since the 1990s, for the first time in international history, victims have appeared as witnesses before international courts; perpetrators, both direct and indirect, have been successfully prosecuted; and sexual violence has been tried as a crime of genocide, a war crime and a crime against humanity. These past two decades can be starkly contrasted to the silence and neglect that has previously encumbered the issue since – and long before – the end of the Second World War. Mass media documentation in diverse geographical locations has since revealed both the gravity and extent of wartime sexual violence; truth and reconciliation commissions have heard harrowing victim narratives; and books, documentaries and films have captured the unceasingly common horrors of rape, forced impregnation and sexual slavery. However, despite the growing attention to wartime sexual violence and the codification of rape as a serious violation of international criminal law, rape remains an 'unspeakable' crime of war. Victim accounts of rape have not featured prominently in post-conflict collective memory and yet, paradoxically, rape has been manipulated by and through political debates that have pitted nations against each other. Thus when rape is 'remembered', it is often the subject of political controversy and heated debate, and victims are often caught in the crossfire of these disputes.

In part, the establishment of the two *ad hoc* tribunals – the International Criminal Tribunal for the Former Yugoslavia (ICTY) in 1993 and the International Criminal Court for Rwanda (ICTR) in 1994 – were in response to the extent and perceived gravity of war crimes against women in both the former Yugoslavia and Rwanda. And yet despite the international shock surrounding mass rapes and the subsequent prosecution of these crimes, thousands more women suffered a similar fate during the decade-long war in Sierra Leone from 1991 to 2001, the 1998 Kosovo conflict and the 1999 Timorese war of independence. Patterns of rape and sexual enslavement were also rife in conflicts in Liberia, Haiti, Iraq and many other locations during the latter part of the twentieth century. In more recent times, the use of sexual violence as a method to humiliate, control and displace women has been widespread in the conflicts in the Democratic Republic of Congo and the Darfur region of the Sudan.

In wars of sovereignty, territory, conquest, religion, ideology and liberation, sexual violence has brought about long-lasting physical, psychological, emotional, communal, national, international, as well as intergenerational impacts. We now know that the taboo, silence and shame of sexual violence can have significant repercussions on a woman's psychological wellbeing, identity and livelihood. Moreover, these crimes can destroy the social fabric of post-conflict communities well after the cessation of violence. As Kai Erikson (1994: 233) states, traumatic events can administer 'a blow to the basic tissues of social life that damages the bonds attaching people together and impairs the prevailing sense of community'. The intergenerational cycle of unresolved trauma, violence and vengeance obstructs the fulfilment of post-conflict peace and justice, contributing to the perpetuation of conflict and suffering. Victims are often dealing with economic deprivation, displacement, homelessness, cultural property destruction and the deaths of friends, family and people within their communities. The burden of carrying a child under these devastating circumstances is quite simply unthinkable.

The mass rapes that have occurred in recent history contribute to some accepted 'truths' about wartime rape. First and foremost, sexual violence has been prolific throughout the history of warfare. Wartime rape and sexual enslavement have been well captured by mythical, artistic and historical representations: from the abduction/rape of Helen of Troy described in Homer's *Iliad*, and the rape of the Sabine women as a legendary tale of early Roman history; to the story of systematic rape in the Scottish Highlands during the eighteenth century by English forces, the rape of Belgian women during the First World War, and of course, the many contemporary examples of mass rape that have occurred during and since the Second World War (see Brownmiller 1976).

A second accepted certitude of wartime rape is that women suffer disproportionately from these crimes. While the torture, rape and sodomy of male prisoners held at the Iraqi Abu Ghraib prison in 2004 has vividly imprinted on public memory images of female-perpetrated wartime sexual violence (see e.g. Hersh 2004), and there are many other wars where men have been subjected to horrific forms of sexual violence, few would disagree that women bear the brunt of wartime sexual violence. For the majority of these crimes, it is men who are the perpetrators of wartime sexual atrocities

(Bourke 2008; see also Engle 2005 for a critical discussion of this issue). Third, there is little dispute that impunity for wartime rape has been the rule rather than the exception. Although there have been formal prohibitions of rape in national and international legal jurisdictions at various historical junctures (see Khushalani 1982; Krill 1985), and many individuals have been tried for crimes of rape by domestic or international tribunals (Meron 1993a; Piccigallo 1979),[2] the prosecution of sexual violence against women has been traditionally both selective and sporadic, and wartime rape continues to be demarcated by both impunity and silence.

While few would challenge any of these largely accepted historical truths, the subject of wartime rape has caused, and continues to cause, heated debate. I was quite shocked when someone commented to me last year that they did not see what the big deal was about wartime rape. I could not stop thinking about this remark and where it belonged in the wider discourse on this topic. Although very few people dare challenge the gravity of sexual violence in this way, in scholarly writing new questions about whether or not rape is the worst thing that can happen to women during wartime have been increasingly raised. Atina Grossman (1995), for instance, discusses how rape was not the worst of horrible experiences for German women at the end of the Second World War. Janet Halley (2008a: 80) also argues that the superior 'badness' of wartime rape 'can be deployed in an alarming number of ways to advance contested ends, ends which one might well want to resist' (see also Engle 2005).

The point that these scholars are trying to make, I imagine, is that the focus on wartime rape can have a range of implications, including obscuring the other harms that occur against women and men during armed conflict (Gardam and Jarvis 2001; Halley 2008b; Nikolič-Ristanovič 2000); prioritizing rape above other human rights violations; positioning women solely as helpless victims of sexualized atrocities (Engle 2005); failing to account for the sheer heterogeneity of survivors of mass atrocities; and treating wartime rape as a universal example of women's oppression (Halley 2008b). Indeed, in this book I do focus exclusively on wartime sexual violence (whether that be penetrative rape or other forms of sexual violation – and the reader should note that I do not always make a distinction between 'rape' and 'sexual violence').[3] I am aware that such exclusive attention may make me guilty of some or all of the above problems. However, what is concerning to me is the fixation on hierarchies of suffering that are increasingly popular in the current war crimes literature. On the one hand, rape is often included on an actual or metaphorical list of the worst possible crimes, and the recent push of rape up the international criminal hierarchy reflects this perceived gravity. Even as far back as 1919, a post-war commission was set up to investigate breaches of law and customs of war committed by Germany and its allies in the First World War, and out of 32 war crimes, rape was listed at number five and the 'abduction of girls and women for the purposes of enforced prostitution' at number six (murders and massacre made the number one spot) (Adatci and Tachi 1920).

On the other hand, although wartime rape has been repeatedly condemned as the 'worst of crimes' throughout history in political rhetoric, in practice these crimes have very much been neglected, disregarded, denied and downplayed. The debate about whether or not rape is a fate worse than death ('Better a Russki [Russian] on top than a Yank overhead' – quoted in Halley 2008a: 104) not only contributes to a problematic suffering hierarchy, but may also lead to complacency and inadvertently position rape yet again as an inevitable by-product of armed conflict.

It is important to note that there is a distinction between suffering hierarchies within the minds of victims and what I believe is the futility of these comparisons within political and scholarly discourse. We often find similar historical analogies and hierarchies of atrocities constructed in relation to genocide. The Nazi Holocaust, for example, is often taken as the benchmark and epitome of the crime of genocide and heated debate inevitably arises when the Holocaust is compared to other historical examples of genocide (see e.g. Moses 2005; Moshman 2001). Like the Holocaust, past narratives of wartime sexual violence have also been subjected to revisionism and denialism in contemporary political discourse. For example, former sex slaves from the Second World War – euphemistically known as 'comfort women' – began to talk about their experiences in public from the 1980s, leading to the celebration of women's lost and silenced voices; however, as a consequence, voracious debate ensued as revisionists sought to question the veracity of the entire 'comfort system' in Japan.[4] Of course, these debates form a key part of the collective memory of past atrocities – and this is what this book is about.

Most of the literature to date on wartime rape and international criminal courts is from a more practical, legalese perspective. For example, there has been much discussion about whether the establishment of *ad hoc* and permanent international war crimes courts since the 1990s have adequately dealt with rape crimes, and whether the definition of gender-specific crimes under international humanitarian law provides an adequate framework for prosecuting war crimes against women (for excellent books on the application of international law, see Askin 1997; de Brouwer 2005; Quénivet 2005). My approach to examining wartime rape deviates from the more narrow, disciplinary location of international law. My book is instead situated within the interdisciplinary field of memory, and more specifically the understudied yet growing body of literature on collective memory and the law.

I am inadvertently asserting or underscoring the gravity of wartime sexual violence in the same way perhaps that other law and memory scholars have done in relation to other examples of mass atrocities. While I certainly want to avoid comparing and contrasting the array of crimes and whether or not international law should prioritize their prosecution, I nonetheless hope that this book will stress the significance of law, the limitations and harms of legal institutions for responding to crimes of gendered violence, and the importance of documenting rape crimes within these institutional sites of memory.

The purpose of the book, therefore, is not to document victim experiences of rape *per se*, nor to document the rules, procedures or institutions of law, but rather to provide a conceptual analysis of the political, cultural and historical impact of law and its attention to wartime sexual violence throughout the past 65 years. I do not set out to evaluate the most appropriate form of justice for victims of rape, nor examine the vast array of legal and non-legal responses to wartime rape. Rather, my aim is to examine the power of memory through three interrelated issues: the historical silencing of rape throughout international legal history; the potential of law to restore these silenced histories; and the violence of law and the obstacles to individual and collective redemption.

The book is essentially about the pivotal relationship between law and memory. I look at memory from both the personal and collective perspective. My main concern is with how law shapes or produces a history of wartime rape, and how law reproduces hegemonic relations of power that in turn shape how wartime rape is remembered. In other words, how is memory used as a tool of power in the discourse on wartime sexual violence, and whose memories are privileged? What are the didactic aims or consequences of legal prosecution for wartime rape?

While there have been some momentous achievements within international war crimes law,[5] there have also been some worrisome outcomes emerging from this shift. Because of the power and 'selective memory' of law, not only is history clarified and proclaimed, but law can also obscure and distort crimes of the past (Douglas 2001). This book examines the contribution that international courts make in shaping historical consciousness about wartime sexual violence. In addition to exploring the potentials and limitations of law in 'collective memory' terms, the book also explores the 'violence' of law in addressing gendered crimes. I am not suggesting that international criminal justice for these crimes is undesirable, but rather, I am interested in the nature and limitations of this justice, and how it contributes to, or distorts, memory, both interpersonal and collective. A subset of questions therefore concerns the emergence of the 'counter-memory', namely memories that challenge dominant or pre-existing memory, in both law and politics. In what way has law facilitated the celebration of the counter-memory? And in what way does law subvert or distort these counter-memories?

In Chapter 2, I critically examine the concept of 'memory' and more specifically the dynamics and problematic of 'collective memory'. The chapter will thereafter consider the role of law in the formation of collective memory, provide a framework to think about not only the way in which law – as a repository or site of *traumatic memory* – contributes to a historical consciousness of the past, but also the ways in which law may obscure or distort such consciousness through its method and mode of selection.

Chapter 3 focuses on the silence of law at the Nuremberg and Tokyo trials following the Second World War, and the didactic legacy of these historic trials in relation to wartime rape. Rape was not enumerated as a war crime or a crime against humanity in either the Nuremberg or Tokyo charters. Both tribunals were fixated on vilifying the aggressor nations of Germany, Japan and their allies, and victims played a small role in the prosecution of offenders. At Nuremberg, evidence of rape was presented but rape was not formally prosecuted. At Tokyo, some defendants were prosecuted for rape crimes, but rape was tried only alongside other crimes and the sexual enslavement of comfort women was all but completely ignored. The chapter goes on to examine wartime rape as a terrain of contestation, illustrating how law and collective memory are deeply intertwined, and how the politics and power of memory inform this relationship. Most pertinently, the chapter looks to the 'stories' of wartime sexual violence told and *not told* by law. The chapter will thus examine the contemporary relevance of historical war crimes trials and the notion of 'contested memories', seeking to understand the political manipulation of memory and wartime rape.

Chapter 4 examines the role of law in shaping collective memories of wartime rape. According to Lawrence Douglas (2001: 112–13): 'The trial ... must be seen not simply as a procedural device whose legitimacy is governed by rules generated within the system of legality itself, but as a complex ritual which *produces* and *suppresses* narrative and *clarifies* and *obscures* history' (emphasis added). The chapter critically evaluates three international courts: the International Criminal Tribunal for the Former Yugoslavia (ICTY); the International Criminal Court for Rwanda (ICTR); and the International Criminal Court (ICC). In the chapter, I discuss the most 'legally' significant rape trials that have gone before the ICTY and ICTR (*Tadič*, *Čelebiči*, *Foča* and *Akayesu*) in order to assess the contribution that such trials (and other rape trials at the international level) may make to collective memory: whether they produce, suppress, clarify or obscure both narrative and history.[6] In particular, I will focus on witness testimony,[7] the nature of cross-examination, prosecution and judgment to identify the power potential and 'violence' of law.

The intersection of personal and collective memory is examined in Chapter 5. Specifically, the mediation of trauma and memory through law is addressed, looking at the way in which witness memory in the courtroom communicates the pain or trauma of gross human rights violations, and the way in which legal actors in turn use personal memory to undermine witness authenticity, credibility and reliability. In this chapter, I examine the vulnerability and inexpressibility of human pain to develop a deeper understanding of the inexpressibility of wartime rape within war crimes courts, and the complex array of reasons for the silencing of victims, including the political complications that arise out of the difficulty women experience disclosing their experiences of sexual violation.

Finally, Chapter 6 will explore the ways in which international criminal justice has contributed to a collective memory of wartime rape. To what extent does the law do 'representational justice' (Douglas 2001) to wartime rape? How is the past history of wartime rape through law made to matter?

*Just read him :)*

A question that has beleaguered scholars and practitioners within the growing multidisciplinary field of transitional justice is how societies come to terms with a violent past of political conflict, totalitarianism and genocide.[8] Justice has increasingly been sought via war crimes trials (international and domestic), truth-telling commissions, apologies, memorials, forgiveness and other forms of redress in post-conflict reconstruction. These various forms of justice are viewed as important avenues for international peace and stability, societal reconciliation and victim vindication. More recent investigations into the efficacy of transitional justice mechanisms, such as war crimes trials, have exposed the gap between the promise and reality of justice. This confirms what John Rawls (1971) proclaimed about justice; that it is universal, inviolable, sacrosanct and morally imperative, but also fragmentary, incomplete, elusive and deeply personal. Rawls famously declared that justice is the first virtue; an intuitively natural right. Historically in practice, however, victims of wartime rape have been alienated and excluded from any form of justice. Even today, in conjunction with hostile community reactions to rape survivors and the lack of acknowledgment for rape crimes, denialism most of all serves to deeply entrench silence and stigma, and victims typically suffer multiple layers of pain, grief and loss when their experiences are neglected, distorted, questioned and they are told they never happened. It is thus not simply the trauma of the rape that devastates notions of self and the world, but the reactions of others to rape in the aftermath of conflict that may be equally damaging.

Each chapter of the book implicitly or explicitly recognizes the impossibility of full justice and vindication for gross human rights violations in the aftermath of armed conflict, as well as the heterogeneity of rape victims within their communities and their differing conceptions of justice. In each chapter I aim to explore the political skirmishes that take place over wartime rape in the post-conflict period, whether they be *nationalistic* (e.g. historical denialism; competing versions of historical truths); *interpersonal* (e.g. the inexpressibility of wartime rape); or they cross the divide of the *public and private* (e.g. the repetition of gendered biases within criminal justice institutions). Because of their influence, scope and authority, international criminal trials are capable of contributing to, or even defining, a 'historical consciousness' of past events through authoritatively declaring what constitutes crimes worthy of international recognition and justice, who should be prosecuted and which groups are deserving of justice.[9] In part, the long overdue legal attention to wartime rape and the courageous achievements of victims who have overcome enormous social, cultural and political barriers to bearing witness are celebrated in this book, but my aim is more focused on the relationship between law and memory, and between law, memory and politics, in order to assess the significance of wartime rape – for not simply the past, but also the present and the future, both inside and outside the law.

# 2    Traces of truth

## Collective memory and the law

> Contest, conflict, controversy – these are the hallmark of studies of collective memory.
>
> (Schudson 1997: 361)

In late September 2004, Bosnian Muslim women were reportedly pelted with eggs, stones and insults by 200 protestors as they attempted to erect a memorial plaque to honour the memory of Foča women who were raped, tortured and sexually enslaved during the 1992–95 conflict in Bosnia-Herzegovina (BBC News 2004). This is a stark reminder of the tensions, hostilities and controversies that arise when memories of the past, particularly 'unspeakable memories', are invoked in the present. Indeed, much controversy typically surrounds the invocation of memory. This is likewise exemplified in heated debates about the Holocaust, including controversial questions about Polish and German complicity in the extermination of Jews (Goldhagen 1996; Gross 2001); the nature of Jewish resistance in concentration camps; the collusion of the Jewish Council in assisting with the 'Final Solution' (Arendt 1994; Hilberg 1961); and the likewise vexed debate about the exclusivity of Jewish Holocaust memorials and whether sites of memory exclude the experiences of other victims of the Third Reich (Adam 2009). The unspeakability and contestation of traumatic histories reveals the complexity of memory and the nature of competing truths in the aftermath of conflict. And yet at the same time, the memorialization of the past also provides and sustains social cohesion and solidarity, serving as an antidote to amnesia and silence; a potent marker of trauma, justice and injustice. Memory validates the experiences and identities of victims and may bolster conceptions of national, religious, community and personal identity. We thus indubitably live in an age of memory. Even war crimes courts have begun to acknowledge their own unique contribution to collective memories of war crimes, genocide and crimes against humanity, and some courts have established legacy officers with the aim of extending the didactic and historical reach of these courts.

Over the past two decades, there has been escalating fascination and interest in the phenomenon of memory; what Andreas Huyssen (1995) calls 'memory fever'. This analogy is derived (but distinct) from Friedrich Nietzsche's (2003: 67) concern about a 'consuming historical fever'. Nietzsche (1980: 47), for example, believed that human beings suffer from an excess or arrogance of history, a 'naked admiration for success' and a worship of the factual. He viewed the historical past as a scourge on the human condition, comparing this obsession to blissfully unaware and forgetful cattle, grazing in paddocks: 'Man ... braces himself against the great and even greater pressure of what is past: it pushes him down or bends him sideways, it encumbers his steps as a dark, invisible burden which he can sometimes appear to disown' (Nietzsche 2003: 61).[1] This led Nietzsche (1980: 10) to famously declare that the past – when used or viewed as scientific, dialectical and rational – is destined to be the 'gravedigger of the present'. He argued there was a critical balance between selective forgetting and selective remembering, and that this forms the basis of 'socially worthwhile history' (Posner 2000: 578).

On the other hand, Huyssen (1995) saw 'memory fever' in contemporary culture as distinct from Nietzsche's historical fever. While historical fever is more concerned with complacency, helplessness and despair based on the past, and the superficiality, distortion, glorification and arrogance of 'moral progress' in the present, Huyssen (1995: 7) argues that the present-day preoccupation with memory is an important reaction to the currents of a rapidly changing society in which there is a need for 'some anchoring space in a world of puzzling and often threatening heterogeneity, non-synchronicity, and information overload'. Indeed, memory has become the ultimate catchphrase in contemporary times for remembering and validating collective narratives of mass suffering. Modern memory, therefore, seeks to fight 'the virus of amnesia' which constantly threatens to 'consume memory itself' (ibid.).

Memory fever can be seen through the dramatic rise in memorialization in recent times.[2] The contemporary interest or fascination with memory extends to individualized as well as collective, cultural or social forms of memory. Huyssen (1995) attributes this obsession in contemporary culture not only to postmodernism, but also to the notion and crisis of time: both the temporal nature of memory (memory that is continually on the brink of amnesia due to the passage of time) and the speed of technological innovation and modernization. A fundamental shift in intellectual culture has instigated greater interest in the social construction of the past, through the rise in postmodernist thought and the critique of hegemonic metanarratives of historiography (Schwartz 1996). More pragmatically, Michael Kammen (1995) attributes the growth in memory studies to the following factors: an increase in official commemoration; the rise of multiculturalism; Holocaust denial; delayed memory syndrome or 'repression'; the increasing role of films and documentaries as 'authoritative' sources of the past; the shift in places of memory preservation; commercial, state-sponsored tourism; the liberation for forgotten victims of past wrongs; and the end to the Cold War.

We might therefore think of three concurrent developments that explain both the fascination with memory and the increased prevalence of mnemonic devices for memory preservation. First, globalization and advances in technology have not only contributed to the growing interest in memory, but these forces have also facilitated diverse mnemonic forms, for example transitional justice mechanisms such as truth commissions and war crimes trials; commemorative sites and rituals such as memorials and museums; and emerging technologies such as the Internet and other expeditious modes of communication for the preservation of memory.[3] Second, the study of trauma and the 'return of the repressed' (Klein 2000: 145) has arguably contributed to the rise in memory sites and studies. Particularly since the 1980s, psychology, psychiatry and interdisciplinary scholarship have helped develop specific understandings of the individual in reaction to traumatic events, although this discourse has attracted criticism for its western-centric focus (see Chapter 5 for a discussion of trauma). And third, related to the recent popularity of both memory and trauma studies, the study of transitional justice and how societies come to terms with a violent past has led to the conceptualization of collective dimensions of suffering, promulgating entirely new ways of understanding the problematic of memory.[4]

These trends may be contextualized within pivotal political and social currents, such as the end of the Cold War, the modern human rights movement, and the general struggles of minority or marginalized groups to claim recognition and vindication for past injustices. The recollection of the past has thus become a powerful tool for the powerless and 'formulations of memory [act] as alternative to the discourses of objectivity and legitimizing history, and as cure to the pathologies of modern life' (Huyssen 1995: 6).[5] The point here is that previously silenced or repressed histories now inform, to a much greater degree, how the past is being remembered. Thus while official, nation-state memory may continue to glorify the past in ways that Nietzsche would have found contemptible, both contemporary sites and studies of memory tend to represent the past as a struggle of forgotten histories.

*ie. history by women, minorities etc.*

The origins of contemporary studies of memory and the interrelationship between individual and cultural forms can be located in studies of the Holocaust (see e.g. LaCapra 1998; Novick 2000; Yerushalmi 1982; Young 1993). While the Holocaust continues to function as a central Jewish narrative of victimization, empowerment and resistance (Huyssen 1995), there is growing concern about the ubiquitousness of Holocaust memory, including the commodification and distortion of the Holocaust within popular culture (see e.g. Abramovich 2009; Finkelstein 2000). This concern interlinks with the belief of many scholars that the Holocaust simply defies representation; that it goes far beyond human comprehension and a language for interpreting it (see e.g. Agamben 2002; Friedlander 1992; Levi 1987; Lyotard 1988). There is also concern about the extent to which the Holocaust is used as the benchmark by which all other atrocities are measured and remembered (see e.g. Alexander 2002; Moses 2005; Moshman 2001; Rosenbaum 1998; Rothberg 2006). While these debates continue to rage, and indeed are now part of the rich scholarship in this area, the study of memory encompasses a wide range of past, historical events beyond the Holocaust, spanning a variety of academic disciplines particularly within interdisciplinary scholarship.

In the sociological tradition, contemporary studies of memory fundamentally recognize the interrelationship between the individual and society.[6] As Jeffrey Olick (1999) has noted, individual memory cannot exist without social interaction, nor can collective memory exist without the communal participation of individuals. Katharine Hodgkin and Susannah Radstone (2003: 5) likewise claim that memory is both individual and cultural, because even when we have a private experience, it is drawn from the 'countless scraps and bits of knowledge and information from the surrounding culture, and is inserted into larger cultural narratives'. Both individual and societal forms of memory are fundamentally concerned with *memory preservation*; namely, what we use to perpetuate, maintain and sustain our past memories so they are not forgotten (photography is a good example of this). Memory is thus integral to understanding and interpreting the past, present and future; it has become an important vehicle for the construction of identity and meaning, and a central way of confronting the legacy of a traumatic past. Indeed, memory is absolutely central to the human condition; writes Luis Buñuel, 'Our memory is our coherence, our reason, our feeling, even our action. Without it, we are nothing' (quoted in Huyssen 1995: 1). Huyssen adds: 'It does not require much theoretical sophistication to see that *all representation* – whether in language, narrative, image, or recorded sound – is based on memory' (ibid.: 2, emphasis added). But due to its very nature, memory – both personal and social – is inherently problematic, unstable and transformative. In order to understand why and how the invocation of memory incites and invites contestation and to understand the power of memory as a political and legal tool, it is important to examine some problematics of memory: first, the nature of individual memory; second, the debates about social, collective or cultural memory; and third, the gendering of memory.

## The problematic of memory

### *The fragility of memory*

The first problematic of memory relates to the nature of individual memory. Memory is often treated as mere perception, an imperfect 'imprint' of the past at risk of being branded erroneous and false. Paul Ricœur (2004: 5) argues that the phenomenology of memory is located in the realm of the imagination and that individual memory through the process of recall is 'at the lowest rung of the ladder of modes of knowledge, belonging to the affections that are subject to the connection governing things external to the human body'. He adds that there is a problem between phenomenological knowledge and scientific knowledge and that the 'conjunction between (external) stimulation and (internal) resemblance will remain, for us, the crux of the entire problematic of memory' (ibid.: 17).

As memory is 'the modality of our relation to the past' (Terdiman 1993: 7), and because it is 'simply perception', it serves as a trace, remnant or fragment of the actual 'real' experience (Agamben 2002; Nora 1989; Ricœur 2004). Memory is not a thing or an object, but an action, deeply connected to the problematic of time (Ricœur 2004) and, as such, memory unsettles our chronological sensibility (Terdiman 1993). This puts memory at risk of disappearance when a person dies or if the ability to remember is no longer possible due to psychological will or deterioration (Hodgkin and Radstone 2003). Psychologists and psychiatrists further claim that memory may be repressed, altered or corrupted by psychological trauma and thereby impossible to translate into narrative memory (van der Kolk and van der Hart 1995; see also Chapter 5). The fragility and ambiguity of memory (the 'crisis of representation') therefore poses problems for the science of various rationalist and chronological disciplines, such as psychology, history and law. Law, for example, relies on memory for the construction of 'truth' and the delivery of justice, yet memory is at odds with law's claim to knowledge and rationality, and its method of abstraction. In part this explains the contestation that arises as a result of the nebulous, malleable and fluid nature of memory, and yet despite the inherent and intractable deficiencies of memory, as Ricœur (2004: 21) states, 'To put it bluntly, we have nothing better than memory to signify that something has taken place, has occurred, has happened *before* we declare that we remember it' (emphasis original).

The fragility and perceived authenticity of memory, it may be argued, enables the 'renewal and redemption' of the past (Sturken 1997: 17) within contemporary social, cultural, institutionalized or collective means of preservation. Marita Sturken (1997: 2) argues that the instability of memory means that the past is constantly being 'verified, understood and given meaning' but that our focus should not be on reliability, rather, we need to think about the way in which the past affects the present. This can happen once personal memory is shared in a social context. Because of the inherent power and fragility of memory, it functions in the present as something deeply contested and fundamentally omnipresent. As a consequence, memory is also manifestly political.

### Collective memory

Inextricably connected to the instability of individual memory is the second problematic of memory; that is, the range of debates – including the conceptual and the methodological – relating to the study of 'collective memory'. The French sociologist Maurice Halbwachs (1992) first developed the concept of 'collective memory' in the early twentieth century to refer to the social construction of memories. Importantly, he examined the role of social institutions in the preservation or transmission of memory. Halbwachs was inspired by the theories of his mentor Émile Durkheim (1982), who coined the term 'social facts' to describe the existence of societal forces beyond and independent of the individual. Halbwachs (1992: 38) argued that over time individual memory becomes generalized within a social framework: 'There exists a collective memory and social framework for memory; it is to the extent that our individual thought places itself in these frameworks that it is capable of the act of recollection'. In other words, human memory only makes sense in a social context: 'the idea of an individual memory, absolutely separate from social memory, is an abstraction almost devoid of meaning' (Connerton 2003: 37). This is reminiscent of Durkheim's (1984: 38) notion of the 'collective conscience', defined as 'the totality of beliefs and sentiments common to average citizens of the same society'.

The study of memory raises a number of methodological and conceptual challenges. First, there is a tendency for scholars to use the term 'collective memory' without clarifying its meaning or deficiencies. Jay Winter (2000: 13), for example, states, 'The only fixed point is the near ubiquity of the term. Just as we use words like love and hate without ever knowing their full or shared significance, so are we bound to go on using the term "memory", the historical signature of our generation' (see also Berliner 2005). There is also conceptual disagreement over terminology within memory studies and scholars use a range of concepts, including (among others): public memory (e.g. Bodnar 1992); collective memory (e.g. Halbwachs 1992); social memory (e.g. Fentress and Wickham 1992); national memory (e.g. Nora 1989); and cultural memory (e.g. Assmann 1995). Collective memory is sometimes used so broadly that it could be seen as constituting both culture and identity (Berliner 2005; Klein 2000).

The conceptual confusion is in part due to the disagreement among scholars over personal memory (memory that is not shared socially); collected memory (aggregated individual recollections); and collective memory (socially constitutive memories) (see Kansteiner 2002; Olick 1999). Olick (1999) argues that it is the latter two types of memory where the confusion most often lies. He refers to *collected memory* as the aggregated sum of individual memories. For example, we could think about collected memory as a collection of stories, experiences and emotions of a group of survivors, such as the collected narratives of former comfort women. *Collective memory,* on the other hand, has its own dynamic and is independent of the individual because there are ways, other than the human brain, of providing representations of the past (Olick 1999). Using again the example of the comfort women, for instance, the stories of women may be preserved in various mnemonic forms, such as film, books, protests, law suits and other commemorative sites or practices. An overarching narrative might be that the plight of the comfort women has been thoroughly distorted and ignored in post-war narratives and as such it constitutes a massive injustice. This narrative of injustice may be considered part of the collective memory of the Second World War, and commemorative forms may be utilized to highlight the memory of this injustice. It is important, therefore, to differentiate between different forms of memory so there is some clarity over the frame of reference in memory studies.

Second, and related to the conceptual issues mentioned above, the reification of collective memory as a metaphor raises methodological and epistemological challenges because memory and the act of remembering are predominantly individualized, human functions. In other words, the study of collective memory begs the question: is it possible for *societies* to 'remember' and is it possible for societies to have 'memories'? Susan Sontag (2003: 85–6) calls collective memory a 'spurious notion', adding that 'All memory is individual, unreproducible – it dies with each person'. Amos Funkenstein (1989: 6) likewise states:

> consciousness and memory can only be realized by an individual who acts, is aware, and remembers. Just as a nation cannot eat or dance, neither can it speak or remember. Remembering is a mental act, and therefore it is absolutely and completely personal.

The reification of memory has been prevalent within transitional justice studies on how societies can transcend collective suffering; however, extrapolating individual psychological and emotional responses to the societal level may not be a particularly useful strategy for dealing with a violent past. For example, notions such as 'traumatized nation', 'collective guilt' and 'societal healing' have been widely used to explain post-conflict societies in the aftermath of warfare and politicized violence. Notions of society-wide 'repression' and 'disassociation' are further examples of the tendency towards reification. These may be nothing more than 'extravagant metaphors' (Ignatieff 1996), but they may also foster inappropriate or unrealistic responses to gross violations of human rights (e.g. that a nation plagued by collective guilt can experience national 'catharsis' or 'healing').

Essentially, the key task for memory scholars is to come up with befitting ways to analyze the phenomenon of collective memory in light of these methodological pitfalls and conceptual confusions (Kansteiner 2002).[7] We might usefully think of the separation between personal and collective memory through Jan Assmann's (1995: 125) distinction between cultural memory and oral history. Assmann describes oral history as 'communicative memory' or 'everyday memory' that is inherently unstable and disorganized and that does not have cultural characteristics (even if it is essentially socially mediated, as Halbwachs claims). Cultural memory, on the other hand, may be distinguished from oral history because of its distance from everyday memory and because it is maintained through cultural forms and institutionalized forms of communication (Assmann 1995).[8]

Because collective memory cannot be empirically measured or validated in a concrete sense, some have suggested that it can only ever be used in a metaphorical sense. Noa Gedi and Yigal Elam (1996: 43), for example, write: '[Collective memory] has the advantage of being a vivid and illustrative description, but as an explanatory tool it is useless and even misleading'. Other scholars disagree, seeing collective memory as more than just a metaphor, as such memories do arguably exist within families, groups, institutions and nations, even if these memories 'have no organic basis and do not exist in any literal sense' (Kansteiner 2002: 188).

A useful way to think about the relationship between personal and collective memory may be to examine the 'transcultural' and 'transnational' context of memory; namely the way – using a very loose definition – memory can transcend geography, culture and time. For example, Olick (2007) claims that the Vietnam War is 'traumatic' for Vietnamese survivors and American veterans, as well as for American and Vietnamese citizens (and others) in general. In a similar vein, the memory of Auschwitz 'will not disappear with the death of the last survivor; nor is it carried only through those – mainly their children – who suffered its personal ripple effects: Auschwitz remains a trauma for the narratives of modernity and morality, among others' (ibid.: 32). Of course, memory across different groups, time periods and geographical distances is by no means uniform or consensual. It is important to note also that the notion of transcultural memory raises issues about ownership of the past and claims to authenticity. In other words, the vicarious invocation of the past is likely, of course, to be thoroughly different from the act of remembering by those who directly experienced the event (and in strict definitional terms, the former is not really 'remembering' at all).

Despite the questions and complexities that are raised in memory studies, collective memory, as a concept, is useful for thinking through constitutive narratives about past historical events. In response to some of the concerns identified in critiques of collective memory, Olick (2007) deconstructs a variety of misconceptions about the term by stating the following: (1) memory is multiple and contested rather than unifying and consensual; (2) remembering provides an imperfect representation of the past rather than a 'mirror' of the past; (3) memory is intangible, a process or an activity as opposed to tangible and measurable; and (4) memory is interdependent, not distinct and separable. Collective memory is therefore useful as a heuristic device for understanding the critical relationship between the individual, social, political and cultural: 'The beauty of memory is that it is imprecise enough to be appropriated by unexpected hands, to connect apparently unrelated topics, to explain anew old problems' (Confino 1997: 1403). Thus, the way I use the term is both as a *representation* and as a *narrative* of the past that takes place in the present:

> Collective memory is substantiated through multiple forms of commemoration … Each act of commemoration reproduces a *commemorative narrative*, a story about a particular past that accounts for this ritualized remembrance and provides a moral message for the

group members. In creating this narrative, collective memory clearly draws upon historical sources. Yet it does so selectively and creatively.

(Zerubavel 2004: 5–6, emphasis original)

To repeat what Olick (1999: 342) has argued, 'there are mnemonic technologies other than the brain'. Collective memory, adds Olick (1999: 346), may therefore be used as:

a sensitizing term for a wide variety of mnemonic processes, practices, and outcomes, neurological, cognitive, personal, aggregated … It means remembering that 'memory' occurs in public and in private, at the tops of societies and at the bottoms, as reminiscence and as commemoration, as personal testimonial and as national narrative, and that each of these forms is important; it also means remembering that these different forms of remembering are not always equally important for each other.

Drawing on this conceptualization, different mechanisms and mediums of memory may include the news media, art, cinema, literature, education, law and other commemorative institutions, traditions and practices. Using the example of wartime sexual violence, collective memories may be shaped by (and may include) diverse sites for memory preservation, including paintings and sculptures of the *Rape of the Sabine Women*; the collection of newspaper articles during the 1990s documenting the mass rapes in the former Yugoslavia and in Rwanda; the published anonymous diary – *A Woman in Berlin* (2006) – based on a woman's experience of rape at the end of the Second World War;[9] the award-winning film *Grbavica* by Jasmila Žbanič about the life of a single mother in Sarajevo after the systematic rapes in the former Yugoslavia; and the testimonies collected from former comfort women for the mock, NGO-initiated Women's International War Crimes Tribunal in the early 1990s. A range of other mnemonic forms for ensuring that wartime rape is no longer a 'forgotten crime of war' may also be included in this list, including international humanitarian law and war crimes courts.[10] It is the latter commemorative form which this book focuses upon, in order to make sense of how past narratives of wartime rape are made to matter in the present (and how they might be thought about in the future).

If we apply a rather broad understanding of collective memory to wartime rape, the mechanism of a war crimes court may be seen as preserving memory when rape is prosecuted as a serious violation of international humanitarian law (although I will critically examine this presumption in the subsequent chapters). Institutionalized mechanisms such as international courts, therefore, preserve and transmit memory, and may contribute to a certain narrative about past historical events. The important task is then to examine the nature of such institutions as sites of memory preservation and to assess the extent to which these mnemonic forms faithfully or adequately construct a narrative (but not necessarily whether they should). For the purpose of this book, I am not so much concerned with *what* memories exist (since I don't actually think agreement on this is possible due to the sheer diversity of memories in the first place); rather the way I use the term 'collective memory' is to think critically about the nature of institutional mechanisms as *sites of traumatic memory preservation.*[11]

I would go further by stating that these mechanisms, mediums, processes, practices and outcomes also form part of the collective memory of pivotal historical events *in and of themselves.* For example, not only has the prosecution of crimes at the Nuremberg and Tokyo trials after the end of the Second World War shaped the way in which we remember the war itself, but the development and existence of these tribunals *per se* are part of the collective memory of the war (e.g. why they were set up in the first place; how they operated; their limitations and potential; as well as their short- and long-term consequences). What interests me is how the past is made to matter: 'To trace how – and which – past is made to matter, we also need to ask: by whom, to whom, when, where, and why' (Irwin-Zarecka 2009: 7).

Collective memory scholars often refer to memory as the shared past; however, this implies consensus and social solidarity and may neglect the *BUT* contested aspects of memory and how memory operates within relationships of power (see Zerubavel 2004). Postmodernist approaches, for example, have drawn attention to the conceptual linkages between history, memory and power, and a number of memory studies have examined conflicting narratives and the ways in which marginalized memories have been excluded from dominant understandings of past events. Understanding the political decisions regarding which memories are retained and which memories are discarded or ignored is thus important for understanding the politics of memory. *Foucault* Likewise, understanding whose memories are privileged gives us insight into *looking @ how we remember* these dynamics.

*This is all so M. Foucault*

## Gender and memory

The politics of memory can be seen through the third problematic of memory; namely, the gendering of memory. In her work on the Holocaust, memory and gender, Anna Reading (2002: 5) argues that there is a gender gap in most of the key studies on collective memory.[12] She underscores the importance of examining the 'ways in which gender is a factor in the collective construction, mediation and articulation of memories of historical events'. Although gender may be neglected or overlooked in memory studies, on the other hand, it is paradoxically and vividly apparent in official, nationalistic recollections of the past (perhaps to such an extent that it is rendered invisible). For example, Mark Osiel (2000: 4) states that all societies have 'founding myths' commemorated in 'the form of "monumental didactics", ɔlic recountings of the founders' heroic deeds as a national epic'. These numental myths are often based on remarkably overt gendered narratives of heroism, masculinity and martyrdom (for critiques of such myths, see e.g. Damousi and Lake 1995; Lake 2009; Levinger 1995). The hyper-masculinity of warfare and the perpetration of gross human rights violations are no new revelation; indeed, the history of warfare is a history of masculinity. As 'former comfort woman' Jan Ruff O'Herne said, 'men are not the only victims in the war, women are victims too, the men get all the medals and the women wear the scars' (Personal Interview, 6 August 2003). Typically, women's experiences of warfare, particularly as victims of gendered crimes, do not sit comfortably with such recountings since they fundamentally challenge hegemonic, state-centric versions of heroic battle. One example, which occurred during the late 1970s and 1980s in Australia, was the threatening and banning of anti-ANZAC Day protestors who staged protests to challenge masculine glorification and the rape of women during armed conflict (Braithwaite 2006; Howe 1983).

Conversely, while the memory of wartime rape may at certain points in time cause great outrage and denial, at other junctures wartime rape is quite purposefully woven into the collective narrative of nations. This occurred, for example, in Belgium during and after the First World War when 'the German Army cut a swath of horror. Houses were burned, villages were plundered, civilians were bayoneted, and women were raped' (Brownmiller 1976: 41). Likewise, since the 1990s in China and Korea, rape has been used to construct a narrative of nationalistic victimization. The invocation of rape as memory under these circumstances (e.g. 'the Rape of Belgium'; 'the Rape of Nanking') is essentially premised on the ulterior motive of expounding a nation's virtue in opposition to another nation's barbarity. The issue here is that the role of women and their memory of sexual violence play a subsidiary part in these competing, conflicting versions of collective memory. Susan Brownmiller (1976: 37–8) powerfully captures the ways in which nations surreptitiously solicit the memory of rape:

> An aggressor nation rarely admits to rape. Documentation of rape in warfare is something the *other side* totals up, analyzes and propagandizes when the smoke has cleared after defeat. Men of a conquered nation traditionally view the rape of 'their women' as the ultimate humiliation, a sexual *coup de grace*. Rape is considered by the people of a defeated nation to be part of the enemy's conscious effort to destroy them. In fact, by tradition, men appropriate the rape of 'their women' as part of their own male anguish of defeat … rape by a conqueror *is* compelling evidence of the conquered's status of masculine impotence. Defense of women has long been a hallmark of masculine pride, as possession of women has been a hallmark of masculine success … The body of a raped woman becomes a ceremonial battlefield, a parade ground for the victor's trooping of the colors. The act that is played out upon her is a message

passed between men – vivid proof of victory for one and loss and defeat for the other.

(emphasis original)

Moreover, while it is correct to add that marginalized memories of the past, such as the Holocaust and other traumatic pasts, serve to challenge state-centric memory, often gender is a neglected factor in *what* is to be remembered and *how* is it to be remembered. Marianne Hirsh and Valerie Smith (2002: 6), for example, claim that the way in which memory operates – the technologies for preservation, the mode of interpretation and the act of transfer – are inherently gendered.[13] They write:

> gender, along with race and class, marks identities in specific ways and provides a means by which cultural memory is located in a specific context rather than subsumed into monolithic and essentialist categories. Moreover, gender is an inescapable dimension of differential power relations, and cultural memory is always about the distribution of and contested claims to power. What a culture remembers and what it chooses to forget are intricately bound up with issues of power and hegemony, and thus with gender.

My focus for the rest of the book is on the gendering of law; specifically focusing on international criminal courts and the way in which women's experiences of wartime rape become part of the legacy of these institutions. In the subsequent chapters, I will examine the modes of preservation, interpretation and transfer within these institutional mechanisms of memory.

## Collective memory and the law

The extent to which law plays a pedagogical or didactic function has become part of an absorbing debate among scholars seeking to explore the link between law and memory. The creation of memory through official 'storytelling' has assisted – to some extent at least – in the recognition and validation of gross human rights violations. Through adjudicating on past injustices, war crimes courts, truth commissions and other approaches help to create a public record of wrongdoing so that denial and amnesia do not obliterate the experiences of victims and their communities in the past, present and future. Osiel (2000), for example, argues that a criminal trial is a significant public opportunity for the collective mourning of victims that can help them and the general public come to terms with a traumatic and violent past. As mentioned earlier, Osiel also argues that ideally law functions to create compelling stories about past historical events capable of generating society-wide debate about the past and the lessons for the future. This requires an active deliberation on the part of courts and legal actors to adopt 'dramaturgical license' in order to construct a coherent narrative:

If courts could find a way to tell the tale as a genuine tragedy, alternately eliciting a measure of sympathy and antipathy for each side, dramatic tension would be enhanced, evoking more attention from the public. Such sustained attention would help stimulate the public discussion and collective soul-searching that is the primary contribution of criminal prosecution to social solidarity at such times.

(ibid.: 135)[14]

Likewise, Lawrence Douglas (2001: 2) argues that trials do more than simply resolve questions of guilt. Robert M.W. Kempner, the junior prosecutor at Nuremberg, for example called the trial 'the greatest history seminar ever held in the history of the world', while the British Chief Prosecutor, Sir Hartley Shawcross, declared that Nuremberg would 'provide ... an authoritative and impartial record to which future historians may turn for truth'. In 1945, Henry Stimson and Edward Stettinius (respectively US Secretary of War and Secretary of State), drew upon a broader conception of law when they said that 'The use of the judicial method will ... make available for all mankind to study in future years an authentic record of Nazi crimes and criminality' (quoted in ibid.: 18).

The Nuremberg trial, writes Douglas (2001: 6), was one of the 'most spectacular trials of the century', due to the innovative nature of the proceedings, the gravity of crimes and the global attention devoted to them. He argues that some high drama moments characterized Nuremberg, including the showing of the documentary film *Nazi Concentration Camps*; the shrunken head of Buchenwald presented during the trial; Justice Jackson's opening statement, regarded as one of the most momentous courtroom speeches in history; and the rare 'testimonial spectacle' when witnesses and defendants took the stand. Douglas (2001: 15) concedes, however, that the Nuremberg trial was 'drained' of drama, leaving the spectators 'puffy with boredom' due to the fixation on judicial process and the charge of crimes against peace (as opposed to crimes of the Holocaust), as well as the predominant use of documentary evidence as opposed to eyewitness testimony. According to one journalist reporting on the Nuremberg trial at the time:

It was the largest crime in history, and it promised the greatest courtroom spectacle. [But] with their cheap suits and hungry faces, these indistinguished men did not look like the archcriminals of the age. What ensued was an excruciatingly long and complex trial that failed to mesmerize a distracted world.

(quoted in Osiel 2000: 91)

However, the legacy of the Nuremberg trial is that it did eventually capture the world's attention, at least in the years to come, and despite its shortcomings, Nuremberg arguably did therefore serve didactic ends.[15] The trial was the first in international history to try individuals for alleged crimes, signalling the internationalization of criminal justice (see e.g. Blumenthal and McCormack 2008; Ferencz 1998; Fogelson 1989). Nuremberg thus significantly broadened the scope of international humanitarian law and provided a legal basis for the *ad hoc* tribunals for the former Yugoslavia and Rwanda in the early 1990s. However, the important point here is that the Nuremberg trial, as well as the Tokyo trial and contemporary courts for the prosecution of international crimes, constitute *selective memory*. In other words, the legacy of these trials is contingent, based on the specific nature of the proceedings, the prosecution of particular crimes, the appearance of selected perpetrators and witnesses, and the nature of judicial outcomes. While it is impossible to predict what memories will later emerge in public consciousness, or what lasting legacies will be transmitted to future generations, it is nonetheless possible to identify the distortions, interpretations and manipulations of law when examining the way in which particular crimes are dealt with by these monumental institutions. As such, Douglas (2001) was able to argue in his study of Holocaust trials that the pedagogic deficiencies and the failure of the Nuremberg trial to make sense of an extraordinarily traumatic moment in history were due to the absence of the human element in the trial. Douglas (2006) concludes, therefore, that collective memory and didactic legality are enabled through law when the voices of survivors and witnesses are heard.

In fact, the role of victims and witnesses in legal contexts has become a focal point for debate in the few studies on the relationship between law and collective memory. The Eichmann trial and Hannah Arendt's (1994) fascinating study of the trial have been at the centre of this analysis (see e.g. Douglas 2001; Felman 2002; Osiel 2000). I will briefly discuss this here to demonstrate the debate that has ensued regarding this issue (and I believe this has relevance for examining other war crimes trials, for example rape trials at the international level).

Eichmann was a high-ranking Nazi who had the task of managing the forced migration and then later the mass deportation of Jews to ghettoes and concentration camps. Eichmann was captured by Israeli agents in Argentina on 11 May 1960 and taken to a rented house in a remote suburb of Buenos Aires where he was tied to a bed for eight days while the Israelis waited for a plane to take him to Israel to be tried for crimes against the Jewish people, crimes against humanity and war crimes. The trial, which began on 11 April 1961, was carefully orchestrated by the prosecutor, Gideon Hausner, to depict the Holocaust in terms of a dichotomy between Jews as 'helpless sheep on the one hand and the venal survivor on the other' (Douglas 2001: 156). This narrative of both Jewish victimization and survival has predominated in collective memory accounts since, and perhaps because of, the Eichmann trial. Shoshana Felman (2002: 127) writes, 'Prior to the Eichmann trial, what we call the Holocaust did not exist as a collective story'.

The Prime Minister of Israel at the time, David Ben-Gurion, saw the Eichmann trial as a lesson in history to the whole world: 'We want to establish before the nations of the world how millions of people, because they happened to be Jews, and one million babies, because they happened to be Jewish babies, were murdered by the Nazis' (quoted in Arendt 1994: 9). The trial was thus an opportunity to elucidate why Jews allowed themselves to 'go to their death like lambs to the slaughter' (ibid.: 5). Hausner encouraged witness testimony and urged witnesses to tell their stories largely uninterrupted in narrative form, even if they were less relevant to the actual case itself. An Israeli scholar commented that 'Eichmann rather swiftly became peripheral to his own trial, which was deliberately designed to focus more comprehensively on the Nazi crimes against the Jews' (quoted in Osiel 2000: 60).

Arendt (1994) saw the trial as a legal failure because legal neutrality and impartiality were sacrificed for pedagogical aims. She argued that centring a trial on the victim narrative of mass atrocity was highly problematic, going far beyond the purpose of a criminal trial. In addition to discussing, controversially, the role (collaboration and betrayal) of the Jewish Council during the Holocaust and conducting a character evaluation of Eichmann himself (where she asserted her theory on the banality of evil),[16] Arendt reflected on the legitimacy of post-conflict justice mechanisms for trying individuals for the worst crimes against humanity. She famously declared (1994: 253) that the criminal law should focus exclusively on the prosecution of the accused:

> The purpose of a trial is to render justice, and nothing else; even the noblest of ulterior purposes … can only detract from the law's main business: to weigh the charges brought against the accused, to render judgment, and to mete out due punishment.

Arendt also reflected on the impossibility of justice, arguing that the crimes of the Nazis were so abhorrent that they tested the very limits of the law, and as such, law was quite simply ill-equipped to deal 'on a human, political level, with a guilt that is beyond crime' (quoted in Douglas 2001: 39). Arendt's study of the Eichmann trial has been so widely discussed since the 1960s that it has very much become a shared and divisive 'collective memory' itself – of both the Holocaust and a character study of Eichmann as the embodiment of human 'evil' – and even of Hannah Arendt herself as an enormously influential literary figure.

In contrast to Arendt's formulation of international criminal justice, Douglas (2001) views the Eichmann trial as contributing to the greater good of collective memory, even if the trial itself deviated significantly from the traditional aims of criminal justice. The trial, he writes (2001: 174), demands 'to be viewed as a legal success insofar as it transformed understandings of what the law can and should do in the wake of traumatic history'. Felman (2002: 121) comments that justice for Arendt is 'ascetic, disciplined, conceptual experience, not an emotional stage for spectacular public expression'. Felman further argues that law repeats trauma through the dramatic explosion of interruptions to the legal process and framework (citing the fainting of a witness in the Eichmann trial). Douglas (2001: 2) likewise contends that although the primary responsibility of criminal trials may be to ascertain the guilt of the accused in a fair manner, 'To insist ... as Arendt does, that the *sole* purpose of a trial is to render justice and nothing else, presents ... a crabbed and needlessly restrictive vision of the trial as legal form' (emphasis original).

Indeed, sociologists and socio-legal scholars for a long time have looked beyond the traditional aims of the law to examine ulterior functions of criminal punishment (see e.g Simpson 2007). Savelsberg and King (2007) cite Garfinkel's (1956) notion of courtrooms playing the function of 'degradation ceremonies' and Durkheim's conceptualization of law as a ritual practice reflective of social solidarity (see Lukes and Scull 1983). Other contemporary legal scholars view law as a narrative through which cultural and social understandings of human relations are constructed and suppressed (see e.g. Brooks and Gewirtz 1996; Douglas 2001; Minow, Ryan and Sarat 2004; Patterson 1990). Many transitional justice scholars too have emphasized the necessity of criminal prosecutions as a tool to secure deterrence and the prevention of future atrocities. Carlos Santiago Nino (1996) argued, for example, that criminal trials in the aftermath of politicized violence are not only necessary for victims to reclaim their self-respect, but also important for the collective conscience of society and for reawakening a nation's ethical foundations. Likewise, Diane Orentlicher (2007: 15) observes that while many victims of gross human rights violations have been disappointed in international criminal courts, they generally agree that trials are necessary for restoring 'fundamental norms of human decency ... to secure the moral integrity of future generations'.

In response to the current debates over prioritizing the retributive function of criminal justice, in recent years contemporary war crimes courts have increasingly looked beyond the perpetrator, judgment and punishment in a modified vision of post-conflict justice. For example, the International Criminal Tribunal for the Former Yugoslavia (ICTY), on an earlier website, listed its tasks as follows:

> To bring to justice persons allegedly responsible for serious violations of international humanitarian law; to render justice to the victims; to deter further crimes; [and] and to contribute to the restoration of peace [and reconciliation in the former Yugoslavia].
>
> (quoted in Henry 2009: 117–18)

It appears that the addition of less conventional criminal justice goals, such as victim vindication and societal reconciliation, was partially in response to a shifting conception of the retribution/restoration dichotomy that has begun to influence modern criminological and legal studies. Legal practitioners and transitional justice scholars have argued that criminal trials *should* embrace rehabilitative or therapeutic goals, particularly if peace is to be achieved in post-conflict societies (interestingly, peace is not a goal normally attributed to domestic criminal jurisdictions). The former President and ICTY Judge, Gabrielle Kirk McDonald (2000: 7), stated that by acknowledging the suffering of victims, international war crimes courts can 'help the healing process and begin to lay the groundwork for reconciliation', adding that this is a revolutionary change to the way international criminal tribunals operate in the protection of human rights. While there is little doubt that improvements have been made to procedural mechanisms to allow victims a greater role in the prosecution of serious violations of international laws (and perhaps these trials do contribute more to collective memory than their predecessors), the focus of international courts *in practice* nonetheless continues to be retribution and the prosecution and punishment of perpetrators.

What is at issue, therefore, is the *rhetoric* of restoration within international criminal justice. More recent critiques, for example, point to the lack of empirical evidence to substantiate the claim that criminal trials can in fact lead to victim vindication, offender rehabilitation and societal reconciliation (Fletcher and Weinstein 2002; Stover 2005). We might add to this list the contribution of war crimes courts to collective memory since courts are now claiming this as one of their goals (for example, the Special Court for Sierra Leone has a legacy officer; the ICTY held a legacy conference in February 2010; and the ICTY states on its website that it has made important contributions to collective memory). Critical responses within transitional justice studies demonstrate that unrealistic expectations underpin international criminal justice, from punishment and deterrence to reconciliation and victim restoration (Henry 2009). Interestingly, the goal of reconciliation has since been removed from the ICTY's website (ibid.), presumably due to more recent scholarship critiquing the therapeutic model of international criminal justice (see e.g. Pupavac 2004) or the incapacity of law to respond to some complex goals of post-conflict justice.

Michael Marrus (2002: 235) cautions that 'we should not look to trials to validate our general understanding of the Holocaust or to provide a special platform for historical interpretations'. Others warn that we must avoid treating war crimes courts as drama theatres, educational devices and as therapy centres. Power (1998: 38), for example, states, 'it is worth remembering also that there is a difference between theatres and courts, between therapy and justice, between a story and a truth'. While I agree with the array of pertinent critiques on the function of law and judicial process, there is a distinction between, on the one hand, advocating a normative function of law and legal process (e.g. to assert what law *should* do) and, on the other hand, analyzing what law *does do in practice.* Thus my aim is to depart somewhat from the debate started by Arendt in *Eichmann in Jerusalem* about whether or not law should perform a therapeutic, didactic, collective memory or otherwise function, and rather focus more specifically on the narratives that inadvertently *do* unfold through law (Brooks and Gewirtz 1996), and the way in which law does justice to the memory of wartime sexual violence in the aftermath of armed conflict.[17]

An understanding of the relationship between law and memory helps to elucidate the way in which law shapes narratives about genocide, war crimes and crimes against humanity; how law shapes or produces history; and how law reproduces hegemonic relations of power that in turn shape how historical events are to be remembered. Despite the inherent deficiencies and limitations of the concept of collective memory, it can be said to nonetheless exist independently of, and dependent on, the individual. As Wulf Kansteiner (2002) highlights, collective memory continually escapes one's conceptual grasp. This is particularly so when we are dealing with transcultural memory and mass atrocities like genocide, torture and wartime rape, where the collective 'mind' is amorphous, vast and extremely diverse. This means it is difficult to come up with a coherent or agreed-upon grand narrative of various international crimes and their aftermath. As such, and in sum, collective memory – metaphorically speaking or not – consists of the stories or narratives that are told at particular points in time in particular spaces about past historical events. Collective memory is also about the interpretations of these narratives. Collective memory does not necessarily imply a shared and solidifying consensus of the past because memory is not fixed or static, but rather it is in a state of constant transformation (Hodgkin and Radstone 2003). In addition, memory is constantly within the grasp of politics and so it is crucial to look at the 'politics of memory' and how this informs the current discourse on wartime rape. It is thus important to recognize that collective memory is 'drastically selective' and certain memories gain credence at certain points of time (Yerushalmi 1982).

# 3 A history of silence
## The Nuremberg and Tokyo trials

We must establish incredible events by credible evidence.
(Justice Robert H. Jackson, Chief Prosecutor at the
Nuremberg trial, quoted in Taylor 1955: 498)

Rape, sexual enslavement, forced sterilization and other forms of sexual violence were extremely widespread during the Second World War. In the late
1930s, the spree of violent rapes against the Chinese population of Nanking by
the Imperial Japanese Army was later coined 'the Rape of Nanking' due to the
horrific numbers of women raped during the six-week invasion. Women were
raped in occupied German areas and in street mobs, where 'the ideology of
rape burst into perfect flower as Hitler's armies goosestepped over the face of
Europe' (Brownmiller 1976: 48–9). Women were humiliated, mutilated and
tortured in brothels and in Nazi concentration camps, undergoing rape, forced
sterilization and other forms of gruesome experimentation on their reproductive organs. And thousands of comfort women were kidnapped, coerced, lured
and sold into forced prostitution in Japanese military-style brothels scattered
across Asia, suffering from repeated forms of sexual violence on a daily basis.

In 1944, the Red Army entered East Prussia and Silesia, committing a
frenzy of rapes, culminating in the final major offensive in Berlin in January
1945, where vengeful Russian soldiers raped an estimated 2 million German
women.[1] Cases of Allied rapes were relatively undocumented; however, rapes
occurred in the liberated areas and Allied soldiers visited Japanese-established
'comfort stations' where women once again faced repeated violation from
all sides of the conflict. Given the enormity and extent of wartime sexual
violence during the Second World War, it is striking how these crimes quickly
entered into oblivion at the cessation of the conflict.

At the end of the Second World War, the Allies agreed that two inter-
national criminal tribunals be established to prosecute and punish those
responsible for atrocities committed in violation of the laws of armed conflict.
From this agreement, the Charter of the International Military Tribunal
(IMT) and the Charter of the International Military Tribunal for the Far
East (IMTFE) established the Nuremberg and Tokyo tribunals respectively.
The tribunals were the first of their kind in international history.[2]

Together, the Nuremberg and Tokyo tribunals failed to adequately address sexual violence. In both their respective charters, rape was not enumerated as a 'war crime' or as a 'crime against humanity', and no rape victims were called to testify at either trial. At the Nuremberg trial, evidence of rape was submitted, but not formally prosecuted, while in contrast at the Tokyo trial defendants were convicted for rape crimes committed during the Nanking invasion, although the sexual enslavement of the comfort women was all but completely ignored.

The failure of the Nuremberg and Tokyo tribunals to adequately prosecute rape crimes is reflective of two interconnected factors: first, the status of war crimes against women within international humanitarian law and second, the scant attention towards victims generally in the aftermath of conflict. Both the attention to and the silence of these crimes are deeply connected to the politics of wartime rape and the gendered nature of legal discourse.[3]

## Silence at Nuremberg

The First World War initiated the emergence of a new consciousness about war and atrocities, but the cataclysm of the Second World War was the decisive event that culminated in a discernible international human rights discourse.[4] The repudiation of 'libertarian, humanitarian, and internationalist ideals' in Nazi ideology was manifested in the corruption of the rule of law, indiscriminate imprisonment, executions, the expulsion of Jews and the existence of concentration camps (Taylor 1992: 21). The condemnation of the totalitarian dictatorship of Nazism, in conjunction with the proliferation of international agreements after the First World War, led to international outrage and called for the weight of the law to address the horrors (ibid.), resulting in the establishment of the International Military Tribunal (IMT), or the Nuremberg Tribunal as it is also known. The Tribunal was officially established to try the major war criminals of the European Axis.

The trial of the major war criminals took place between November 1945 and August 1946, in total trying 22 German defendants for individual responsibility for three distinct categories of crimes: crimes against peace; war crimes; and crimes against humanity. Crimes against peace included the planning, preparation, initiation and waging of an aggressive war. War crimes covered violations of the laws or customs of war, which included murder, ill-treatment, deportation, plunder and other forms of devastation not justified by military necessity. Crimes against humanity included murder, extermination, enslavement and deportation when committed against any civilian population before or during the war, as well as 'persecutions on political, racial, or religious grounds in execution of or in connection with any crime within the jurisdiction of the Tribunal, whether or not in violation of domestic law of the country where perpetrated'.[5]

Susan Brownmiller (1976) argues that rape played a pivotal role in the Nazi quest to conquer, humiliate and destroy 'inferior peoples' – in the over-arching aim of creating a master, Aryan race. Jewish women were raped in secretly ordered street riots across Germany (ibid.). Russian and Polish women were also raped in large numbers by advancing German soldiers. Rape, however, was not explicitly listed as a crime in the Nuremberg Charter, nor was it formally prosecuted, although rape was actually implicitly pro-hibited under international humanitarian law (e.g. the 1863 Lieber Code and the 1907 Hague Conventions). Rape could have been prosecuted as 'ill-treatment' and 'other inhumane acts' according to the respective war crimes and crimes against humanity categories (Askin 1997; Bassiouni 1999; Meron 1993a). As verification of a systematic Nazi campaign of terror and genocide, rape was, however, entered into evidence at Nuremberg based on various Russian, German and French documents that reported rape in the occupied areas.

The most substantive evidence of rape submitted to the Tribunal on 14 February 1946 was the 'Molotov Note', prepared in 1942 by Vyacheslav Molotov, the People's Commissar for Foreign Affairs in the Soviet Union. This official document catalogued a litany of atrocities committed by the Nazis during the German invasion of 1941. It began:

> As and when the Red Army, in the course of its continued and victorious counter-offensive, liberated numerous cities and rural committees which had, for a certain time, been in the hands of the German invader, an incredible picture emerged more clearly with every passing day – a picture of the looting which took place in every community, of general devastation, of *revolting acts of rape*, ill-treatment, and mass murder – all committed against peaceful citizens by the fascist German occupa-tional forces during their advance, during the occupation, and during their withdrawal.
>
> (IMT, 1946: 7: 456–7, emphasis added[6])

The Molotov Note was compiled to convey a horrifying picture of systematic rape and slaughter by the Nazis, while portraying the Red Army in compar-ison as both civilized and victorious. In specific reference to rape:

> In the village of Semenovskoe, in the region of Kalinin, the Germans bound with twine the arms of Olga Tikhonova, the 25-year-old wife of a Red Army man and mother of three children, who was in the last stage of pregnancy, and raped her. After violating her the Germans cut her throat, stabbed her through both breasts, and sadistically bored them out.
>
> (IMT, 1946: 7: 456–7)

The Note further made reference to the 'bestial acts of violence perpetrated against the women everywhere':

Women and young girls are vilely outraged in all the occupied areas.

In the Ukrainian village of Borodayevka, in the Dnepropetrovsk region, the fascists violated every one of the women and girls.

In the village of Berezovka, in the region of Smolensk, drunken German soldiers assaulted and carried off all the women and girls between the ages of 16 and 30.

In the city of Smolensk the German Command opened a brothel for officers in one of the hotels into which hundreds of women and girls were driven; they were mercilessly dragged down the street by their arms and hair.

Everywhere the lust-maddened German gangsters break into the houses, they rape the women and girls under the very eyes of their kinfolk and children, jeer at the women they have violated, and then brutally murder their victims.

In the city of Lvov, 32 women working in a garment factory were first violated and then murdered by German storm troopers. Drunken German soldiers dragged the girls and young women of Lvov into Kesciuszko Park, where they savagely raped them. An old priest, V. I. Pomamew, who, cross in hand, tried to prevent these outrages, was beaten up by the fascists. They tore off his cassock, singed his beard, and bayoneted him to death.

Near the town of Borissov in Bielorussia, 75 women and girls attempting to flee at the approach of the German troops, fell into their hands. The Germans first raped and then savagely murdered 36 of their number. By order of a German officer named Hummer, the soldiers marched L. I. Melchukova, a 16-year-old girl, into the forest, where they raped her. A little later some other women who had also been dragged into the forest saw some boards near the trees and the dying Melchukova nailed to the boards. The Germans had cut off her breasts in the presence of these women, among whom were V. I. Alperenko, and V. H. Bereznikova.

On retreating from the village of Borovka, in the Zvenigorod district of the Moscow region, the fascists forcibly abducted several women, tearing them away from their little children in spite of their protests and prayers.

In the town of Tikhvin in the Leningrad region, a 15-year-old girl named H. Koledetskaya, who had been wounded by shell splinters, was taken to a hospital (a former monastery) where there were wounded German soldiers. Despite her injuries the girl was raped by a group of German soldiers and died as a result of the assault.

(*IMT*, 1946: 7: 456–7)

In an effort to reveal the 'characteristic features of Hitlerite terrorism' (*IMT*, 1946: 7: 61) and the decree of terror from the German leaders tried before the Nuremberg trial, L.N. Smirnov, the Chief Counselor of Justice for the USSR, referred to a report of the Extraordinary State Commission for the investigation of the 1941 German atrocities in the town of Kerch:

> Many women and girls in their teens were separated from the rest of the internees by the fascist blackguards and locked in separate cells, where the unfortunate creatures were subjected to particularly outrageous forms of torture. They were raped, their breasts cut off, their stomachs ripped open, their feet and hands cut off, and their eyes gouged out. After the Germans had been thrown out of Kerch, on 30 December 1941, Red Army soldiers discovered, in the prison yard, a formless mass of bodies of young girls, naked, mutilated, and unrecognizable, who had been savagely and cynically tortured to death by the fascists.
>
> (*IMT*, 1946: 7: 62)

In concentration camps and in brothels across the eastern front, thousands of women were also reportedly forced into prostitution for German soldiers, the SS and male slave labourers. The Tribunal entered into evidence a secret letter from Heinrich Himmler regarding the brothel in Dachau (dated 16 November 1942):

> Only such prostitutes are to be selected for the Camp brothel who from the beginning can be taken for granted as not being able to be saved for a later regulated life, judging from their previous living and bearing. Also, that we are not guilty of spoiling a person who could still be saved for the German people. Such women can only be released from the Concentration Camp if they according to their age, do not constitute a destruction to the youth, to health (by contagion), or to the public welfare and security.
>
> (Nazi Conspiracy and Aggression Volume IV, 1946, Document No. 1583–PS)

In this letter, Himmler was referring to German women who were used as prostitutes in the camps. Overall, though, little evidence of forced prostitution was actually presented at the Nuremberg trial. According to Insa Eschebach, the director of the Ravensbrück Memorial Museum, 'Hardly any other topic from the history of the concentration camps has ... been kept so quiet and repressed and is ... so tainted with prejudice and distortion, as the forced prostitution of female camp inmates for male camp inmates by the SS' (quoted in Spiegel Online International 2007; see also Beck 2002; Snyder 2007; Szobar 2002). One of the few female witnesses at Nuremberg, Marie Claude Valliant-Couturier, however, did testify about forced prostitution and the behaviour of the SS towards the women in Auschwitz and Ravensbrück concentration camps. Valliant-Couturier was a member of the French Resistance. She was arrested and taken to Auschwitz in 1943, and later transferred to Ravensbrück. In her testimony (dated 28 January 1946), she described the horrors inflicted on the women in the camps:

MME. VAILLANT-COUTURIER:   At Auschwitz there was a brothel for the SS and also one for the male internees of the staff, who were called 'Kapo'. Moreover, when the SS needed servants, they came accompanied by the Oberaufseherin, that is, the woman commandant of the camp, to make a choice during the process of disinfection. They would point to a young girl, whom the Oberaufseherin would take out of the ranks. They would look her over and make jokes about her physique; and if she was pretty and they liked her, they would hire her as a maid with the consent of the Oberaufseherin, who would tell her that she was to obey them absolutely no matter what they asked of her.

M. DUBOST:   Why did they go during disinfection?

MME. VAILLANT-COUTURIER:   Because during the disinfection the women were naked.

M. DUBOST:   This system of demoralization and corruption – was it exceptional?

MME. VAILLANT-COUTURIER:   No, the system was identical in all the camps where I have been, and I have spoken to internees coming from camps where I myself had never been; it was the same thing everywhere. The system was identical no matter what the camp was. There were, however, certain variations. I believe that Auschwitz was one of the harshest; but later I went to Ravensbruck, where there also was a house of ill fame and where recruiting was also carried out among the internees.

M. DUBOST:   Then, according to you, everything was done to degrade those women in their own sight?

MME. VAILLANT-COUTURIER:   Yes.

(*IMT*, 1946: 5: 189)

In addition to this scattering of various documents reporting on rape and forced prostitution, the French prosecutor, Charles Dubost, presented evidence of rape at the trial on 31 January 1946. The exhibit was based on the interrogation of the German consul in Marseilles, Von Spiegel, in reference to the German occupation of France during 1944 about the rape of a 21-year-old maid by a German soldier. During his reading, Dubost remarked, 'I will not mention any more of the atrocities described in this document' (*IMT*, 1946: 6: 403). It is unclear whether his reference was to rape or to other atrocities; however, he briefly returned to the subject of rape moments later when he presented the exhibit describing the June 1944 atrocities committed against the population of St Donat: 'The Marquis had evacuated the town several days earlier ... 54 women or young girls from 13 to 50 years of age were raped by the maddened soldiers' (*IMT*, 1946: 6: 404). Yet no further details of these rapes were given. The French prosecutor then declared: 'The Tribunal will forgive me if I avoid citing the atrocious details which follow', describing a couple more rapes in Crest and Saillans, and then saying, 'A medical certificate from Doctor Nicolaides, who examined the women who were raped in this region – I will pass on' (*IMT*, 1946: 6: 404). Moments later, though, the prosecutor described another exhibit, concerning the operation of the German Army in Nice in July 1944, where he again mentioned rape, and then again in another exhibit describing the looting, rape and burnings at Saillans in July and August 1944.

The prosecutor thus explicitly referred to rape on a number of occasions but his seeming indifference and offhand remarks regarding rape crimes have attracted criticism from feminist scholars (Askin 1997; Brownmiller 1976). The suggestion is that at the Nuremberg trial rape was not considered worthy of detailed, serious attention like other atrocities presented in these exhibits. However, reading through the transcript further, it is quite possible that the sheer length of the exhibits made it an onerous task to read all documents into evidence (and at some point during the trial, for instance, Dubost asked the President whether it was necessary to read through whole documents in their entirety). Nonetheless when one considers overall the references to rape at the Nuremberg trial, it does appear that rape was treated in a very similar way to pillaging and looting. In other words, these crimes were viewed as heinous, but not enough on their own to warrant formal prosecution.

The horrors experienced by women during the war were not simply restricted to rape and forced prostitution, and women also experienced other forms of sexual violence. Sterilization, for example, of non-Aryan subjects, formed part of the eugenics ideology of National Socialism and Nazi laws were introduced in January 1934 to sterilize those with hereditary defects or those who were enemies of the state to ensure they would not reproduce.[7] In concentration camps women were sterilized through toxic chemicals secretly placed in their food, the use of x-rays to burn and destroy women's ovaries, and through injections given during general gynecological examinations (see Bock 1983). Between 120 and 140 Roma and Sinti women were sterilized at Ravensbrück in January 1945, duped into signing consent forms after being told that German authorities would release them if they agreed to sterilization (Morrison 2000). Experiments were also carried out at Auschwitz at the Block 10 laboratory by the infamous Dr Carl Clauberg to further the 'racial purity' ideology of National Socialism, with horrifying results. Rosalinde de Leon, a Jewish woman from the Netherlands, for example, testified against Dr Clauberg during the Doctors' trial (held before US military courts after the war) regarding the mass sterilization of women. She told the court that if women did not agree to the scientific experiments, they were told they would be sent to the gas chambers. She herself was sterilized by an injection of a substance into her vagina about three times with breaks of between three and four months (Benedict and Georges 2006). Other women too were sterilized without their knowledge.

The practice of sterilization was captured, albeit briefly, at the Nuremberg trial through Marie Vaillant-Couturier's testimony:

M. DUBOST:  Will you tell us about experiments, if you witnessed any?

MME. VAILLANT-COUTURIER:  As to the experiments, I have seen in the Revier, because I was employed at the Revier [a barrack for sick inmates], the queue of young Jewesses from Salonika who stood waiting in front of the X-ray room for sterilization. I also know that they performed castration operations in the men's camp. Concerning the experiments performed on women I am well informed, because my friend, Doctor Hade Hautval of Montbeliard, who has returned to France, worked for several months in that block nursing the patients; but she always refused to participate in those experiments. They sterilized women either by injections or by operation or with rays. I saw and knew several women who had been sterilized. There was a very high mortality rate among those operated upon. Fourteen Jewesses from France who refused to be sterilized were sent to a Strafarbeit kommando, that is, hard labor.

M. DUBOST:  Did they come back from those kommandos?

MME. VAILLANT-COUTURIER:  Very seldom. Quite exceptionally.

M. DUBOST:  What was the aim of the SS?

MME. VAILLANT-COUTURIER:  Sterilization – they did not conceal it. They said that they were trying to find the best method for sterilizing so as to replace the native population in the occupied countries by Germans after one generation, once they had made use of the inhabitants as slaves to work for them.

M. DUBOST:  In the Revier did you see any pregnant women?

MME. VAILLANT-COUTURIER:  Yes. The Jewish women, when they arrived in the first months of pregnancy, were subjected to abortion. When their pregnancy was near the end, after confinement, the babies were drowned in a bucket of water. I know that because I worked in the Revier and the woman who was in charge of that task was a German midwife, who was imprisoned for having performed illegal operations. After a while another doctor arrived and for 2 months they did not kill the Jewish babies. But one day an order came from Berlin saying that again they had to be done away with. Then the mothers and their babies were called to the infirmary. They were put in a lorry and taken away to the gas chamber.

(*IMT*, 1946: 5: 188)

Despite evidence that corroborated the use of sexual violence, rape, sexual slavery, mutilation and sterilization by German troops, the founding statute of the Nuremberg Tribunal made no specific reference to rape or sexual violence. Most significantly, these crimes were not formally prosecuted (Askin 1997; Tompkins 1995) and the word 'rape' does not appear once in the 179-page Nuremberg judgment (in contrast, the judgment does refer repeatedly to looting and pillaging).[8] The failure of the Nuremberg Tribunal to prosecute sexual violence not only is indicative of the fixation on crimes of aggression, but also points to the status of crimes against women and specifically to crimes of sexual violence during this period. From a historical perspective, there are three ways to interpret this treatment. The first is that while rape and other forms of sexual violence were not prosecuted, a story of sexual violence during the reign of the Nazis, albeit a severely abridged one, nonetheless was told and concretized into public record. The second interpretation is that the Nuremberg Tribunal failed dismally to create a public record of these crimes due to the status of women and rape, and the failure to adequately address the extent of these crimes. As a result, no juridical basis for subsequent international prosecutions was established (Askin 1997). While I accept both these interpretations, there is a third interpretation that may be considered; that is, the silence surrounding sexual violence at the Nuremberg trial *itself tells a story* about war crimes against women. This silence forms part of the collective memory or public narrative of wartime sexual violence which has since – in much later years – been instrumental in putting rape on the international agenda (see Chapter 4).

In comparison to the IMT, at the Tokyo trial the rape of Chinese women during the Nanking invasion was formally prosecuted and explicitly referred to in the judgment. And yet, as at Nuremberg, sexual enslavement was all but completely neglected. As a consequence, the Tokyo trial also failed to adequately address the extent and gravity of wartime sexual violence, despite its prevalence, and despite the general official and public awareness surrounding these crimes. Again as at Nuremberg, this neglect has created a legacy of silence, and has left an indelible mark on the lives and memory of many survivors.

## The Tokyo trial: the Rape of Nanking and the 'comfort women'

On 3 May 1946, the Tokyo trial was convened at Ichigaya Court in Tokyo to try 28 military and political leaders of the Japanese Empire for the same three types of crimes that were tried at Nuremberg (crimes against peace, war crimes and crimes against humanity).[9] Only defendants accused of crimes against peace were tried, although there were numerous other trials for lesser Japanese war criminals (see Piccigallo 1979).

Although rape was not explicitly listed in the Tokyo Charter as a crime against humanity, in contrast to Nuremberg, it was included among the crimes listed in the Tokyo indictment. Also in contrast to Nuremberg, rape charges were in fact brought against Tokyo defendants, tried as 'war crimes' under the 1907 Hague Convention and 1929 Geneva Convention.[10] At the trial, the infamous 'Rape of Nanking' was made known to the world, and numerous witness accounts were heard of mass rapes against Chinese women. Excerpts from one witness's diary were read out:

It is a horrible story to try to relate; I know not where to begin nor to end. Never have I heard or read of such brutality. Rape! Rape! Rape! – We estimate at least 1000 cases a night, and many by day. In case of resistance … there is a bayonet stab or a bullet. We could write up hundreds of cases a day.

(*IMTFE*, 1946: 11: 4467)

Other depositions regarding rape were entered into evidence. According to Wong Pan Sze in her affidavit:

At the time, the Japanese entered the city on December 13, 1937, I and my father and my sister had already been removed to live in a house on Shanghai Road No. 100 which was in the refugee zone. There were about 500 persons living in that house, and I often saw the Japs come to the house asking and searching for women. On one occasion one woman was raped in the open yard. This happened in the night, and all of us could hear her cry while she was being raped … Twice I saw the Japs' truck come to the house and round up women living in the house. These women were taken away by the Japs and none of them returned with the exception of one girl who managed to get back home after having been raped … At this time I was about 15 years of age. I hid every time … and this is why the Japs never caught me.

(*IMTFE*, 1946: 11: 4467–68)

One of the witnesses for the prosecution, Mr John G. Magee, had been a member of the International Committee for the Nanking Safety Zone and the International Red Cross Society. At the trial, he too mentioned rape on numerous occasions:

It was again the same story, unbelievably terrible. The rapings continued day by day. Many women were killed and even children. If a woman resisted or refused, she was either killed or stabbed. I took pictures, moving pictures of the wounds of many of these women – women with their necks slit, stabs all over their bodies … It seemed to us that there were Japanese soldiers in every house after women … If there had been any real effort to stop this conduct, it could have been stopped; but it was looked upon entirely too lightly.

(*IMTFE*, 1946: 11: 4501)

Other parts of Mr Magee's evidence are replete with horrific stories of rape. Evidence submitted by other witnesses told similar stories:

girls dragged off by gangs of four or five men in uniform; abducted women forced to wash clothes for the Army units by day and to 'service' as many as fifteen to forty men at night; women forced to perform sex shows for troops at play; fathers forced at gunpoint to rape their own daughters. Many of the stories had similar endings. When a group of soldiers was finished with a captured woman, a stick was sometimes pushed up into her vagina; in some cases the woman's head was severed.

(Brownmiller 1976: 59)

While no evidence was presented from rape victims specifically, one woman, a victim of attempted rape, gave a statement that was presented as an exhibit to the court. It reads as follows:

four Japanese soldiers came to my home ... about four in the afternoon. They were about to rape me and three of them forcibly unclothed me, as to upper part of my apparel, and at that time my husband came to protect me and he was instantly kicked to death. My children were in the same room, and were crying. My children were 2 months and 4 years of age. They did not rape me after killing my husband but left the house.

(*IMTFE*, 1946: 11: 4498)

Several defendants were found guilty of war crimes, which included rape. Serving as Commander-in-Chief of the Central China Area Army (CCAA) during the Nanking invasion, General Matsui was sentenced to death for the atrocities committed under his command. The Tribunal concluded that Matsui was guilty of war crimes, because he 'knew what was happening ... [but] did nothing, or nothing effective to abate these horrors' (IMTFE Judgment, 1948: 103: 49815–16; see also Parks 1973).[11] Matsui's defence was to claim lack of responsibility for the 'discipline and morals of the troops'. He declared that the reports of rape were mere rumours – of 'Chinese passing on the information, perhaps in fun' (quoted in Brownmiller 1976: 61).

The evidence regarding the brutal rapes that occurred during the invasion was sufficient to lead the Tribunal to find approximately 20,000 cases of rape occurring during the first month of occupation:

There were many cases of rape. Death was a frequent penalty for the slightest resistance on the part of a [victim] or the members of her family who sought to protect her. Even girls of tender years and old women were raped in large numbers throughout the city, and many cases of abnormal and sadistic behavior in connection with these rapings occurred. Many women were killed after the act and their bodies mutilated. Approximately 20,000 cases of rape occurred within the city during the first month of the occupation.

(*IMTFE* Judgment, 1945: 103: 1012–19)

A number of scholars have since praised the Tribunal's treatment of rape crimes. For example, despite her scathing critique of the political and legal discourse on wartime rape, Brownmiller (1976: 58) writes:

Rape in Nanking might have passed out of history then and there, relegated in typical fashion to the dubious area of unsupported wartime rumor. But as it turned out, the Allied Powers elected to hold an International Military Tribunal for the Far East once the global war was finished.

She adds, 'Had it not been for the Tokyo war-crimes tribunal, who would have believed the full dimensions of the Rape of Nanking?' (ibid.: 61–2). Likewise, Kelly Askin (1997: 202) reasons that 'One of the most positive aspects of the Tokyo Trials was its inclusion of rape, albeit secondarily, as a serious war crime meriting inclusion in the prosecution's cases'.

The prosecution of rape at the Tokyo trial no doubt marked a symbolic deviation from the historical silence surrounding these crimes. It stands in contrast to the Nuremberg Tribunal's failure to prosecute rape. This attention signified that rape was a crime of historical importance. However, while it is necessary to acknowledge this juridical outcome, it is also important to focus on the shortcomings or silences of both the Tokyo and Nuremberg trials in reference to rape crimes. There are essentially two silenced narratives that can be identified through a close examination of both trials. The first is the silence surrounding the systematic sexual enslavement of hundreds of thousands of comfort women across Asia by the Japanese military, and the silence around Nazi, Russian and Allied rapes. And the second silence refers to the fact that no victims of rape were called to testify before either trial.

## The silent witness

International humanitarian law regulates the rules of armed conflict and thereby purports to protect civilians and combatants against the scourge and savagery of warfare. Although international courts try individuals for serious violations of these laws, generally justice for victims is not the priority of courts in the aftermath of armed conflict. This was most certainly the case for the Nuremberg and Tokyo trials, where the very architecture of 'justice' was premised on victory for the victors and punishment for the vanquished. Justice was located in 'the outcome of the conflict' (Kant quoted in Bass 2002: 9) and power politics – both nation-state politics and gender politics – determined the entire configuration of both trials (see Kirchheimer 1961). Political factors thus contributed to the absence or failure of prosecution for crimes of sexual violence. From the outset, for example, the Tokyo trial was committed to trying major Japanese war criminals for crimes against peace. As a result, the trial has been heavily criticized as an imperialist exercise of 'victor's justice'.[12] At the beginning of the trial, the Chief Prosecutor of the Tokyo Tribunal, Joseph B. Keenan, issued a press statement, saying: 'it is high time … that the promoters of aggressive, ruthless war and treaty-breakers should be stripped of the glamour of national heroes and exposed as what they really are – plain, ordinary murderers' (quoted in Schick 1947: 55). This statement reflected a myopic focus on vilifying Japan for waging an aggressive war, which, in the process, served to vindicate the Allied powers for their part in the war. In 1948, Tojo Hideki, the former Prime Minister of Japan (and Tokyo defendant) declared, 'In the last analysis, this trial was a political trial. It was only victors' justice' (quoted in Bass 2002: 8).

Justice Robert H. Jackson's epic opening speech at the Nuremberg trial also captures the essence of victor's justice:

> The privilege of opening the first trial in history for crimes against the peace of the world imposes a grave responsibility. The wrongs which we seek to condemn and punish have been so calculated, so malignant, and so devastating, that civilization cannot tolerate their being ignored, because it cannot survive their being repeated.
>
> (quoted in Taylor 1955: 503–4)

For a number of interconnected reasons, rape was also a victim of victor's justice at Tokyo and Nuremberg, even though the Tokyo Tribunal did actually prosecute rape crimes.[13] An examination of both trials reflects the political nature of successor proceedings during this period. In both trials, rape did not fit the dominant discourse of post-conflict justice, nor did it conform to the political will of the victors. The systematic sexual enslavement of the comfort women, for example, may not have been – at least in the eyes of the prosecutors – 'political enough' to warrant serious attention at these proceedings. Because victory in warfare is an overly masculinized concept, victor's justice was also marked by the absence of gender justice. Women were thus the silent witnesses of this historic period, and although narratives of rape were sometimes utilized (as shown above), this was usually only as a way to bolster political and often nationalistic goals from all sides of the conflict.[14]

The victor's justice narrative forms part of the collective memory of the Nuremberg and Tokyo trials, to such an extent that it has become somewhat of a cliché – a phrase that many scholars have since interrogated and critiqued (see e.g. McCormack 1997; McCormack and Simpson 1997). Gary Jonathan Bass (2002: 16) argues that the term is not a particularly informative one and he asks 'not whether we are looking at victors' justice [we probably are] ... But *which* victor? And what justice?' (emphasis original).

### The victors

The nationality of the victors, specifically those nations that were represented at both trials, helps to explain attention or lack thereof to rape crimes. Some scholars have argued that the prosecution of sexual violence was avoided because this would bring attention to similar crimes committed by the Allied troops (Neier 1998). Askin (1997: 163) too argues that rape crimes were not effectively prosecuted at either Nuremberg or Tokyo trial because:

> the Allies wanted to limit the prosecution of the Nazis and Japanese for crimes which were not likewise committed by the Allied troops, namely, mass extermination and crimes against peace, and not for crimes which were regularly committed by Axis and Allied troops alike – most notably rape crimes.

*[handwritten margin note: cannot prosecute rape because it is not unique to one side as genocide was...]*

As mentioned above, the lengthy depositions submitted by the Russian foreign minister regarding German rapes of Russian women challenge the notion that rapes were purposely ignored because all parties were guilty of similar atrocities. This is particularly relevant since the Russians committed wholesale rapes against German women towards the end of the war, suggesting that rape was only considered abhorrent if committed by the defeated powers. Reference to rape was also relatively frequent throughout the Tokyo trial, and as such it is unlikely that avoidance was due to the Allies' own complicity in such crimes (Dolgopol 1995). My interpretation is rather that distinctions were made between *different forms* of rape. In other words, rape was seen as qualitatively different when committed by aggressive defeated nations, as will be further argued below.

There was a somewhat frenzied attention to rape during the Second World War, but afterwards at the historic trials the fixation on defendants and their culpability meant that victims and the crimes committed against them were granted minimal consideration in general (Taylor 1992). Victims were over-looked because the Allies were committed to vilifying German and Japanese military and political personnel of the highest ranks. The purpose behind the establishment of these tribunals was criminal responsibility and not victim rehabilitation.[15] Moreover, women's experiences of sexual violence were treated as peripheral not only to the main defendants, but also to the war in general.

When rape was mentioned at both trials, it was often used as an instrument to highlight the heroism of one side, pitted against the barbarity of the enemy. The metaphor of the 'raped nation' during the Nuremberg trial for example was used to describe the invasion of European nations and cities (e.g. the 'rape of' Czechoslovakia, Prague, the Netherlands, Belgium and Austria). In a similar vein, the rape of women was also raised to expound the gallantry of armed forces. As mentioned above, the Molotov Note at Nuremberg appeared to specifically use rape to highlight the barbarity of the enemy and the heroism of the victor nations. Here is another example:

> In the fight by our troops for the liberation of the city of Kalinin, units of the German 303rd Regiment, 162d Division, attempting to launch a counter-attack, assembled the women of one of the suburban villages,

placed them in the vanguard of their troops, and then went into action. *Fortunately the Soviet troops succeeded, when beating off the attack, in driving a wedge between the Hitlerites and their victims thereby saving the lives of the women.*

> (*IMT*, 1946: 7: 40, emphasis added)

The topic of rape was also used to defend the Nazis on trial at Nuremberg. For example, defence counsel Dr Laternser asked the defence witness Erich von Manstein how military discipline was observed. His response was as follows:

We exercised military jurisdiction as we had to do according to our training, in other words, according to the right and law and as decent soldiers. I should like to quote as an example that the first two death sentences with which I had to deal were imposed at the beginning of the Russian campaign on two German soldiers in my corps for the rape of Russian women, and it was the same everywhere.

> (*IMT*, 1946: 20: 609)

Similarly, the Nazi defendant Hermann Goering was examined by defence counsel Dr Stahmer at Nuremberg and the following reveals his deliberate effort to condemn the crime of rape:

DR STAHMER:  What was your attitude as the highest judicial authority of the Luftwaffe with regard to punishable acts committed by the soldiers under you in occupied territory?

GOERING:  As highest judicial authority I had all the bad cases referred to me and spent many hours examining them. That is why I attach particular importance to the highest legal counsel of the Air Force by being heard here on this point. In many cases I rescinded sentences because they were too mild, *especially if it was a matter of rape*. In these cases I always confirmed the death sentence which had been handed down by the court, unless an appeal for mercy was made by the injured party in exceptional cases. I thus confirmed the death sentence of a number of members of the Air Force who took part in the murder of inhabitants of the occupied territories in the East as well as in the West.

> (*IMT*, 1946: 9: 360, emphasis added)

On another day during the trial, Goering remarked: 'as regards rape … I always punished with death even if committed against citizens of enemy states' (*IMT*, 1946: 9: 563). Although of course Goering belonged to the defeated nation, in general the treatment of rape as one of the most serious crimes deserving the most serious of punishments stands in stark contrast to the failure of the historic trials to try crimes in this same way.

At the Tokyo trial, lawyers for the defence also expressed disgust at the crime of rape, but used a different strategy – that of minimization, denial and blame. For example:

> As to the charge of raping, we admit that there were some imprudent youths among the troops then in China, who committed this shameful crime during the existing excitement. Among the cases so reported, some were, however, *the result of approach by Chinese girls to the Japanese soldiers.* When discovered, they accused the Japanese of forcing them. The Japanese Army was strict in the punishment of violators of women, and it is unthinkable that, though there might have been some who were imprudent enough, it was done systematically by a large number.
>
> (*IMTFE*, 1946: 128: 46969–7347, emphasis added)

In another example that likewise blames Chinese women, an affidavit of Sekijiro Ogawa, the Chief of Legal Affairs Section of the Tenth Army, was read into evidence:

> Before I came to Nanking, I dealt with about twenty cases of offenses on military discipline and public morals. In the course of my dealing with the crimes of public morals, I found it very difficult to decide whether the cases were fornication or violation. *The reason was that it was not rare on the part of the Chinese women to take a suggestive attitude towards Japanese soldiers, and when they were found as having committed adultery with Japanese soldiers by their husbands or other people, they suddenly changed their attitude and asserted exaggeratedly that they had been raped.*
>
> (*IMTFE*, 1946: 32676, emphasis added)

The strategy of blaming the victim for complicity in sexual violence has been all too familiar in both domestic and international courts, and this is dealt with in greater detail in subsequent chapters. My point here is that rape throughout history has been drawn upon not simply to raise the status of victim nations during armed conflict, but to construct a narrative of victorious masculinity, as opposed to any concern or understanding for women's human rights (Brownmiller 1976). In the aftermath of the Second World War, the exploitation of wartime rape as propaganda consolidated the idiosyncratic status of rape during this era. Propaganda was employed specifically to rouse up old antagonisms against enemy forces, yet paradoxically rape ultimately served to undermine the credibility of reports of sexual violence (ibid.). At the end of the Second World War, when scholars sought to define the truth of atrocities, rape was often viewed as unsupported wartime rumour and propaganda assisted in denying that women had been raped, combined with the understandable reluctance of women to come forward with their stories (ibid.). As Brownmiller (1976: 47) remarks, 'The crime that is by reputation "the easiest to charge and the hardest to prove" has traditionally been the *easiest to disprove* as well' (emphasis original). This is part of what I will call (to use a cliché) the 'politics of wartime rape' because these examples point to the use and manipulation of rape for explicit political purposes, such as nationalism and the further entrenchment of victory and of victor's justice, regardless of side.

Victor's justice must also be explained through the lens of colonialism, racism and the self-interest of the victorious nations. This too played a large part in determining which crimes were addressed at both trials. This was particularly so at the Tokyo trial, evidenced by the fact that women who were sexually enslaved in military brothels were mainly Asian women whose countries were not represented at these proceedings. The 11 male prosecutors and the panel of 11 male judges that presided over the Tribunal were representative of the following Allied powers: Australia, Canada, China, France, India, the Netherlands, New Zealand, the Philippines, the Soviet Union, the United Kingdom and the United States. According to Richard Minear (1971: 75–6), 'the principle that stood firm was that the justices were nationals of the countries that had suffered from Japanese activity. There were no justices from neutral nations'. The hundreds of thousands of rape victims across Asia, on the other hand, came from Korea, China, Japan, the Philippines, Thailand, Vietnam, Malaysia, Taiwan, the Dutch East Indies, the Netherlands, Burma, Indonesia and some other Japanese-occupied territories. The vast majority of victims were Korean women, and yet Korea, as well as most of the countries listed here, was not represented at the Tribunal. Had women from the Allied power countries been sexually enslaved in brothels, it is quite possible that forced prostitution would have received more attention at Tokyo.

A large number of comfort women came from China; however, in the Tokyo judgment there is only one reference to forced prostitution in the Chinese city of Kweilin, which reads as follows:

> After the Japanese forces had occupied Changsha, they also freely indulged in murder, rape, incendiarism and many other atrocities throughout the district. Then they drove further down southward to Kweilin and Liuchow in Kwangsi Province. During the period of Japanese occupation of Kweilin, they committed all kinds of atrocities such as rape and plunder. They recruited women labor on the pretext of establishing factories. They forced the women thus recruited into prostitution with Japanese troops.
>
> (*IMTFE* Judgment, 1948: 103: 1022)

Thus, for Chinese representatives at Tokyo, the focus was on the rapes of Nanking and not on the sexual enslavement of women in brothels. In relation to the Philippines, Minear (1971: 86) argues that the Filipino judge 'was so totally Americanized'[16] and, as such, the crimes committed against the Filipino population were largely ignored during the trial. This may explain the similar lack of attention to rape crimes against Filipino women.

*[handwritten margin note: Victims not represented by authorities at trials]*

Also, while in fact evidence of sexual slavery was actually presented before the Tokyo trial, the Netherlands failed to ensure the prosecution of these crimes. This is most likely because such crimes took place in the Dutch colonies and not in the Netherlands proper. Interestingly, two years later in 1948, the Netherlands did in fact institute its own proceedings against forced prostitution in Batavia, but only in relation to Dutch women and not native Indonesian women. This trial concerned the treatment of 35 Dutch women living in Indonesia who had been forced into sexual servitude by the Japanese. It was the only known trial for forced prostitution and no such trial was conducted for the thousands of other local Indonesian women also forcibly recruited to service the Japanese soldiers. According to George Hicks (1995: 228), 'Indonesian women who were also captured for comfort stations did not figure in the Batavia trials, a reflection of racist bias just as the failure of the Allies to try those responsible for the comfort system is a reflection of sexism'. The Batavia trials and the Tokyo trial thus created a hierarchy of victims based on gender, class, race and national identity.

In April 2007, historian Yoshiaki Yoshimi and the Center for Research and Documentation on Japan's War Responsibility (JWRC) uncovered several official documents revealing evidence of forced sexual slavery and direct Japanese military involvement presented before the Tokyo Tribunal (see Center for Research and Documentation on Japan's War Responsibility 2007).[17] Yoshimi's findings challenge the prior assumptions about the trial: that no evidence was presented at the Tokyo trial regarding sexual enslavement. The documents identified by Yoshimi were used for the sentencing of defendants for war crimes. In one of the exhibits submitted by the Dutch prosecution, the brothels in western Borneo were documented as follows:

> The brothel for Naval personnel [was] run by the garrison. Under the C.O. the signal Officer, Lt. SUGASAWA AKINORI was placed in charge and the daily business was attended to by the duty warrant ... Women who had had relations with Japanese were forced into these brothels, which were surrounded in barbed wire. They were only allowed on the streets with special permission. Permission to quit the brothel had to be obtained from the garrison commander. The Special Naval Police (Tokei Tai) had ordered to keep the brothels supplied with women; to this end they arrested women on the streets and after enforced medical examination placed them in the brothels.
> (Tribunal Exhibit No. 1702: Prosecution Document No. 5330)

This exhibit clearly points to sexual enslavement since these women were arrested in the streets and thereafter underwent forced medical examination before being placed in the brothels. In another exhibit:

> In their search for women the Tokei Tai ordered the entire female staffs of the Minseibu and the Japanese firms to report to the Tokei Tai Office,

undressed some of them entirely and accused them of maintaining relations with Japanese. The ensuing medical examination revealed that several were virgins. It is not known with certainty how many of these unfortunates were forced into brothels. Women did not dare to escape from the brothels as members of their family were then immediately arrested and severely maltreated by the Tokei Tai. In one case it is known that this caused the death of the mother of the girl concerned.

(Tribunal Exhibit No. 1702: Prosecution Document No. 5330)

In yet another exhibit based on a statement from Lt Ohara Seidai, the commander of Moa Island in Indonesia in September 1944, sexual enslavement was once again used as part of the evidence:

Q:  How were the men killed?
A:  They were lined up in threes in column of route and then the 21 soldiers mentioned above charged them with bayonets, killing three at a time.
Q:  A witness has said that you raped women and that women were brought to the barracks and used by the Japs. Is this true?
A:  I organized a brothel for the soldiers and used it myself.
Q:  Were the women willing to go into the brothel?
A:  Some were willing, some were not.
Q:  How many women were there?
A:  Six.
Q:  How many of these women were forced into the brothel?
A:  Five.
Q:  How were these women forced into the brothel?
A:  They were daughters of the men who attacked the KEMPEI TAI.
Q:  Then these women were forced into the brothels as a punishment for the deeds of their fathers.
A:  Yes.
Q:  For how long were these women kept in the brothel?
A:  For eight months.
Q:  How many men used this brothel?
A:  Twenty-five.

(Tribunal Exhibit No. 1794: Prosecution Document No. 5591)

In sum, these recently uncovered exhibits clearly point to a system of forced prostitution within the Japanese military, challenging previously held notions that sexual enslavement was completely ignored at the Tokyo trial. Nonetheless, the evidence of sexual enslavement was presented by the victor nations (France, the Netherlands and China) only in relation to *their* colonies/nations; namely, Vietnam (Fr), Indonesia (N), East Timor (N) and China (Ch). This of course did not in any way amount to justice for the war's many rape victims since sexual enslavement was not prosecuted as a crime before the Tokyo trial.

*Whose justice?*

In addition to examining the ways in which victory determined which crimes were prosecuted and the very nature of these prosecutions, the second component of the victor's justice equation concerns the question of 'whose justice?' The first thing to note is that the prosecutors relied heavily on written documentation as opposed to live victim testimony at both trials. Since the 1990s, transitional justice mechanisms for dealing with past atrocities have embraced restorative justice approaches that have placed victims at the centre of justice (e.g. truth commissions and even war crimes courts). However, the prosecutors at Nuremberg and Tokyo had little interest in providing a space for victims to disclose their traumatic experiences. Mark Osiel (2000) argues that the emphasis on prosecuting the top political elites meant that courts bypassed the personal stories of victims, including those having experienced rape, biological warfare and vivisection. In other words, the failure of historical war crimes trials to prosecute rape crimes reflects not only a failure to appreciate the impact of injury on rape victims, but a lack of appreciation concerning the injuries inflicted on *victims in general*. Witnesses were overlooked because 'they did not factor into the larger political debates at the time, especially in Germany and Japan, where the very legitimacy of the trials was hotly contested' (Stover 2005: 18).

In total there were only 30 prosecution witnesses who gave evidence of the atrocities in Nanking at the Tokyo trial and 20 of these individuals had submitted written affidavits and were thus absent witnesses (Sedgwick 2008). At Nuremberg, the prosecutors had full access to 100,000 captured German archives (4,000 of which were entered as trial exhibits), as well as reports from national commissions that had heard approximately 55,000 witnesses, of which the Tribunal used 143 written interrogations (Douglas 2001). In total there were only 33 prosecution witnesses and 61 defence witnesses (in addition to 19 of the defendants) called to give evidence at the Nuremberg trial out of a total of 94 witnesses. Significantly, no victims of rape were called to testify at either of these proceedings.[18] Witnesses, especially female witnesses, played a small role at both the Nuremberg and Tokyo trials. As mentioned above, one of the few female witnesses at Nuremberg who testified to the atrocities in the concentration camps was Marie Claude Vaillant-Couturier.

Second, the politics of prosecuting leading Nazi and Japanese war criminals for crimes against peace was a determining factor in the inclusion and exclusion of various crimes at these proceedings. The categories of both war crimes and crimes against humanity were given less attention than the crimes against peace (crimes of aggression) charges. Crimes against humanity were considered distinct from 'war crimes' since crimes of the former could be committed before *and* during armed conflict, whereas the latter could occur only during conflict. Crimes against humanity thus potentially covered those crimes committed by a sovereign state against its own citizens, regardless of whether or not the domestic laws of that state at the time permitted these crimes, as was the case in Nazi Germany. In a sense then, writes Lawrence Douglas (2001: 47), the labelling of crimes against humanity was an innovative response 'to the unprecedented nature of Nazi crimes against the Jews'. But crimes against humanity were actually given little attention at the Nuremberg trial. Hannah Arendt's (1994) explanation was that there was difficulty in connecting these crimes to war, since these atrocities took place before the war had even begun. Arendt (1994: 258) states that in effect crimes against humanity conflicted with the war crimes and crimes against peace categories 'gauged by the fact that the only defendant to be condemned to death on a crime-against-humanity charge alone was Julius Streicher'.[19]

Thus, rigid restrictions applied to prosecuting individuals for crimes against humanity, and under the jurisdiction of the Nuremberg Tribunal, crimes against humanity, such as murder and extermination, needed to be connected to either crimes against peace or war crimes. According to Douglas (2001: 196), while the Final Solution was treated as 'a kind of war crime, an offense born of the poisonous business of aggressive war', the Nuremberg Tribunal 'reached the famous conclusion that prewar atrocities against the Jews did not fall within its jurisdictional competence' (ibid.: 49).

There was potential scope for the prosecution of rape crimes under the categories of crimes against humanity and war crimes, but rape was not considered a characteristic Nazi crime since rape violated the Nuremberg racial laws that forbade sexual intercourse between Gentiles and Jews (see Burds 2009). Hitler expelled men who raped Jewish women from the Nazi party and turned them over to civil courts (Shirer 1960). This did not mean, however, that rape and other forms of sexual violence did not occur against Jewish women, as indeed they did; rather, it is likely that the Allies did not consider rape by the Nazis in the same way as rape by Japanese soldiers. Moreover, as mentioned above, given the difficulty in prosecuting the crimes of the Holocaust, proving rape crimes were intricately connected to crimes against peace presented another major obstacle. This was in large part also because rape had historically been treated as an incidental by-product of warfare.

Similarly, at Tokyo, although some defendants were charged with conventional war crimes, all were primarily on trial for planning or waging an aggressive war.[20] Conventional war crimes – ordering, authorizing or permitting atrocities (Count 54), or disregarding the duty to uphold the laws of war (Count 55) – played a *secondary* role to that of crimes against peace. Rape was considered politically and legally significant only where it could be used as part of the evidence against the accused. Subsequently, rape was prosecuted only alongside other war crimes perpetrated during the Nanking invasion. And most significantly, of course, the systematic sexual enslavement of comfort women was not prosecuted at all. This was arguably because it was seen as altogether separate from the charge of waging an aggressive war.

In summary, political factors determined the process and outcome of the two war crimes trials. This helps to explain why rape victims did not appear as witnesses at the proceedings; why rape was not tried as a separate crime in relation to the Nanking invasion and in other areas throughout Europe and Asia; and why the sexual enslavement of comfort women and the rapes of many other women during the Second World War were ignored. The victor's justice thesis cannot alone explain this silence, and the deeply entrenched patriarchal and gendered nature of legal discourse must also be examined here to get a clearer story of wartime rape within this historic context.[21]

## The unspeakability/inevitability paradox of wartime rape

Rape has the curious and somewhat paradoxical status of being considered both an unspeakable and inevitable crime. Paradoxically, unspeakability and inevitability are part of the silence that continues to envelop rape and the experiences of victims. On the one hand, rape is seen as shocking the conscience of humanity; for example, Arnold Brackman, a 23-year-old United Press staff correspondent covering the Tokyo trial, asked: 'Is gang rape worse than beheading? Given the evidence I listened to at the IMTFE, the answer would appear to be *yes*' (quoted in Askin 1997: 164, emphasis original). On the other hand, the prevalence of rape has frequently been minimized as merely part of the usual conduct of soldiers in war and the scant attention to rape at both trials is indicative of this status. For centuries, women have been viewed as 'booty' or as reward for soldiers fighting in battles. According to Brownmiller (1976: 32):

> Women ... are [seen as] simply regrettable victims – incidental unavoidable casualties – like civilian victims of bombing, lumped together with children, homes, personal belongings, a church, a dike, a water buffalo or next year's crop.

She adds, 'It's funny about man's attitude toward rape in war. *Unquestionably* there shall be some raping. Unconscionable, but nevertheless inevitable' (ibid.: 31, emphasis original).

While it is heartening that the Tokyo judgment refers explicitly to rape (especially compared to Nuremberg), the judgment nonetheless reflects the paradox of unspeakability/inevitability:

> Death was a frequent penalty for the slightest resistance on the part of a victim or the members of her family who sought to protect her. Even girls of tender years and old women were raped in large numbers throughout the city, and many cases of abnormal or sadistic behavior in connection with the rapings occurred. Many women were killed after the act and their bodies mutilated ... The barbarous behavior of the Japanese army *cannot be excused as the acts of a soldiery which had temporarily gotten out of hand when at last a stubbornly defended position had*

*capitulated* – rape, arson and murder continued to be committed on a large scale for at least six weeks after the city had been taken.

(*IMTFE* Judgment, 1948: 103: 1012–19, emphasis added)

My argument here is that both tribunals adopted a hierarchical stance toward different types of rape; between what may be labelled as 'unjustifiable rape' and 'justifiable rape'. The judgment above represents the Tokyo Tribunal's view that, after capitulation, rape might be expected or even excused under these special circumstances. This would constitute 'justifiable rape', whereas large-scale forms of rape as part of an aggressive war constitute 'unjustifiable rape'. This sets up a hierarchy of victims based on the timing and nature of the rapes. In other words, those men who rape due to out-of-hand soldiery in advance of final surrender are to be excused for their behaviour. Presumably this would encompass the Russian rapes of German women at the end of the war, as well as the rapes committed by the Allied soldiers in the occupied areas. On the other hand, using the Tribunal's logic, if after capitulation women continue to be raped, these rapes must then be considered 'barbarous' and inexcusable. This is part of the victor's justice phenomenon mentioned above: while the Allies did not set up military brothels or conduct rapes on the scale of the Japanese military (Brownmiller 1976), what Japanese soldiers did to women in Nanking was viewed as qualitatively different to the rapes perpetrated by Russian and Allied troops during the war.

In addition to a hierarchy of victims based on race, gender and national identity, class also played a role in the determination of the gravity of crimes. For example, the civilians left behind in Nanking during the Japanese invasion were mostly from the poorer classes. Indeed, the reports filed at the time and then entered into evidence during the Tokyo trial rarely mentioned the names of Chinese victims. The evidence at the trial reveals a hierarchy of victims based on both class and race. For example, Items No. 13 and 12 may be compared:

At 10 p.m. on the night of December 14, a Chinese home on Chien Ying Hsiang was entered by 11 Japanese soldiers who raped four Chinese women. On December 14, Japanese soldiers entered the home of Miss Grace Bauer, an American missionary, and took a pair of fur-lined gloves, drank up all the milk on the table, and scooped up sugar with their hands.

(quoted in ibid.: 60)

Moreover, the Tokyo judgment set up a victim hierarchy based on victim characteristics and behaviour. Women forced, lured and coerced into brothels against their will were arguably considered less authentic or worthy victims. Examining the words contained within the judgment above, the 'authentic victim subject' (Kapur 2002) includes the 'girls of tender years', older women, as well as women who were killed after being raped. But scores of women had been rounded up, put into brothels and then repeatedly gang-raped for prolonged periods of time, some suffering multiple rapes per day over many years. This hierarchy of victimhood in part helps to explain the subsequent judicial silence regarding rape and sexual enslavement within both courts.

The failure of the Nuremberg and Tokyo trials to prosecute rape and sexual enslavement, and the significant omission of women's voices at these proceedings, is also indicative of the public/private status of rape. Rape and other forms of sexual violence were frequently viewed as 'private' experiences and, particularly in the post-Second World War environment, rape was not considered an appropriate subject for a public forum, let alone an international war crimes trial (Bassiouni 1999) – unless used for political and nationalistic purposes. The taboo and silence surrounding sexual violence were a product of a code of morality and chastity (Hicks 1995). This was despite the widespread knowledge of rape during this period. While a minority opinion, Justice Pal's dissent to the verdict of the Tokyo trial regarding allegations of rape in Nanking is illuminative of prevalent attitudes surrounding reports of rape. Pal stated in his dissent: 'I am not sure if we are not here getting accounts of events witnessed only by excited or prejudiced observers' (quoted in Askin 1997: 184). Pal found a number of witnesses unreliable, citing that instead of rape these incidents may 'be accepted as instances of misbehaviour on the part of the Japanese soldiers with the Chinese women' (quoted in ibid.: 184). Askin writes that this attitude was 'consistent with the patriarchal notion that gender crimes, including sex crimes, are mere minor infractions [to be blamed on] … promiscuous women' (ibid.). Of course, dissenting and incongruous positions are also part of the overall story or collective memory of traumatic histories (Simpson 2007).

The legal necessity to prove consent in historical and contemporary contexts represents a persistent judicial obstacle for women seeking justice in both domestic and international jurisdictions. During war, there may be a blurred distinction between rape and prostitution, what Brownmiller (1976: 75) calls the 'murky line that divides wartime rape from wartime prostitution'. The establishment of comfort stations across Asia and the label of 'military prostitutes' had the effect of morally reconstructing the reprehensible act of sexual enslavement into complicit victim participation and collaboration. And so in order to avoid problems of rape, the Tokyo Tribunal heard evidence that company commander instructions for rape in Nanking were as follows: 'In order that we won't have problems, either pay [the women] money or kill them in some obscure place after you have finished' (*IMTFE*, 1948: 1023). Askin (1997) argues that because the comfort women were incorporated into a prostitution system, their experiences were not considered as serious as other forms of rape and in fact some Allied documents referred to the comfort women as 'camp followers' (Dolgopol 1995).

The status of rape and wartime rape cannot be separated from the status of women during this period. This helps to explain why the historic tribunals failed to adequately prosecute rape crimes. In war and in law, women were peripheral, or, as Brownmiller (1976: 32) claims, 'irrelevant to the world that counts, passive spectators to the action in the center ring'. Not only was discrimination against women strikingly evident during the Second World War itself, but in the aftermath of the conflict and during the post-war trials the gendered nature of law meant that the international community appeared more concerned with violations against men than harms typically experienced by women (Askin 1997). It may be argued that even when the evidence of sexual violence was heard at Nuremberg and Tokyo, it was based on the damage done to masculine conceptions of identity and nationhood. Vesna Nikolić-Ristanović (2000: 79), for example, argues that 'rape is understood as a crime against a particular ethnic community, against women as a form of male property, and not as a crime against the female body, against the woman as an individual'. The exclusion or absence of women as witnesses, and from policy and judicial decision-making mechanisms, further contributed to this gender inequality and to the ensuing silence on rape.[22]

It was not until the feminist movement from the 1960s that women began talking about their experiences of rape and other forms of gender violence. The lack of conceptual formulation regarding rape due to the 'invisible' physical and psychological wounds inflicted by acts of sexual aggression has assisted in historically diminishing the gravity of sexual crimes (Bassiouni 1999). Vera Mackie (2000: 49) argues that there was a failure to recognize that such private matters were in fact 'deeply implicated in political relationships'. As a consequence, following the Second World War most rape survivors were afforded no avenue for justice and, for a time, the stories were relegated to the abyss of history (see Chinkin 2001; Dolgopol 1995; McDougall 1998). In the words of one survivor: 'I felt like a living corpse. When soldiers came to my room and did it to me one after another, it was done to a lifeless body. Again. And again. And again … All these years I have lived in secret, in shame and in pain' (quoted in Schellstede 2000: 51). That it has taken 50 years for women to come forward about their experiences of rape and enslavement demonstrates the resilience of the culture of silence surrounding wartime sexual violence.

## History under siege

Rape is a profoundly private, individualized experience of bodily violation, and yet it is also highly politicized and collectivized at certain points in time. In some contexts, rape has been used as a way to build a shared or communal tragedy that binds a nation or group of people. Therefore, although a staggering silence has come to define wartime rape, nonetheless that has not precluded the subject of rape from forming part of collective memory or memories in a variety of complex ways. The mass rapes that occurred during the Nanking invasion in 1937, for example, have become part of the national memory in China. Likewise, the systematic sexual enslavement of Korean women now forms a dominant narrative of Korean suffering at the hands of the Japanese during the Second World War. In a different way, the rape of Berlin women by Russian soldiers has also become part of the collective memory of the Second World War.[23] In all these examples, much controversy surrounds the memory of wartime rape. Rape is often viewed as a private experience, and yet paradoxically it has exceptional political ramifications, particularly in collective memory terms. The main question I am interested in here is the role that the war crimes trials play in the formation of these collective memories.

Wartime rape enters the realm of the political when it becomes utilized for the explicit political purposes of nation building. This should come as no surprise since the politicization of memory is evident in most other shared tragedies that both connect and divide certain groups of people, yielding intense political controversies over historical 'truth' and accuracy. Specifically, a number of studies have documented the ways in which unspeakable memories or 'difficult pasts' are repressed or suppressed in post-conflict societies (many of which are Holocaust studies). Studies have explored the notion of contested memories; the divisive memories which stir controversy and emotion, for example the genocide of Armenians by Turks during the Ottoman Empire (Hovannisian 1998); the systematic rape, slaughter and pillage of the Nanking population in 1937 (Li, Sabella and Liu 2002), and the 1995 Srebrenica massacre in Bosnia (Judah 2009), to name a few. Examples of both unspeakable and contested events demonstrate the complexity of memory and competing truths in the aftermath of conflict (see Hodgkin and Radstone 2003). In particular, rape is one of the many highly contested and divisive issues that continue to cause much political animosity, despite having been perpetrated a half-century ago. My aim is not to invalidate survivor narratives or memories of rape, torture and mass murder, but rather to point out that memory – because of its tenuous and temporal nature – is vulnerable to much contestation and controversy. This explains why survivors of wartime rape, for example, often suffer their memories in silence for fear that their stories will not be believed. Thus below I aim to reflect on the legacy of silence to make sense of contemporary understandings of wartime rape as they have been shaped by the Nuremberg and Tokyo trials.

### The rape wars

A war crimes trial, writes Osiel (2000: 2), 'indelibly influence[s] collective memory of the events they judge'. Collective memory 'consists of the stories a society tells about momentous events in its history, the events that most profoundly affect the lives of its members and most arouse their passions for long periods' (ibid.: 18–19). Osiel adds that victims want an authoritative, official narrative as a remedy for the suffering they have experienced. Likewise, in his work on the Holocaust and collective memory, Douglas (2001) argues that law inescapably contributes to a narrative about the past.

There has been much debate about whether or not trials should serve pedagogical purposes in the aftermath of armed conflict (see Chapter 2). Indeed, many warn against such ambitious goals. According to Justice Louise Arbour:

> We must determine whether it is realistic for a criminal prosecutor to undertake the task of a historian … History leaves room for doubt. It is a fluid project, a story in motion, which strives for a reconstruction of the past informed, understood, and therefore revised in the light of the present and even of the future. Justice, in contrast, imposes irreversible conclusions. It binds itself to a permanent and official interpretation of facts, often followed by irreversibly harsh consequences.
>
> (quoted in Sedgwick 2008: 1229)

However, whether we *should* look to law as history is a different question to whether we in fact *do* so. The imposition of irreversible conclusions, to use Arbour's words, means that although, for example, the Tokyo trial did prosecute rape crimes and did accept some evidence of forcible prostitution, the following factors ultimately circumvented an *official* narrative of wartime sexual violence against women: first, the absence of rape victims at these and the Nuremberg proceedings; second, the diminutive role of rape crimes in the prosecutions for serious violations of international law; and third, the failure of the tribunals specifically to prosecute sexual enslavement. The perceived absence of evidence of rape and sexual enslavement at the Tokyo trial may in part be responsible for the intense history wars that have ensued since the 1990s over Japan's responsibility for the sexual enslavement of the comfort women. This silence has inflicted irreparable damage, not only on the lives of the victims, but also by hindering a full recognition of the harms suffered by women during war in general.

But is it possible for a collective memory of wartime rape to emerge when a story is not told in law? And what are the ramifications of legal silence? International criminal proceedings have a powerful, authoritative claim over historical consciousness in ways that are not always apparent until decades later. This means that certain historical events where legal silence prevails will struggle to form part of historical consciousness, unless some uncovering of 'truth' emerges consequently. Douglas (2001) argues that the Nuremberg trial, for example, failed to tell the story of the Holocaust, which contributed to subsequent conceptual, institutional and political silences surrounding it, although memory was later redeemed through subsequent Holocaust trials, such as the Adolf Eichmann trial (see also Bass 2002). Likewise, in relation to Tokyo, Osiel (2000: 183) states: 'Had the Tokyo trial focused not on Japanese wrongs inflicted on those who dropped atom bombs on Hiroshima and Nagasaki, but rather on the industrial rape of the Asian comfort women … the trial's impact on Japanese memory would likely have been quite different'. My argument here is that the failure of the Tokyo and Nuremberg trials to tell a comprehensive story about sexual violence has thwarted historical consciousness and contributed (at least partially) to contemporary forms of revisionism and denial.

To illustrate my point more clearly, the present-day controversy surrounding the issue of the comfort women is at least in part due to the silence of the Tokyo trial. After the Second World War, little was said of the comfort system until women began speaking out in the early 1990s. Although Japan formally apologized to the comfort women in August 1993,[24] young nationalist politicians led by former Prime Minister Shinzo Abe subsequently lobbied for the removal of this acknowledgment. In 1994, Justice Minister General Nagano Shigeto told a newspaper that Korean comfort women were 'licensed prostitutes' (Chang 1997). Then when Abe became the Prime Minister of Japan in 2006, he publicly declared that there was no evidence of Japan's military involvement in forcing women into military brothels. To quote him here: 'it is a fact that no evidence has been found to support coercion as initially defined' (quoted in Hayashi 2008: 123). The recently uncovered exhibits from the Tokyo trial, discussed earlier, are important because they form part of the official documentation of the trial. Because Japan accepted the Tokyo Tribunal and its judgment in the peace treaty in 1952 (which was reaffirmed by Abe in 2006), this should mean that Japan accepts the evidence of sexual enslavement because it was actually presented before the Tribunal (ibid.: 14).

The issue of the comfort women until the early 1990s was, by and large, excluded from the history books. It is interesting to note that Susan Brownmiller's comprehensive chapter on rape in war, originally published in 1975, does not mention the comfort women. Brownmiller (1976: 76) alludes to the system of forced prostitution on only two occasions: first, when she mentions the evidence at the Tokyo trial regarding the forced prostitution of Chinese women for the Japanese troops; and second, when she briefly [*comfort women disappearing in history.*] mentions 'Japanese military brothels, into which conquered women were forcibly placed'. However, these are the only references to the comfort system in Brownmiller's book. Her study of wartime rape is no doubt comprehensive and she does discuss the 'murky line' between prostitution and rape, so this omission is striking. I can only guess that because the Tokyo trial did not deal with this issue and because it remained so deeply hidden until very recently, public knowledge of the comfort women was likewise lacking (see also Mackie 2000).[25]

Legal silence does not completely explain the history wars surrounding other historical examples of wartime rape. The Rape of Nanking, for example, was well documented at the Tokyo trial and yet remains a deeply controversial and divisive issue between Japan and China, particularly since the 1980s and the release of Iris Chang's 1997 book *The Rape of Nanking*.[26] The *subsequent silences* after the Tokyo trial, and the politics of diplomacy and immunity, provide a more accurate explanation for controversy and denial. Not only was Japan reluctant to accept any responsibility immediately after the war crimes trials, there was little pressure from western governments based on diplomatic and trade reasons following the defeat of Japan. Furthermore, in his attempt to stabilize post-war Japan, General Douglas MacArthur helped to ensure the Japanese Emperor remained immune from prosecution, and Cold War politics prevented any serious diplomatic pressure being placed on Japan. Osiel (2000) further notes that the Tokyo trial was absent in public discourse at least until the 1970s. Since this period, a lot of attention has focused on the failings of the Tribunal, most notably the Emperor's immunity and the charge of victor's justice, which essentially has challenged both the authority and legitimacy of the Tribunal and remains a subject of intense debate. Timothy Brook (2001: 673) summarizes the connection between the Tokyo trial and the current history wars over memory:

> Within this controversy, the IMTFE trial in Tokyo has been used as a touchstone to confirm or deny all manner of claims concerning the incident. Those who feel aggrieved over Japan's conduct towards China cite the evidence produced at the trial to authenticate the scale and brutality of the massacre. Those who feel that Japan and the emperor system have been unfairly blamed for the war in East Asia scour the trial proceedings for failures of logic and evidence that demonstrate to their satisfaction that the 'Tokyo trial view of history' is nothing but anti-Japanese distortion and fabrication. For both sides, the Tokyo judgment is fuel for ideological fire.

There was silence too within China, until recently, due to internal factors such as governmental repression and what some have labelled 'Chinese pride' (Link 2002). Recently, however, much attention has been paid to the memory of Nanking and the sentences of the Tokyo defendants over their role in the Nanking invasion are a sore point for many Chinese survivors (particularly compared to the sentencing of Nuremberg defendants) since many were released by the end of 1948 in the trials of lesser war criminals in Tokyo (ibid.). In addition, Japan was never required to pay reparations to China compared to Germany's payment of reparations to Israel. According to Perry Link (2002: xi):

> Chinese people have often felt, and with good reason, that the 1945 war crimes trials in Tokyo did not address the atrocities of World War II as squarely as did the parallel trials in Nuremberg.

Due in part to the circumvention of an official narrative embedded within the authority of international law, the Rape of Nanking, like the issue of the comfort women, has been repeatedly questioned by revisionists who claim that the massacre is an over-exaggerated or fabricated form of Chinese propaganda. In 2007, for example, a group of protestors from the Liberal Democratic Party of Japan denounced the Nanking massacre as Chinese propaganda, declaring there was no evidence to prove the mass killings and rapes by Japanese soldiers (Nishiyama 2007). According to Higashinakano Shudo (quoted in Sedgwick 2008: 1223), 'seven cases of rape was the entire scope of the Nanking Incident'. In a similar way to Holocaust denial and the dispute over the numbers of people exterminated (see Lipstadt 1993), rape deniers also point to the veracity of numerical calculations to support their often unsubstantiated claims.

Gerry Simpson (2008) has argued that the Tokyo trial has been subject to more historical contestation than the Nuremberg trial. However, while the memory of wartime rape and generally women's experiences during the Holocaust might not be embroiled in a history warfare on the same scale as both the Nanking massacre and the sexual enslavement of comfort women, nonetheless sexual violence and the Holocaust has been a matter of some controversy. Some scholars of the Holocaust, for instance, have been reluctant to pay attention to gender and women's specific experiences for fear of minimizing or trivializing the mass extermination of millions of victims (for a discussion, see Baer and Goldenberg 2003; Ofer and Weitzman 1998; Rittner and Roth 1993). Whether or not this is partially due to the silence at Nuremberg over gender crimes is of course debatable, yet my point is that a past that remains undocumented and unaccounted for constitutes a past that is vulnerable to speculation and controversy in the present. As I mentioned at the beginning of the book, there is a tendency to construct suffering hierarchies, and some scholars have asked whether or not rape is the worst of crimes. Of course, this may be partially explained by what is known as 'survivor guilt' and survivor shame. For example, in her interviews with 20 female survivors of the Holocaust, Joan Ringelheim (1985: 745) observes:

> Although there are many stories about sexual abuse, they are not easy to come by. Some [survivors] think it inappropriate to talk about these matters; discussions of sexuality desecrate the memories of the dead, or the living, or the Holocaust itself. For others, it is simply too difficult and painful. Still others think it may be a trivial issue.

The mass rapes of German women by advancing Russian soldiers at the end of the war have likewise ignited much controversy in post-war collective memory, particularly since the fall of the Berlin Wall and reunification after 1989. Helke Sander, a German feminist and filmmaker, produced a 1992 documentary called *Liberators Take Liberties* in an attempt to document the extraordinary nature of the rapes and expose the 'void' surrounding this issue (Sander 1995). This film was the subject of an entire journal publication in 1995. Sander's exposure of and approach to these rapes has polarized commentators. On the one hand, some view the attention to rape as a construction of a highly problematic post-war German narrative of victimization that is 'borrowed from a revisionist discourse' (Koch 1995: 38).

Atina Grossman argues (1995: 48) that while there is no doubt German women were victims of rape, it is important to evaluate the political motivations for this attention. She asks how and why

> the (eventually privately transmitted and publicly silenced) collective experience of rape of German women in the absence of (protective) men insinuated itself into postwar Germans' view of themselves as primarily 'victims' and not 'agents' of National Socialism and war.

Likewise, Gertrud Koch (1995: 33) takes issue with German women being presented as 'solely and incontestably war victims' whose participation in Nazism is obscured. But the controversy does not simply lie among German scholars. Russian veterans, as well as historians and academics, continue to deny or overlook the prevalence of the rapes (see Beevor in Anonymous 2006). Commenting on the potential as 'cinematic gunpowder' of the film *Woman in Berlin* (2008) (based on the anonymous diary of a woman who suffered rapes at the hands of the invading Soviet forces), Andrew Roberts (2008) writes:

> For Russia, the episode besmirches the fine name of the Red Army that had fought so hard and suffered so much in its four-year campaign against the Wehrmacht ... When the historian Antony Beevor wrote about it in his book ... the Russian ambassador to London, Grigory Karasin, accused him of 'an act of blasphemy', saying: 'It is a slander against the people who saved the world from Nazism'.

The Russian rapes of German women received no attention at the Nuremberg trial, compared to the evidence presented of German rapes against Russian women by Soviet prosecutors. Furthermore, there was a conspiracy of silence surrounding the Allied rapes of women during the war. Brownmiller (1976: 74) writes: 'when their side does it, it's exquisite proof of the bestiality of the enemy; when our side does it, it's bad politics to bring it up'. The Allies had extensive knowledge of the comfort stations (Dolgopol 1995); however, they failed to prosecute the Japanese leaders for these crimes at Tokyo, perhaps in part due to the fact that the Allies themselves visited the comfort stations and paid women for sex during the war (Tanaka 1995). The comfort station visits for Allied soldiers were organized and managed by the Kempeitai, which was founded in 1881 as Japan's military force:

*[margin annotation: exactly]*

> On the days of Japanese surrender to the United States after the devastation of World War II and the bombing of Hiroshima and Nagasaki, records show that Japan's Ibaraki Prefectural Police Department, the Kempeitai, which had been in charge of forced prostitution during the war, set up numerous 'comfort stations' for US GIs by order of the

office of Japan's Ministry of Interior on August 18, 1945 ... One brothel called Yasu-ura House 'comfort station' in Yokosuka, Kanagawa Prefecture was set up immediately by the Japanese Kempetai and Japan's RAA – the Recreation and Amusement Association using Japanese government funds. This brothel was used for US military men flooding Japan at the end of the war on August 18, 1945.

(Anzia 2007)

Tanaka (1995) writes that the post-war Japanese brothels for US military men operated for almost a year after the end of the war, until General Douglas MacArthur, who led the post-war occupation of Japan, closed the programme in 1946. Again, according to Brownmiller (1976: 65):

those who judged at Nuremberg and Tokyo were those who had emerged from the war victorious. It was the *other side* that was held accountable. No international tribunals were called to expose and condemn Allied atrocity, no war-crimes depositions were taken from 'enemy' women, no incriminating top-secret documents from our side of the war were held up to merciless light. A theorist of rape must admit that the evidence has been unfairly weighted.

(emphasis original)

She adds:

I am not suggesting that an equality of rape existed in World War II ... But Allied soldiers did commit rape, with gusto ... I rather suspect that Allied rape, for the rapists, was often joyous – a sporadic, hearty spilling over and acting out of anti-female sentiment disguised within the glorious, vengeful struggle, an exuberant manifestation of the heroic fighting man who is fighting the good fight.

(ibid.)

While there were prosecutions and heavy punishments for rape crimes that were committed by Allied soldiers, the absence of international prosecutions for these crimes has, at least in part, contributed to the silence and subsequent controversy surrounding wartime rape. The power of an international war crimes trial, like at Nuremberg and Tokyo, is formidable to the formation of a collective memory of wartime rape. Silence then forms a central part of the memory of wartime rape during the Second World War, due to the driving force of victor's justice; a justice that spared little room for women or victims in general.

It is worth noting though that silence can also be constructive and sometimes very powerful. Shoshana Felman (2002: 79), for example, argues that the failure of a trial and that which is not seen may indeed be 'at the story's heart'. She adds (ibid.: 166), 'Great trials are perhaps specifically those trials whose very failures have their own necessity and their own literary, cultural, and jurisprudential *speaking power*' (emphasis original). The upshot of the Nuremberg and Tokyo trials' legal amnesia regarding rape and sexual enslavement, therefore, is that the silence – or at least the collective memory of silence – has helped create a powerful political counter-memory, particularly since the 1990s when women began to speak out publicly about their horrific experiences.

In addition to the diminutive role of victims at the historic Nuremberg and Tokyo trials, explanations for the inadequate attention to crimes of rape and sexual enslavement can be seen through the political and gendered nature of legal discourse. The interconnected forces of colonialism, classism, racism and sexism contributed to a legal amnesia based on a number of related outcomes, including: the exclusive focus on the defendants and the waging of an aggressive war; the fixation on crimes committed against the victor nations; the hierarchy of victims based on national identity, race, class and gender; the 'inevitability' and 'unspeakability' of rape and war; the status of women during this period; the exclusion of 'private' matters from the public realm; and the taboo and stigma of rape.

Law has been complicit in this silence. Looking back at the trials it is possible to unmask a complex relationship between silence, justice and memory, not only uncovering the reasons why rape and sexual enslavement were inadequately addressed, but also identifying the ways in which this silence has ultimately blocked justice for victims. Although this historical 'judicial blindness' (Felman 2002: 5) may have helped to place rape firmly on the international agenda in later years, the silence has, I believe, served to bolster revisionist claims of denialism. Denialism through 'official memory' serves to further marginalize victim experiences, adding a further layer of insult and  injustice for the surviving victims of wartime rape. In sum, it can be argued that rape was, and continues to be, a victim of victor's justice at the historic trials after the Second World War. This is a reminder about the power of law to dictate how the past is remembered.

# 4 Casualties of law

## Wartime rape and war crimes courts

Q. The gang-rape you described, was it painful?
A. Yes.
Q. How did this make you feel?
A. I felt dead.

(Foča Transcript, 30 March 2000: 1391)

On 30 March 2000, a young woman known only as 'Witness 75' gave evidence before the International Criminal Tribunal for the Former Yugoslavia (ICTY) in The Hague. In conjunction with the testimony of other witnesses, Witness 75 helped piece together a disturbing account of the mass rapes and sexual enslavement that took place between July 1992 and February 1993 in the Foča region during the armed conflict in Bosnia-Herzegovina. Her testimony described how she was hiding in the woods with her mother, father and brother after her village was attacked in July 1992. On the day of her capture, Serb soldiers shot her mother and three other villagers as they tried to flee. Witness 75 was rounded up with other Muslim villagers, she was separated from the male members of her family, and was then taken to Buk Bijela detention centre, where she was gang-raped. According to her testimony, 'I just counted up to ten, because that was the order they made. I counted up to 10, and I don't know how many there were after that number. There could have been about 20 of them. I don't know' (*Foča* Transcript, 30 March 2000: 1389–90). During the rapes, she heard her uncle being shot and later she would learn that her 20-year-old brother had also been murdered.

Witness 75 was taken to Foča High School the same day as her capture, where she was detained with approximately 50 other women, children and elderly people. Almost every night she was removed to local apartments and sexually assaulted by many soldiers. After 15 days, she was relocated to the Partizan Sports Hall, where again she was taken out at night to various apartments to be raped. From 2 August 1992, she was kept in captivity in different apartments over several months, where she was forced to perform domestic duties and was again continually raped and humiliated. In her testimony before the ICTY, she described how she and the other women were forced to strip off their clothes and dance naked in front of the soldiers, and how they were forced to walk through the town where they were told that their throats would be slit and their bodies thrown into the river Drina. After eight months of rape and sexual enslavement, the young woman was able to flee Foča with the help of two Serbs on 5 March 1993.

This harrowing story of wartime sexual violence was recorded and preserved through an international war crimes court as an 'institutional site of memory'. The appearance of sexual violence survivors as legal witnesses before international criminal courts marks a new era within the history of international humanitarian law. Significantly, rape is no longer seen as merely a by-product of warfare, but as a serious crime that had finally transcended its problematic union with looting and pillaging.[1] This can be juxtaposed with the silence that has traditionally enveloped sexual crimes and the experiences of victims within the international judicial realm. After the Second World War, the Nuremberg and Tokyo war crimes tribunals failed to address sexual violence adequately: rape was not enumerated as a war crime or as a crime against humanity in either charter, and no rape victims were called to testify at either of these trials. In stark contrast, contemporary international criminal proceedings have resulted in successful prosecutions for sexual violence as genocide, war crimes and crimes against humanity.

## Victims' justice: wartime rape and the rise of the counter-memory

During the Second World War, the invention of gruesomely efficient technological methods of mass extermination in concentration camps and on the battlefield, combined with the enormous number of civilian and combatant casualties, culminated in an emerging consciousness regarding the imperative of protecting human rights. The atrocities instigated the development of the modern human rights movement, characterized by universalism and the inherent dignity of the human person (see e.g. Donnelly 2003). In conjunction with the emerging concept of human rights and the subsequent 'rights revolution' since the Second World War (Ignatieff 2000), the genesis and evolution of a global victims' movement inspired newfound attention to victims of violent crime.[2]

Gilbert Geis notes that for centuries victims 'aroused little comment or interest'. He adds, 'Suddenly, they were "discovered", and afterwards it was unclear how their obvious neglect could have so long gone without attention and remedy' (quoted in Strang 2002: 27). The victim movement has taken on many forms, yet the common characteristic is a shared sense of injustice (Strang 2001). The victim movement might thus include: the American Civil Rights movement, the feminist movement, the anti-war lobby, the human rights revolution, the restorative justice movement, as well as the evolution of a modern trauma discourse. The ever-increasing role of the media and the war correspondent (see e.g. Allan 2004; Knightley 2000; Neier 1998; Neuffer 2001) and the growth of non-governmental organizations (NGOs) (see e.g.

Afsharipour 1999; Halley, Kotiswaran, Shamir and Thomas 2006) further promoted reactivity and sensitivity towards victims of violent crime and unjust discrimination, particularly in geographical locations of conflict and violence.

From the 1960s, a great deal of attention focused on the narratives of Holocaust survivors as victims of state-sponsored genocide. Moreover, various socio-political events, such as the end of the Cold War, the fall of the Berlin Wall, the transition of communist and post-colonial states to democracy and independence, global capitalism, shifting migration patterns, the expansion of technological innovation, as well as a whole range of other pivotal events, essentially led to a greater focus not only on victims, but also on the massive problems facing post-conflict communities in transitional periods. Essentially the notion of the 'counter-memory' as a challenge to and shift from state-centric versions of the past, and the general growth of commemoration of traumatic histories, has been a decisive force behind greater recognition of marginalized histories in various legal, political and social realms. Michel Foucault (1977) used the notion of the 'counter-memory' to exactly describe challenges to official history through subjugated or disqualified knowledge. Counter-memories of previously silenced memories thus provide an alternative, subjective – and some argue more authentic – account of past events. The counter-memory thus stands in contrast to the posited objectivity in traditional historiography. The rise of the counter-memory and the significant impact of oral or eyewitness history since the second half of the twentieth century (see e.g. Perks and Thomson 2006; Tonkin 1992) is very much connected to the increasing attention towards victims of past historical events, in both peacetime and wartime. This development has contributed enormously to the rise of memorialization and commemoration of 'forgotten' histories, and the contiguous popularity of collective memory studies.

Andreas Huyssen (1995: 9) sees the boom in memory as a 'healthy sign of contestation … of the informational hyperspace'. Katharine Hodgkin and Susannah Radstone (2003: 4) likewise state that memory

> laid claim precisely to an authentic truth excluded from the historical record. It solicited the voices of those who have been silent and ignored throughout the centuries: the poor and powerless, workers and women, who seldom have speaking parts in the historical drama. It attended to the private, the domestic, the details of daily life, rather than to great events. And it found in the memories evoked a counter-narrative, a corrective to the simplifying and patronising assumptions of the traditional makers of history.

Despite the growth of both the human rights and victims' rights movements since the Second World War, it was not until the early 1990s that counter-memories of wartime sexual violence attracted serious international attention.[3] I argued in the previous chapter that the experiences of women in warfare, particularly of sexual violence, have been co-opted by a nationalist historiography that excluded the authentic voices of the victims and ultimately consolidated them and culminated in an extraordinary silence. This happened to such an extent, I argued, that silence has in and of itself become part of the collective memory of wartime rape. I also argued that the control of the past and the subjugation of subjective knowledge was manifest in the operation of the post-Second World War international war crimes courts. A key question for this particular chapter is whether, and to what extent, the counter-memory is commemorated through contemporary sites of memory. In other words, how do war crimes courts help to nurture or hinder these counter-memories?

## The International Criminal Tribunal for the Former Yugoslavia

The dissolution of Yugoslavia as a communist state began when Croatia and Slovenia declared independence in June 1991 (see Kaplan 2005; Scharf 1997; Silber and Little 1997). On 29 February 1992, Bosnia-Herzegovina followed suit by declaring independence from Yugoslavia by popular referendum. The international community instantly recognized its independence; however, the referendum was boycotted by the Bosnian Serbs, who proceeded to declare their own independence with the self-proclaimed Bosnian Serb Republic, the Republika Srpska. Led by the leader of the Bosnian Serb military forces, Radovan Karadžić, the siege of Sarajevo in April 1992 marked the beginning of civil war. Serb-led attacks against the Croatian and Muslim populations in northeast and southern Bosnia were conducted in a strategic attempt to craft a 'Greater Serbia' by creating a 300 km corridor between Serb populated areas and Serbia proper.[4]

The conflict in Bosnia-Herzegovina simultaneously involved fighting between Bosnian Serbs, Croats and Muslims, and 'ethnic cleansing' came to define the conflict as a whole.[5] Ethnic cleansing, through the perpetration of rape, torture and massacre, was carried out in Bosnia-Herzegovina to remove entire ethnic populations and ensure they would not return. Aryeh Neier (1998: 172) writes that 'For a time, the war in Bosnia became virtually synonymous with rape, acquiring a reputation for uncommon ugliness in the process and helping to create unprecedented awareness of rape as a common method of warfare and political repression worldwide'.

As part of a widespread campaign of ethnic cleansing, most documented cases of rape occurred between 1991 and 1993, with the majority of cases involving the rapes of Muslim women by Serb forces, although Croat and Serb women were also subjected to patterns of sexual violence (Askin 1997; Nikolič-Ristanovič 2000). The United Nations Commission of Experts described five patterns of rape that existed during the conflict: (1) individual and gang rapes in conjunction with looting and intimidation of the target ethnic group; (2) individual and gang rapes in conjunction with fighting, including rapes in public, followed by populations in towns or villages being rounded-up for deportation to camps; (3) rape in detention facilities or camps, involving women being picked out by soldiers, camp guards, paramilitaries and civilians for both individual and gang rapes, beatings and killings; (4) women being detained for the purpose of rape and impregnation in detention facilities in order to carry out a policy of ethnic cleansing; and (5) captivity of women in hotels and similar facilities for the purpose of providing sexual entertainment for soldiers (United Nations 1994).[6]

On 25 May 1993, the Security Council authorized the creation of the first international criminal tribunal since the Nuremberg and Tokyo tribunals in response to the atrocities committed in the former Yugoslavia (which at the time included Slovenia, Croatia, Bosnia-Herzegovina, and later in 1998, Kosovo). The Tribunal, named the International Criminal Tribunal for the Former Yugoslavia (ICTY), is located in The Hague (the Netherlands) with limited powers to undertake 'the prosecution of persons responsible for serious violations of international humanitarian law committed in the Former Yugoslavia since 1991' (see Morris and Scharf 1995). This was the first time a war crimes tribunal was established by a 'neutral' authority as opposed to a military victor (Kaszubinski 2002).[7]

After nearly 20 years in existence, the ICTY has significantly expanded the boundaries of international humanitarian law. The ICTY has become the prototype for the establishment of future war crimes courts, including the International Criminal Tribunal for Rwanda, the International Criminal Court, the special court for Sierra Leone, as well as other hybrid and national war crimes courts in diverse geographical locations. Some of the ICTY's purported achievements (which are explicitly mentioned on its website) include: the repudiation of impunity at the highest levels; the individualization of guilt; the establishment of facts; the expansion and clarification of the legal elements relating to the Geneva Conventions and other instruments of international humanitarian law; and the contribution to procedural law, particularly in the area of witness protection (see: http://www.icty.org). Intentionally or not, war crimes courts like the ICTY contribute significantly to the collective memory of past events. Interestingly, on an updated version of its website, the Tribunal now notes its contribution to collective memory, including specifically the collective memory of wartime rape:

> The Tribunal has contributed to an indisputable historical record, combating denial and helping communities come to terms with their recent history. Crimes across the region can no longer be denied. For example, it has been proven beyond reasonable doubt that the mass murder at Srebrenica was genocide.
>
> *Judges have also ruled that rape was used by members of the Bosnian Serb armed forces as an instrument of terror, and the judges in the Kvočka et al. trial established that a 'hellish orgy of persecution' occurred in the Omarska, Keraterm and Trnopolje camps of northwestern Bosnia.*

While the most significant number of cases heard at the Tribunal have dealt with alleged crimes committed by Serbs and Bosnian Serbs, the

Tribunal has investigated and brought charges against persons from every ethnic background. Convictions have been secured against Croats, as well as both Bosnian Muslims and Kosovo Albanians for crimes committed against Serbs and others.

(http://www.icty.org, emphasis added)

Unlike the Nuremberg and Tokyo charters, the crime of rape was explicitly included in the ICTY's statute as a crime against humanity, albeit several months after its establishment.[8] The late Rhonda Copelon (1993: 199) noted: 'The situation present[ed] a historic opportunity as well as an imperative to insist on justice for the women of Bosnia, as well as to press for a feminist reconceptualization of the role of legal understanding of rape in war'. Whether the ICTY and other international courts are able to not only prosecute war crimes against women effectively but also preserve these crimes within the historical record remains to be seen. In the discussion below, I will predominantly address the *nature* of rape prosecutions before international war crimes trials in order to assess the production of narrative, memory and history.[9]

### The first trial: Tadič

On 7 May 1996 at the first international criminal trial since the Second World War and the first ever case at the ICTY, the trial against Duško Tadič commenced. Tadič was charged with crimes related to the rape, torture and murder of prisoners in and around three prison camps in northern Bosnia-Herzegovina: Omarska, Keraterm and Trnopolje.[10] The son of a Second World War Serbian partisan fighter, Tadič was born in October 1955 in Kozarac, a small town in north-western Bosnia-Herzegovina in the municipality of Prijedor. Divorced with two daughters, he was a café owner and part-time karate instructor. In 1990, he joined the Serbian Democratic Party (SDS) and later became the President of the Local Board of the SDS, which, with the aid of police and military forces, attacked and captured the town of Kozarac in May 1992, expelling the entire non-Serb population by foot or by internment in the three aforementioned detention camps. In February 1994, Tadič was arrested by German police in Munich and then transferred to the ICTY in April 1995 to await trial for his active role in the forcible transfer of Kozarac villagers, the killing of two Muslim police officers and participation in beatings of prisoners.

From about May 1992, Serbs began taking Bosnian Muslim and Bosnian Croat prisoners to the notorious Omarska prison camp, a former mining complex near the town of Prijedor. The prisoners at Omarska were treated brutally, and torture, beatings and sexual assaults were commonplace. Prisoners were virtually starved of food, given very little water, no change of clothing, no bedding and no medical care:

> The camp guards and others who came to the camp and physically abused the prisoners, used all manner of weapons during these beatings, including wooden batons, metal rods and tools, lengths of thick industrial

cable that had metal balls affixed to the end, rifle butts, and knives. Both female and male prisoners were beaten, tortured, raped, sexually assaulted, and humiliated. Many, whose identities are known and unknown, did not survive the camp. After the collection of thousands of Bosnian Muslims and Croats in later May, 1992, groups of Serbs including the accused later entered villages in which Muslims and Croats remained, at which time they killed some villagers and drove others from their homes.

(*Tadić* Indictment, 1996: para. 2.6)

Among other things, the accused was charged with forcible sexual intercourse with 'F'. She was taken to Omarska as a prisoner in early June 1992 and was allegedly subjected to forcible sexual intercourse by the accused. Tadić was charged (under the provisions of the ICTY Statute and Geneva Conventions for 'inhuman treatment' and 'crimes against humanity') for wilfully causing great suffering to 'F' by subjecting her to 'cruel treatment' (*Tadić* Indictment, 1996: para 4.1). A later amendment to the indictment involved the charge of crimes against humanity for Tadić's alleged participation in the torture and rape of a number of other female detainees. He was also charged with the torture of detainees, which included beatings and sexual mutilation of male prisoners.[11]

During the trial, the prosecutor sought various protective measures for witnesses testifying in this case, in which the Trial Chamber considered, among other things, the giving of evidence by victims and witnesses of sexual assault. Although Judge Ninian Stephen opposed the granting of complete anonymity to witnesses or victims of sexual violence because it violated the rights of the accused to a fair and public trial, his separate opinion does contain some important observations concerning the psychological injury inflicted by rape:

> What is special about such witnesses [of sexual violence] is not, of course, that by giving evidence they or their family, more than other victims who give evidence, have reason to fear retaliation. What does make their case special is the combination of possible social consequences of it becoming generally known in communities in the former Yugoslavia that a woman has been a rape victim and also the often acute trauma of facing one's attacker in court and being made to relive the experience of the rape.
>
> (Separate Opinion of Judge Stephen, 10 August 1995)

Judge Stephen's opinion established that rape victims may not have reason to fear retaliation more than any other witness, but confronting the accused in court, reliving the ordeal during the testimony stage and, further, being socially ostracized because of a rape-victim status all have profound implications for potential witnesses.[12] The Trial Chamber considered the application of protective measures for individuals testifying to rape and sexual assault in domestic legal systems in various countries and states. These measures serve

to prevent the retraumatization of sexual assault witnesses and include testifying via one-way closed circuit television, image and voice altering devices,
screens and one-way mirrors so that the witness does not see the accused.
The Trial Chamber granted the use of one-way closed circuit television for
witnesses 'F', 'G', 'H' and 'I' and a 30-day disclosure deadline for the prosecution regarding Witness F, yet denied the request for voice and image
altering devices.[13] This case was historically significant because it not only
demonstrated the international community's commitment to recognizing
and prosecuting sexual violence at the international level, but also acknowledged the particular problems that sexual violence survivors typically experience when disclosing the details of sexual violence. The Trial Chamber
therefore regarded protection as particularly important for victims of sexual
assault. It noted the devastating consequences of sexual assault and that testifying was often difficult in public contexts, recognizing that criminal trials
potentially 'exacerbate the victim's ordeal during the trial' (Decision on
the Prosecutor's Motion Requesting Protective Measures for Victims and
Witnesses, 10 August 1995).

On 7 May 1996, the counts of rape against Tadič were dropped because
Witness F decided to withdraw from the case, reportedly because she was too
frightened to testify. It is unclear whether she was fearful of the trial process,
of encountering the accused in the courtroom, or whether she was concerned
about the possibility for reprisal after she had given her testimony. Towards
the end of the trial she indicated that she felt able to testify, yet by this stage it
was too late as she had already withdrawn from the trial (Kreisler 2001).
However, Witness F did eventually testify in another ICTY case, the *Kvočka*
trial, involving the deputy commanders and shift leaders at Omarska.
Significantly, during this trial, she testified that she was raped by Tadič and
others during her imprisonment; however, this had no legal bearing on the
earlier *Tadič* case, conviction and sentence (but did nonetheless validate the
rapes that Witness F endured at Omarska).[14]

In a later indictment at the *Tadič* trial, the accused was charged with the
torture of several female detainees, including gang rapes between September
and December 1992. Initially Witness L, a protected witness, claimed he
had committed murder and rape together with the accused Tadič.[15] Witness L
was aged 16 years when his family moved to Prijedor in October 1992
as refugees. In closed session, Witness L testified that he got a job at the
Trnopolje camp as a guard to prevent inmates escaping and mingling with
civilians. The witness testified that on 5 November 1992, a girl with her
hands tied behind her back was brought to the cellar in the 'white house' at
the camp, where she was gang-raped by him, the accused and four others.
When asked by the prosecutor whether she was making noise, the witness
stated:

> she was struggling, wrestling, crying, begging not to kill her ... She was
> blindfolded ... struggling and she was trying everything, but she could

not because they held on to her arms and her legs … They were laughing … After that I stood up from the girl and I dressed … [and the others] began to commit rape … [Duško Tadić] threatened her, that he would kill her, that he would slit her throat if anybody in the camp learned … what had happened to her.

(*Tadić* Transcript, 13 August 1996: 5247–9)

Witness L testified again on 14 and 15 August 1996 to committing multiple gang-rapes and murders against the inmates of the camp. This is all graphically described in the trial transcripts. He also testified to the involvement of the accused and how the accused had also committed rapes. However, Witness L later confessed that he had been lying, claiming that the Bosnian authorities where he was detained had forced and trained him to lie in court (IWPR 1997). Subsequently, the Tribunal disregarded Witness L's testimony and the gang-rape charges were dropped.

As a result of F's withdrawn testimony and the various amendments to the indictment, including the dropping of the gang-rape charges due to Witness L's disregarded testimony, it has been incorrectly assumed that the *Tadić* case did not consider crimes of sexual violence (Askin 1999). Rather, the reality was that there was insufficient evidence to convict Tadić for personally taking part in the rapes and sexual assault of prisoners, yet Tadić was in fact indicted for aiding and encouraging the sexual assault of a male detainee through his presence, and for his part in the widespread or systematic attack on a civilian population in which he 'intended for discriminatory reasons to inflict severe damage to the victims' physical integrity and human dignity' (*Tadić* Judgment, 1997: para. 730). Therefore, sexual assault testimony was in fact heard during the trial in order to establish evidence concerning the killings, rapes, assaults and other physical and psychological abuse that took place in the Prijedor region during the war in Bosnia-Herzegovina.

On 18 and 19 July 1996, S.R., a 41-year-old Muslim woman from Prijedor, testified as an unprotected witness to being raped and beaten by various men of Serbian ethnicity.[16] A few days after the town of Prijedor was taken over by Serb forces, she was on her way back from visiting her brother and was stopped at a checkpoint and taken to the police station and interrogated. She was then taken to some military barracks where she was blindfolded and put in a room. S.R. was the first sexual violence survivor in history to testify at an international war crimes tribunal (although, as far as I am aware, no mention of this has been made, possibly because her testimony does not directly refer to any of the rapes allegedly committed by the accused). A section of her testimony is provided below:

WITNESS:   They raped me. They raped me and took me back for interrogation to the same corridor from which they had taken me away.
Q:   Then after that what happened with you?

WITNESS: I was bleeding heavily and the soldier who interrogated me in that room invited me to enter the room. When I entered the room, as I was covered in blood, he said simply: 'What fool did that?' He gave me a blanket and asked me only where I lived and I told him … and he drove me there. After that I called the hospital to see whether they could help me. I asked for Dr. Katzman or Dr. Banovic or nurse Liljia or Jalja or Vikica. Banovic answered my call and I told her what happened. I told her I started bleeding out of fear and she said: 'I cannot help you like this. Come to the hospital'. I went to the hospital. I took a taxi and when I came to the hospital she received me and only said: 'First I have to see what is wrong with you,' and when she examined me she told me I was pregnant, about three or four months, or something like that she said, and said: 'Listen, I have to perform the abortion but I do not have the anaesthetic'. She invited another doctor, Savic, and when he entered the room he started cursing and saying that all balija women, they should be removed away, eliminated, and he also started cursing her because she was helping Muslims and saying that all the Muslims should be annihilated, especially men. She gave me some pills and told me: 'If anything goes wrong, further wrong, I cannot help you any more'.

(*Tadič* Transcript, 18 July 1996: 3745–6)

S.R. a few days later returned to her apartment in Prijedor. Later her house was searched and she was raped in her home by a man she once worked with. He threatened to kill her if she told anybody. The next day she was taken again to the police station and taken to a room which was covered in blood, and was raped and beaten. She spent some time in Keraterm camp and was then detained at the Omarska camp until August 1992. She testified how she had found teeth, hair, clothing and bits of human flesh while cleaning the rooms, and that she would see corpses almost every day which were taken away by a small yellow lorry. She spoke about being called out at night and taken to a room to be raped:

Q: Did any of the women who were called out ever tell you what had happened to them?
WITNESS: No, we never told each other what happened.
Q: Were you yourself called out of the room at night?
WITNESS: Yes.
Q: How often did this happen to you?
WITNESS: Five times …
Q: When this man would called [sic] you out of the room where would he take you?
WITNESS: He would take me downstairs to the first room next to the staircase on the way to the kitchen.
Q: When he took you down there to this room what did he do to you?
WITNESS: Raped me.

(*Tadič* Transcript, 19 July 1996: 3762–3)

After leaving Omarska, the witness was taken to Trnopolje and then back to Prijedor, where she remained until January 1993. She contemplated suicide and had her uterus removed due to the rapes she had endured at all three camps. Her testimony contributes to a particular narrative about wartime rape that may be summed up as follows. First, a woman's gender and her ethnicity are implicitly tied to her victimization during periods of armed conflict. And second, the physical and psychological consequences of wartime rape are incalculable; they may include pregnancy, abortion, surgery, excessive bleeding, not to mention the psychological trauma associated with rape, interrogation and surviving war. These consequences were importantly preserved through S.R.'s testimony, as well the testimony of a doctor during the trial, which reads as follows:

> The very act of rape, in my opinion – I spoke to these people, I observed their reactions – it had a terribly negative effect on them … Somehow they sort of accepted [beatings or killings] in some way, but when the rapes started they lost all hope. Until then they had hope that this war could pass, that everything would quiet down. When the rapes started everybody lost hope, everybody in the camp, men and women. There was such fear, horrible. They had fear from the night because at night there is a danger of being taken away again. One of them told me, I remember, 'Are they going to come for me this night, tonight?' That is the question that is always there. They also knew of some of their neighbours, female neighbours, so they had terrible fear. My personal opinion is that one of the goals of that act was precisely to maintain this fear in the remainder of the Muslim population. That was the goal.
>
> (*Tadić* Transcript, 6 August 1996: 4671)

The doctor's testimony is a comment on the impact of rape not just on the individual, but also on the community. The witness was asked about the consequences for Muslim women within a patriarchal society, to which he commented on the nature of social stigma, in particular for women from Bosnian Muslim communities. Indeed, as mentioned above, the *Tadić* case in general represented the first time an international criminal tribunal has specifically demonstrated the physical, psychological and social impact of sexual violence in the aftermath of armed conflict. Not only does this formally validate women's experiences of sexual violence, but it also judicially condemns the policy of 'ethnic cleansing', to which rape was integral.

Jose Alvarez (1998) argues that some proponents have viewed the *Tadić* trial as closely adhering to a model of 'closure', not only because it gives a definitive historical and geographic account of the war in Bosnia-Herzegovina and it asserts the law's apolitical neutrality, balancing the rights of the accused and witnesses, but because the trial also reflects acknowledgment and respect for the victims who testified at this trial. However, Alvarez (1998: 2053) notes that despite the 'meticulous case presented by the prosecution', providing closure is an inherently unrealistic task for international criminal tribunals. For witnesses, he argues, the trial satisfied few victim-centred goals: '[the] victims were not compensated for lost property, for injuries suffered, or for emotional distress caused. Nor were they able to tell their full stories at trial, during sentencing, or in the bench's record of their testimony' (ibid.: 2069).

In the end, while it could not be proven that Tadić himself personally committed acts of sexual violence, he was nonetheless convicted of persecution and inhumane acts, which included aiding and abetting the sexual assault of female prisoners and the sexual mutilation and humiliation of male prisoners. The evidence was based on the testimonies of other witnesses regarding rape, including S.R.'s testimony. The Trial Chamber importantly found that 'both male and female prisoners were subjected to severe mistreatment, which included beatings, sexual assaults, torture and executions' (*Tadić* Judgment, 1997: para. 154) and that women were 'routinely called out of their rooms at night and raped' (*Tadić* Judgment, 1997: para. 165). The judgment further documented the extensive nature of rape:

> Because [the Trnopolje camp] ... housed the largest number of women and girls, there were more rapes at this camp than at any other. Girls between the ages of 16 and 19 were at the greatest risk. During evenings, groups of soldiers would enter the camp, take out their victims from the dom building and rape them ... In addition, there were women who were subjected to gang rapes; one witness testified that a 19-year-old woman was raped by seven men and suffered terrible pains and came to the clinic for treatment for haemorrhaging.
>
> (*Tadić* Judgment, 1997: para. 175)

The *Tadić* trial was significant because it was the first case at the ICTY and the first time since the Tokyo trial that rape was tried by an international criminal tribunal. Although the rape charges were withdrawn because Witness F was too frightened to testify, the case importantly not only recognized the ramifications of testifying for sexual violence survivors (Askin 1999), but also established that rape was part of a widespread campaign of ethnic cleansing against the Muslim population in Bosnia-Herzegovina. The trial was significant because it demonstrated that even low-level offenders were not exempt from prosecution at the international level. This symbolized a deviation from the international trials at Nuremberg and Tokyo that focused on the major war criminals. The trial thus indicated that even 'ordinary' perpetrators could face prosecution. On 7 May 1997, the Trial Chamber rendered its decision and Tadić was sentenced to 20 years' imprisonment.

### A crime of torture: Čelebići

The 1997 ICTY *Čelebići* case was the first international criminal trial since Nuremberg and Tokyo where more than one defendant was in the dock and the doctrine of command responsibility was used.[17] The defendants on trial were three Bosnian Muslims and one Bosnian Croat who were accused of directly participating in, or were responsible for, atrocities committed against mostly Bosnian Serb prisoners in the Čelebići camp located in the municipality of Konjic in central Bosnia-Herzegovina. The atrocities included murder, torture and rape. The defendants were: Zdravko Mucić, the camp's commander; Hazim Delić, the deputy commander and later commander; Esad Landžo, an 18-year-old guard; and Zejnil Delalić, the top Bosnian Muslim and Croat military officer in Konjic, who had authority over the Čelebići camp and was later a commander in the Bosnian Army. They were charged with grave breaches of the Geneva Conventions and violations of the laws and customs of war. Hazim Delić was the sole defendant charged with individual criminal responsibility for the rape of two Bosnian Serb women.[18]

After fleeing her home and hiding in a cave and in a cellar for seven days, G.C., a 43-year-old Serbian woman, was captured and taken to Čelebići prison camp on 27 May 1992. While she was detained, she suffered 'repeated incidents of forcible sexual intercourse' (*Čelebići* Indictment, 1996: para. 2.4). On 17 March 1997, G.C. testified before the ICTY as an unprotected witness.[19] She testified before the Trial Chamber that after her arrival in the Čelebići prison camp, she was taken to a room in Building 'B', where the accused Delić interrogated her regarding the whereabouts of her husband. She stated that she was then required to go to another room, where the accused raped her in front of two other men. She testified that on her third night in the camp and her first night in Building 'A', she was raped by four men (one of whom was a witness for the prosecution and who denied this allegation during his testimony). G.C. also testified that another man raped her at the end of July 1992. The following is an excerpt from the trial proceedings in which the witness testified against Delić:

> This man with the crutch [Delić]. At that time I didn't know who he was … [he] told me to take my clothes off. I didn't understand what he wanted. I thought he was going to beat me since he had a stick with him. He had a uniform on him. Then he asked me to take off my clothes and then he started taking off clothes from me. It was the trousers, the skirt, the panties, and then he put me on my chest and he started raping me. I didn't realise that this would be happening to me, this at the end of the 20th century, that someone would allow themselves to do.
>
> (*Čelebići* Transcript, 17 March 1997: 492–3)

The witness continued with her testimony:

WITNESS: Then he turned me on my back and then took off everything, everything that was on me, the pants and the boots and I kept the top clothes on me and he raped me. Then—

Q: [Mrs C.], when you say he raped you, can you please tell us exactly what you mean?

WITNESS:   Well, he took off my clothes and he took his penis and he put it in my vagina. He had an erection. As I was lying down he told me to sort of move and he stayed about ten minutes there and Dzajic was lying on a bed next to the window and the little one, Cosic – I think it is Cosic; he is from Ibar – and he told him to stand at the door and he remained there until he was done and then—

Q:   When you say—

WITNESS:   He trampled on my pride.

Q:   [Mrs C.], who was it who raped you?

WITNESS:   The one with the crutch. At that time I still did not know who he was but later I found out. Soon after that I found out who and what he was. Unfortunately he trampled on my pride and I will never be able to be the woman that I was. Then after all there was further misery.

Q:   [Mrs C.], let me just stop you for a moment. When you later on learned who this person was who raped you, who did you learn this was?

(Čelebići Transcript, 17 March 1997: 492–3)

This section of G.C.'s testimony draws attention to the extent that witnesses are permitted to 'tell their stories'. Based on this example, it is possible to make some observations about the telling of a rape story before an international criminal court. The witness began talking about the impact of the rape with statements such as 'He trampled on my pride' and 'Then after all there was further misery', only to be interrupted by the prosecutor, whose purpose is to extract factual evidence, such as the identity of the rapist, thus using questions such as 'who raped you, who did you learn this was?' or 'when you say he raped you, can you please tell us exactly what you mean?' This demonstrates a sharp contrast between what is important for the witness in terms of telling the story and what is important for the prosecution, which is to prove the case in order to secure a conviction. For the witness, legal language can obscure the meaning of rape. Instead of being able to reconstruct the narrative in a meaningful way, witnesses are forced to carve their stories into fragments. In addition to this, the defence team's objective of discrediting the evidence in order to secure a 'not guilty' verdict invariably impacts on the witness and her testimony. This potentially renders the witness in an extremely vulnerable position because she is caught between two opposing sides of the adversarial conflict. The witness and her story thereby become merely a segment of evidence. This reflects an inherent limitation within legal adversarial proceedings and can also be seen during both rape and non-rape trials in domestic contexts (see e.g. Matoesian 1993).

In the *Čelebići* trial, the prosecutor alleged that the rapes constituted torture as a grave breach of the four Geneva Conventions and a violation of the laws and customs of war. For the purposes of international law, one of the required elements of torture outlined by the Convention against Torture and Other Cruel, Inhuman or Degrading Treatment is that the act must be directed towards obtaining information or a confession, or punishing, intimidating, humiliating or coercing the victim or other person. Other required elements include intention and that at least one of the persons involved be a public official, among other things. The witness claimed that she was raped in order to extract information regarding her husband and his whereabouts. This clearly constituted an act of torture based on the above requirements as Delić was the Deputy Commander of the Čelebići camp. The defence claimed, however, that there was no evidence that the purpose of the alleged rapes was to elicit information from G.C. because she gave evidence that the accused had asked about her husband *after* the rape and not before. Therefore, the defence argued that the rapes could not constitute a form of 'torture' as defined by the ICTY Statute, the Torture Convention and the Geneva Conventions.

Under cross-examination, the defence counsel's questions were designed to raise issue with the inconsistencies found in the statements given by the witness. For example, questions regarding her recollection of past events were raised; interestingly, the defence asked the witness nothing about the actual rape. Even the defence lawyer Thomas Moran, whose client Delić was the only defendant accused of actually committing rape, did not ask the witness any questions about the alleged rape. During Moran's cross-examination of G.C., her repeated attempts to bring up the topic of rape were disregarded, as shown here (and can be gleaned elsewhere in the transcripts):

Q:   And the guards would keep it closed also, would they not, because you were a prisoner?
WITNESS:   Yes. When the guards would come in, when they raped me, they would close the door. They would also use the toilet.
Q:   Yes, ma'am, but the toilet that the guards used was at a different place than the room you were kept in, was it not, a different place in the building?

(*Čelebići* Transcript, 18 March 1997: 569)

This example demonstrates the way in which a witness's testimony is completely dictated by the lawyer, who has an unfettered power to exclude particular pieces of evidence, in this case the details concerning the rapes. In the closing statement for Delić's defence, the issue of rape is raised, but this time in order to submit that the witness was not telling the truth:

Hazim Delic was the only accused charged as a direct participant in these counts of the Indictment ... The Defence for Mr. Delic submits that the only direct evidence of the rapes comes from the alleged victim, and that the remainder of the evidence is indirect. It is submitted that the testimony of [Ms. C.] is unsatisfactory and evasive and, if she was in fact telling the truth, her evidence cast severe doubt on her ability to recall and recount past events. In his interview with the prosecution investigators, given on 19 July 1996, Mr. Delic denied having raped [Ms. C.]. He admitted that [Ms. C.] was brought to the Celebici prison-camp because of her husband but that he only ever had coffee with her. Mr. Delic denied that he had heard reports that [Ms. C.] had been raped. The Defence contends that there is no evidence that the purpose of the alleged rapes was to elicit information from [Ms. C.].

(*Čelebiči* Judgment, 1998: para. 930–2)

According to the defence, the 'direct evidence' of the victim was not enough to establish culpability of the accused. Yet again the witness's ability to recall past events – her memory – is questioned. The defence claimed that G.C.'s testimony lacked credibility because she 'made corrections to the statements she had previously made to the Prosecution and was accordingly, contradicting facts she had formerly asserted as being true' (*Čelebiči* Judgment, 1998: para. 934). However, in the discussion and findings of the judgment for the *Čelebiči* case, the Tribunal found that G.C.'s evidence was in fact credible and compelling. The Trial Chamber also decreed that the rapes committed by the accused were, among other things, perpetrated in order to obtain information regarding the whereabouts of the witness's husband, and additionally 'because she is a woman' (*Čelebiči* Judgment, 1998: para. 941). As a result, the Trial Chamber found the accused guilty of torture for the rape of G.C.

On the ICTY website, the story of G.C., in an accessible narrative form, is replicated as an attempt to convey the 'voices of the victims' who have testified before the Tribunal. The following excerpt is taken from the website and I have included it here because it illustrates, in addition to the sexual violence she endured, some of the other harms suffered by women in the camp:

[G.C.] remained in that building for the rest of her time in the Čelebiči camp, sleeping in a room with five to seven other women. They had no place to wash, and no hot water. They had a blue plastic jug that they would wash their underwear in and in which they urinated at night, as they did not dare go out. Throughout the three and a half months she was there, they were given two bars of soap and one and a half cups of detergent to share amongst five to seven of them. However, [G.C.] said that food was what they lacked the most. For 42 days, they were only given a piece of bread. Then they were given soup and some beans that had not been boiled properly. Later the camp authorities allowed food to be brought in, but her sister who brought it did not always succeed in getting it to her. [G.C.] lost 34 kilos, and felt very sick … On 31 August 1992, [G.C.] was released. For the three months that she was in the camp, [she] did not know what had happened to her husband and her son.

*[handwritten margin note: credability of the witness always at issue]*

She learned that her son had left for Serb-held territory. On 5 December 1992, she identified her dead husband's mutilated body.

(http://www.icty.org/sid/196)

Another victim of rape, M.A., who withdrew her protected status a year after the indictment, also testified that Hazim Delič raped her on three occasions at the Čelebiči prison camp. M.A., also of Serbian ethnicity, was approximately 44 years old at the time the shooting started in her village. On the day of her arrest, she was in her garden with her ill, elderly mother, digging potatoes, when three armed soldiers in camouflage uniform appeared. When she arrived at the camp, the women were separated from the men and taken to a room where other women were being held. She told the court how she was then interrogated by the three accused, Mucič, Delič and Delalič. That night, M.A. was called out to be questioned by the commander, Delič:

> Delic started to interrogate me. He questioned me again about my first name, my last name, where I was from, why I was brought there. I did not know what to answer. He started to curse. He said that the Cetniks were guilty for everything that was going on. He started to curse my Cetnik mother. He told me that unless I did whatever he asked from me that he would send me to Grude, where a Croatian camp was, or else I will be shot. I started to cry. He ordered me to take my clothes off. I was constantly imploring and crying and asking him not to touch me, as I was a sick woman. To no avail. He started to threaten me with his rifle, saying that he would kill me. He pointed the rifle at me. I got scared. I was afraid he would kill me. So I had to do what he asked from me. I had to take my clothes off as he pointed the rifle on me, on the upper part of my body.
>
> (*Čelebiči* Transcript, 3 April 1997: 1777–8)

At this point, the prosecutor asked the witness to continue with her story, followed by questions regarding the details of the rape:

WITNESS:  He asked me then why did I not dress more nicely, as I came all torn and dirty from my garden … I did not know what to answer. I said: 'I was not allowed to go into my house'. Then he threatened me. He ordered me to go into the bed and to lie down. Then he raped me. He ordered me to take my tracksuit off. I had a jumper, which I also had to take off. Then I had to go on the bed.

Q:  Sorry to ask you that, but could you please give us some more details about the rape. Did he – can you give us some more details on the very event of the rape, if you don't mind?

WITNESS:  I then had to climb in the bed. Then he took his belt off. On his belt he had a pistol. So he took some of his clothes off and climbed into the bed and then he started to rape me.

Q:   [Mrs A.], did he penetrate your vagina?
WITNESS:   Yes.

(*Čelebići* Transcript, 3 April 1997: 1777–8)

M.A. testified that Delić raped her a second and third time and both accounts are described in detail in the transcripts. After the second rape, the witness was seen by two doctors who were also inmates at the camp. During the trial, she stated that she could not tell the doctors what had happened, nor could she tell anyone else about her ordeal.

Under cross-examination, the defence lawyer, Thomas Moran, attempted to question the number of times the witness was raped by the accused, saying: 'there were only three [rapes]; is that correct, as you testified last week, only three?' (*Čelebići* Transcript, 3 April 1997: 1823). He attempted to discredit her testimony because her previous statement to the Office of the Prosecutor stated she was raped on 'multiple occasions':

> she alleged in her statement to the Prosecutor she was raped on multiple occasions. She has testified here twice that it *only occurred three times.* I am just asking her why she exaggerated and why she told the untruth to the investigator for the Prosecutor.

(*Čelebići* Transcript, 3 April 1997: 1825, emphasis added)

Judge Odio Benito responded: 'Can I ask how many times are for you multiple occasions?' Realizing his error, Moran then proceeded to drop the issue. The inconsistencies were thereafter explained by the witness herself:

> I keep repeating the same thing. I don't know what I can answer – what more I can say. The shock I went through, I had never thought that I would reach a state when I would be able to tell somebody I could trust. I was in a state of shock at the time and maybe I wasn't fully aware of what I was saying.

(*Čelebići* Transcript, 3 April 1997: 1836).

Judge Adolphus Karibi-Whyte admonished Moran for repetitive questioning, stating that it amounted to harassment. This example demonstrates a recurrent defence strategy in both domestic and international criminal trials, designed to undermine the credibility and reliability of the witness. In this example, the power of the defence lawyer over the witness relates to his declaration of relevancy regarding her evidence. Despite these allegations, the Trial Chamber found M.A.'s testimony as a whole 'compelling and truthful, particularly in light of her detailed recollection of the circumstances of each rape and her demeanour in the court room in general and, particularly, under cross-examination' (*Čelebići* Judgment, 1998: para. 957). The Chamber added:

The alleged inconsistencies between her evidence at trial and prior statements are immaterial and were sufficiently explained by [Ms. A.]. She consistently stated under cross-examination that, when she made those prior statements, she was experiencing the shock of reliving the rapes that she had 'kept inside for so many years'.

(*Čelebići* Judgment, 1998: para. 957)

Indeed, it has been widely noted that the distortion of memory is not uncommon in the aftermath of traumatic experiences (Herman 2001). As former ICTY Judge Patricia Wald (2002) has noted, witnesses who come to testify at the ICTY are often testifying years after the conflict. Wald argues that witnesses have often spoken to several people about their experiences, including counsellors, journalists, fellow witnesses, field investigators and humanitarian organizations. She adds that inevitably the stories of witnesses will change in form over the years. The *Čelebići* case importantly validated the nature of traumatic memory; that is, traumatic memories do not function in a linear narrative; 'rather, they are encoded in the form of vivid sensations and images' (Herman 2001: 38). The narrative of traumatic events is told in an emotional, fragmented and sometimes contradictory manner. In the context of private testimony, the victim has the opportunity to reconstruct her story in a meaningful way and fragmented memory is assembled over time. In contrast, at international criminal trials testimonies are often conducted in extremely short time frames, depending on the relative importance of the evidence. This inevitably results in testimonial inconsistencies.

The *Čelebići* trial has been heavily criticized because of the treatment of witnesses. For example, the late Elizabeth Neuffer (2001: 298–9):

Led by three American attorneys – who had earned their legal spurs in Texas and brought the freewheeling, combative style of the Lone Star State to the courtroom – the defense team was aggressive ... [they] submitted witnesses to gruelling – and sometimes pointless – cross-examination in an effort to prove they were lying. 'Texas litigation', said defense attorney Tom Moran, who typically appeared in court in black cowboy boots, 'is a contact sport like football'.

Neuffer interviewed prosecution witnesses, prosecutor Teresa McHenry, defence lawyer Thomas Moran, Judge Gabrielle Kirk McDonald, Louise Arbour, previously the Chief Prosecutor, as well as other ICTY staff who asked to remain unidentified. The presiding Judge Karibi-Whyte, Neuffer (2001: 299) noted, 'rarely stopped defense counsel or witnesses as they droned on' and it was suspected that he had been asleep for segments of the trial 'given his propensity to sit with his eyes closed and breathe with a loud, snorelike rattle'. Based on her interviews, Neuffer (ibid.) concluded that the *Čelebići* trial was:

> a combustible combination: traumatized witnesses who wanted to deliver speeches, earnest prosecutors, lax judges, combative defense attorneys. No wonder Mirko Klarin, an independent journalist who regularly attended the trial, would conclude that *Čelebići* had gained the reputation as 'the trial where everything that could go wrong, did go wrong'.

On 16 November 1998, the Trial Chamber rendered its decision. Three out of the four defendants were found guilty on various counts: Delić was sentenced to 20 years, Landžo 15 years, Mucić seven years, and Delalić was acquitted of all charges. Neuffer (2001: 310) called the case a 'goldmine' for legal scholars. The case was significant because it was the first judgment involving multiple defendants. It was the first elucidation of the principle of command responsibility since the Second World War, emphasizing that this doctrine encompasses not only military commanders, but also civilians in positions of authority. The trial importantly established that the conflict in Bosnia-Herzegovina was 'international' in character. Moreover, this case signified the first time rape was recognized by an international criminal court as a crime of 'torture'. According to the judgment, there can be no question that acts of rape may constitute torture under customary and conventional law. The judgment declared that in addition to the violence suffered by the witness, she was raped 'because she is a woman ... [and] this represents a form of discrimination which constitutes a prohibited purpose for the offence of torture' (*Čelebići* Judgment, 1998: para. 941). This reflects a long overdue gender-sensitive approach to sexual assault that importantly recognizes rape within a broader legal framework.

The *Čelebići* case was also the first case where non-Serbs were put on trial for serious violations of international humanitarian law. This marked a dramatic shift from the 'victor's justice' of Nuremberg and Tokyo, and the neglect and disregard of war crimes against women before both historic tribunals.

### A crime against humanity: Foča

The *Foča* trial was one of the biggest international rape trials in history.[20] According to Kelly Askin (2005b), the decision reached in February 2001 represented 'monumental jurisprudence', a rare opportunity for survivors of sexual violence to hold three defendants accountable for rape, torture and enslavement. In total, 16 women testified to being sexually violated by the three accused during the conflict in the former Yugoslavia. The following discussion will explore some of the events at the *Foča* trial, focusing on a selection of testimonies given by witnesses during the trial process. In addition to the other trials mentioned here, I hope to demonstrate the complex ways in which law helps to both shape and thwart memories of past, traumatic events.

The municipality of Foča, located south-east of Sarajevo near the Bosnia-Herzegovina and Serbia and Montenegro border, was taken over by Serb forces in April 1992. According to the indictment, from mid-July 1992 the Serbs arrested villagers from Foča and the surrounding villages.[21] Thousands of Bosnian Muslims and Croats held in detention facilities or kept under house arrest were 'subjected to humiliating and degrading conditions of life, to brutal beatings and to sexual assaults, including rapes' (*Foča* Indictment, 1996: para. 1.4). The primary detention centre for men was the Foča Kazneno-popravni Dom ('KP Dom'), while women were detained in houses, apartments, motels and short-term detention centres, including Buk Bijela, Kalinovik Primary School, Foča High School and Partizan Sports Hall ('Partizan'). The indictment described how groups of armed soldiers had 'unfettered access' to Partizan and Kalinovik and removed women to houses, apartments or hotels in order to sexually assault and rape them.

In the initial indictment issued on 26 June 1996, Dragan Gagovič, Gojko Jankovič, Janko Janjič, Zoran Vukovič, Dragan Zelenovič and Radovan Stankovič were charged with crimes against humanity and violations of the laws or customs of war. In an amended indictment, the prosecutor brought isolated charges against Dragoljub Kunarac, a commander of a special unit for reconnaissance of the Bosnian Serb Army, and Radomir Kovač, a sub-commander of the military police and paramilitary leader in Foča. They were charged with crimes against humanity and violations of the laws or customs of war for the rape and sexual enslavement of Muslim women and girls. Both Kunarac and Kovač were charged with individual criminal responsibility as direct participants of the alleged crimes. Kunarac was also charged with superior responsibility for the actions of his subordinates, in that he should have known, or must have known, about the perpetration of these crimes, yet did nothing to prevent them from happening. Zoran Vukovič, also a sub-commander of the military police and paramilitary leader in Foča, was tried alongside Kunarac and Kovač in an amended indictment. Of the other defendants, Radovan Stankovič, Dragan Zelenovič and Gojko Jankovič were tried and sentenced in the State Court of Bosnia Herzegovina.[22] Dragan Gagovič and Janko Janjič died in arrest attempts.[23]

The trial began on 20 March 2000, calling a total of 33 witnesses, including 16 women who had been raped. These women testified with protective measures, including the use of pseudonyms, closed sessions and voice/face distortion. Kunarac, Kovač and Vukovič were accused of taking part in the mass rapes of Muslim women and girls in the various detention facilities and local apartments in Foča. Victims were subject to constant individual and gang rapes. One girl was 12 years old and was never seen again. According to presiding Judge Florence Mumba, in a statement read in court:

What the evidence shows, are Muslim women and girls, mothers and daughters together, robbed of the last vestiges of human dignity, women and girls treated like chattels, pieces of property at the time of arbitrary disposal of the Serb occupation forces, and more specifically, at the beck and call of the three accused.

(*Foča* Summary of Judgment)

The prosecutor alleged that the attack on the Muslim population in Foča was part of 'an organised and planned campaign and policy of the Bosnian Serb authorities to ethnically purge the Foca municipality of non-Serbs' (*Foča* Transcript, 20 March 2000: 300). According to Witness 183[24] in her testimony, while she was being gang-raped, the accused Kunarac told her she would have a son 'and that I would not know whose it was, but the most important thing was that it would be a Serb child' (*Foča* Transcript, 22 May 2000: 3683). Likewise, Witness 48 told the court that the accused said to her: 'it was a pity that others should rape me. That he thought I looked like a Montenegrin … He said that we would no longer have Muslim babies, that we would only give birth to Serbs, and that there would be no Muslims in Foča anymore' (*Foča* Transcript, 2 May 2000: 2667). These testimonies contribute to a collective memory of the conflict in the former Yugoslavia, namely one that confirms the use of rape as a form of ethnic cleansing.

· On 30 March 2000, Witness 75 gave evidence regarding the mass rapes that took place in Foča. In part of her testimony she gave a description of one of many occasions where she was taken out and gang-raped. In the following example, the prosecutor asked the witness to describe the rape:

Q:   Where were you taken after you passed your uncle?
WITNESS:   About five meters away, to another room, where an old Chetnik met me. He was 40 or 50 years old, and he pushed me into a room there and made me take my clothes off. And he said that he would be the only one to rape me there.
Q:   At that time were you frightened?
WITNESS:   Of course I was frightened. I was not just frightened; I was completely in a state of shock.
Q:   And did this man rape you?
WITNESS:   Yes, he did.
Q:   Was that the only one who raped you at that time?
WITNESS:   In that hall I just counted up to ten, because that was the order they made. I counted up to 10, and I don't know how many there were after that number. There could have been about 20 of them. I don't know.
Q:   When you say 'rape' what exactly do you mean?
WITNESS:   I don't understand your question.
Q:   You said that this 40 – this elderly man raped you. What exactly did he do?
WITNESS:   He forced me onto the bed to take my clothes off, and then he raped me, he attacked me and raped me.
Q:   Does it mean he put his penis into your vagina?
WITNESS:   Yes.

Q: And these other men, did they do the same thing?

WITNESS: The same thing, yes.

Q: Were you conscious all the time when that happened?

WITNESS: I was conscious up to 10, up to the time I counted 10. Then I lost consciousness, and I know that some of them brought some water to splash over me and that I was all wet from that water when I came to, when I regained consciousness. But that didn't mean anything to them. They continued doing what they were doing.

(*Foča* Transcript, 30 March 2000: 1389–91)

In an interview with Wendy Lobwein and Monika Naslund from the Victims and Witnesses Section at the ICTY, I asked them about the potential for retraumatization because of the necessity for witnesses to describe the details of what happened to them:

There is no way around it, it is not easy for women to be questioned in a court full of dressed-up strange people, around the kinds of words they have to use to describe what happened and so one of the things I have seen is that for many of the women, also in the Rwanda Tribunal and maybe even more so, is unfamiliarity of having to use the language that the court wants to hear. So women will want to say 'he shamed me' and the judge wants to hear 'he put his penis inside my vagina', so using this language, naming these body parts in this way is not something that women are very familiar with and I watch their mouths struggle to spit out the details of what the assaults were or when the prosecutor has to put it very clearly, 'did this event happen?' and spell it out and the strength of these women as they say yes or whatever and to answer these questions there in the courtroom ... it is *never ever* easy for women to testify against sexual assault.

(Personal Interview, 17 October 2002, emphasis original)

Like the other women who testified, Witness 50's story was told through the (albeit limited) structure of trial testimony. Witness 50 was a 16-year-old living in the Foča municipality when war broke out in April 1992. In July 1992, she was captured by four uniformed soldiers while living in the woods with her family. She was taken to a bedroom in a motel and raped by the accused Zoran Vukovič, before then being taken to Foča High School, where she had previously been a high school student. She was picked out by a group of soldiers with seven other girls and raped. The ICTY website has documented the witness's testimony in narrative form, part of which is relayed below:

Witness 50 ... saw Serb soldiers taking other girls out, by pointing at them: 'You, you or you'. She said they would take them out when they wanted to: every night some girl would end up somewhere with some soldier. Witness 50 said that when the girls came back they would all be crying, while some would be bleeding from the nose, screaming, or tearing out their hair.

(http://www.icty.org/sid/188)

At the trial, she told of how she was raped by the accused Vukovič. She told the court that once he had finished, 'he sat down and lit a cigarette, and he said that he could perhaps do more, much more, but that I was about the same age as his daughter, and so he wouldn't do anything more for the moment' (*Foča* Transcript, 29 March 2000: 1263). Her testimony is replete with shocking stories of repeated rape, including when she was raped in a 'beast-like manner' by a Montenegrin soldier who told her, 'You will see, you Muslim. I am going to draw a cross on your back. I'm going to baptise all of you. You're now going to be Serbs' (http://www.icty.org/sid/188).

Although the stories of Witness 50 and other witnesses like her were importantly documented during this trial and do, I believe, contribute to a collective narrative about wartime rape, nonetheless it is important to take into account some limitations and harms associated with giving testimony at an international rape trial. In conjunction with the humiliation of having the private details of bodily violation made public, intrusive cross-examination strategies were a prominent feature of this particular trial. According to the ICTY's Rule 96, the defence is not allowed to raise corroboration, prior sexual history, nor consent if captivity was a factor. However, the rules of evidence and procedure proved inadequate to prevent certain questions designed by the defence to discredit witness testimonies. For example, in cross-examination, the defence raised the issue that Witness 50 failed in her initial statement to tell the ICTY about the first time she was raped. The witness responded that it was because it was her first and most painful experience and she was frightened. In another example of witness credibility being undermined, Witness 205 was cross-examined by the defence counsel about how many times she was raped. According to the defence, there was a discrepancy in the number of times the witness was raped according to her initial statement to the Office of the Prosecutor and her testimony during the trial (*Foča* Transcript, 29 March 2000).

Similar to domestic rape trials in adversarial contexts, one of the most prejudicial cross-examination strategies involves the invocation of consent. The ICTY's Rule 96 states:

> Consent shall not be allowed as a defence if the victim has been subjected to or threatened with or has had reason to fear violence, duress, detention or psychological oppression … or reasonably believed that if the victim did not submit, another person might be subjected to sexual assault, threatened or put in fear.

At the ICTY, the accused has to satisfy the Trial Chamber in camera that the evidence of consent is relevant and credible. This rule relies on the control of the judges in order to protect victims from offensive allegations regarding complicity in rape. However, as Kate Fitzgerald (1997: 641) points out, being subjected to allegations of consent compounds the humiliation: 'Regardless of the control exercised by presiding judges over proceedings, it would be difficult to assure already traumatized witnesses that they would not suffer further attack upon their dignity by unimpeded defence examination as to consent'. In the following example, the defence suggested that one of the witnesses was not telling the truth because she was suffering from a bout of jealousy:

Q:  Will you agree with me that jealousy is a psychological state, when a person imbued by is ready to do certain things [sic] which people which are not imbued by jealousy would not consider doing?

WITNESS:  I'm afraid I don't understand that question at all. What are you talking about? What do you mean by jealousy?

Q:  I'm referring to the fact that you said that after four or five days, Klanfa [Kovač] rejected you. I said yesterday that in my understanding, when a man rejects a woman, it is usually a person he loves and not a person who has been raped.

WITNESS:  How could I possibly be Klanfa's beloved?

(*Foča* Transcript, 4 April 2000: 1624)

These recurrent defence strategies serve as statements of blame, containing 'clear negative evaluations of the witness's behavior' (Conley and O'Barr 1998: 28) regardless of the witness's answer.

Witness 87, another teenage girl at the time of the conflict in April 1992, also testified in great detail about the rapes she endured during the conflict. She was aged 15, living with her father, mother, sister and brother close to Foča when the shooting and explosions began. She too spent time hiding with her family in the woods out of fear of death. On 3 July 1992, her village was attacked by Serb forces and upon hearing shots, she said 'there was panic, and the people started fleeing. Nobody knew where to go, in which direction' (*Foča* Transcript, 4 April 2000: 1666). She was thereafter captured by Serb soldiers in camouflage uniforms and then some time later taken to a hotel building known as Buk Bjela, where she was raped. She told the court that she did not disclose her experiences to anyone, including her mother: 'I think that at that time I didn't have the strength to, to even look her in the eyes. Not only her, but anybody, to look anybody in the eyes … I felt ashamed in a way, and in a way I felt very, very dirty, soiled' (*Foča* Transcript, 4 April 2000: 1675). She was later taken to Foča High School and almost every night, soldiers called out her name and she was taken to an apartment or to a classroom to be raped. After two weeks at the Foča High School, the witness was taken to the Partizan Sports Hall, also in Foča, faced the nightly selections and was taken out to various houses and apartments. The witness, her sister ('DB') and three other girls were later removed to a house where they lived for two months, experiencing repeated rape by the three accused and other soldiers. The trial importantly documents the nature of this sexual enslavement; for example, Witness 87 testified that 'special people had the right to enter that house' and these soldiers were the men who raped them (*Foča* Transcript, 4 April 2000: 1706). When asked if she was able to count how many times she was raped in the house, Witness 87 said, 'I don't think that is possible' (*Foča* Transcript, 4 April 2000: 1703). Her testimony reveals many more months of rape and sexual enslavement and this is described vividly in the trial transcripts.

On 23 October 2000, Witness 87 was recalled to rebut that she was a girlfriend of the accused Kovač. Defence witnesses had testified to seeing Witness 87 with Kovač in several cafés around Foča during the summer of 1992, that she had been introduced as his 'girlfriend', and the couple 'looked to be in love' (*Foča* Transcript, 23 October 2000). Witnesses, including the accused's cousin, also testified that Witness 87 had sent Kovač a letter with a love-heart drawn on it expressing gratitude for all he had done for her and that she had also sent a postcard from Montenegro (*Foča* Transcript, 23 October 2000). One witness told the court that Witness 87 had said she was in love with Kovač. However, this witness later admitted that it was the accused who had told her about the nature of the relationship, not Witness 87. Witness 87 stated that she was raped orally and vaginally almost every night by the accused. In her evidence in rebuttal regarding her alleged relationship with Kovač, she said that she went to the cafés with Kovač because he wanted her to go, that she had not sent him any postcard or letter and denied being in love with him: 'I was not in love, nor did I look like I was his girlfriend. I think that all the people who saw us in the café knew who I was and why I was with him' (quoted in IWPR 2000). The following illustrates the offensive line of questioning put forth by the defence:

Q:   It is a fact that Kovac helped you and rescued you from the hell of war and you are here giving false testimony. So will you tell us why? Why don't you tell us that he helped you?
WITNESS:   To begin—
Q:   And that you were – that you liked him?
WITNESS:   To begin with, I did not like him. Secondly, it's not true that he helped me. To be grateful? There's nothing to be grateful for, because – because – I really don't see why should I be grateful. Because he raped me?
(*Foča* Transcript, 23 October 2000: 6137)

Judith Herman (2001: 75) argues that a perpetrator appears to have 'a psychological need to justify his crimes, and for this he needs the victim's affirmation'. Subsequently, perpetrators may act as though they are in a relationship with their captive subject. One former comfort woman said, for example, that she 'hated the way [the man who raped me] acted as though he was my lover, not my rapist' (quoted in Lusby 1994: 930). In the *Foča* case, despite testifying to repeated rape and categorically denying a relationship with the accused, Witness 87 was nonetheless subjected to cross-examination that suggested complicity in a romantic relationship as opposed to a rela- *[handwritten: RAPE ≠ A RELAT-IONSHIP]* tionship of subjection, exploitation and captivity. Again, this is a recurrent defence strategy in domestic rape trials.

The Trial Chamber, however, ruled that Witness 87 did not send a letter to the accused, noting that none of the defence witnesses actually read the content of the letter and had only heard about it from the accused himself. The Chamber declared: 'The relationship between Witness 87 and Kovac was not one of love as the Defense suggested, but rather one of cruel opportunism on Kovac's part, of constant abuses and domination over a girl who, at the relevant time, was only about 15 years old' (*Foča* Judgment, 2001: para. 762). The Chamber also proved beyond reasonable doubt that the accused had forced Witness 87 and other victims to dance naked on the table while pointing weapons at them:

> The accused Radomir Kovac certainly knew that, having to stand naked on a table, while the accused watched them, was a painful and humiliating experience for the three women involved, even more so because of their young age. The Trial Chamber is satisfied that Kovac must have been aware of that fact, but he nevertheless ordered them to gratify him by dancing naked for him.
>
> (*Foča* Judgment, 2001: para. 773)

The defence did not deny that rapes had taken place; however, they argued that the prosecution had not proved that the three accused had actually 'raped' any of the witnesses. The defence argued that, due to an accident, Vukovič was impotent and therefore could not have physically raped any of the witnesses on the dates specified at the trial, and that Kovač was having a relationship with one of the witnesses (as explained above).

During the trial, Kunarac (the only defendant to testify) managed to raise the defence of consent. He claimed that Witness DB seduced him in order to *[handwritten: asshole]* distract him from further investigation and questioning. Kunarac testified that Gordana Draškovič, a female journalist, had been speaking to some of the detainees at Partizan and had told Kunarac about the allegations of rape and that his name had been mentioned. Kunarac claimed mistaken identity; that someone else had acted in his name.[25] According to his testimony, after speaking with Draškovič, he took Witness 75 and DB to the soldiers' headquarters, the house at Ulica Osmana Đjikica, to find out who was behind the abuse. According to Kunarac: 'That was my most sincere wish and intention: to find out who had mistreated them and who had introduced himself as me and done something in my name, so to speak' (*Foča* Transcript, 10 July 2000: 4675). His testimony is as follows:

> I had insisted so persistently that she gave me the names of these men or to mention any man, even if they were not those who were in the house, then she started beseeching me that I do not ask her. Then she was sitting

next to me. She fell on me. She put her head on my chest and begged me not to ask her anything. This gesture on her part did surprise me. I tried to pacify her, to convince her that there was no reason for her to be frightened, that nothing would happen to her, that she would be protected ... [the accused here goes into detail about the 'seduction'] I tried to refuse this behaviour of hers and to tell her again that I had to find out who these men were, because do I not want my name to be mentioned in such contexts. I don't want this journalist to write such articles that I had nothing to do with ... [more details about the 'seduction'] I remained totally confused ... She did not allow me to say anything. After that, I accepted this behaviour of hers and we had full sexual vaginal intercourse, although I did nothing to give her a reason or pretext for this. And I did not refuse her in any way; I accepted her behaviour.

(*Foča* Transcript, 10 July 2000: 4541–2)

Kunarac was asked by Judge Mumba, 'Is it your position, accused, that DB seduced you?' (*Foča* Transcript, 6 July 2000: 4542). Kunarac replied that he did not give DB any reason to believe that he wanted to have sexual intercourse with her. He therefore claimed that he had sexual intercourse with DB against *his will*. Kunarac then testified in even more detail about the sexual intercourse (again I have decided not to relay this due to the risk that it may come across as voyeuristic).

DB testified in closed session on 23 May 2000. She admitted that she took the initiative with Kunarac because one of his subordinates told her to do so. According to the judgment, DB said she felt terribly humiliated because she had to take an active part in the events' (*Foča* Judgment: para. 219). In rendering its judgment, the Trial Chamber accepted the testimony of DB, stating that it was 'highly improbable that the accused Kunarac could realistically have been "confused" by the behaviour of D.B., given the general context of the existing war-time situation and the specifically delicate situation of the Muslim girls detained in Partizan or elsewhere in the Foca region during that time' (*Foča* Judgment, 2001: para. 646).

In addition to claiming that the three accused did not rape any women and girls, the defence in this case argued that the victims' lack of resistance (their failure to attempt escape and report the crime) undermined the prosecution's case and that there was insufficient evidence that the crime of rape had taken place. In his closing argument, chief defence counsel Slaviša Prodanovič claimed that there were no guards and that all of the prosecution witnesses could move around freely in the building of the secondary school. This argument was based on the testimony of an expert witness who had relied on information given by the Herzegovina Corps of the Bosnian Serb Army, and who had not visited the premises nor talked to detainees. The witnesses in this trial testified that in fact they could not leave the premises and there were guards working in shifts who would permit soldiers to enter the facilities and prevent detainees from escaping (*Foča* Judgment, 2001). The defence counsel asked FWS-51 to explain why she did not try and escape if she was afraid for her life and conditions were bad. The witness explained:

> To escape where? Where could I escape? Did we have any money? Did we have any transport? Did we have any resources? How could I escape? … The last 100 marks they took away from me when I arrived in Foca. How could I go anywhere? Who could I pay for my ticket? Who would take me out? Who would take me on? Where would I go?
>
> (*Foča* Transcript, 29 March 2000: 1205)

The Trial Chamber was in general agreement with the factors put forth by the prosecution determining the crime of enslavement. These factors included: the control of someone's movement; the control of the physical environment; psychological control; measures taken to prevent or deter escape; force and threat of coercion; duration; assertion of exclusivity; subjection to cruel treatment and abuse; control of sexuality; and forced labour (*Foča* Judgment, 2001). This finding importantly affirmed that captivity vitiates 'consent'.

On 28 February 2001, the three accused were convicted of rape, torture and enslavement as a crime against humanity, as a violation of the laws of war, and as outrages upon personal dignity. In rendering the judgment, the Trial Chamber found Dragoljub Kunarac guilty on 11 counts of crimes under violations of the laws or customs of war for torture and rape, and crimes against humanity for torture, rape and enslavement, and sentenced him to 28 years' imprisonment. The Trial Chamber found Radomir Kovač guilty on four counts of violations of the laws or customs of war for rape and outrages upon personal dignity, and crimes against humanity for rape and enslavement. Kovač was sentenced to 20 years' imprisonment. The third defendant, Zoran Vukovič, was found guilty on four counts of violations of the laws or customs of war for torture and rape, and crimes against humanity for torture and rape. Vukovič was sentenced to 12 years' imprisonment.

In collective memory terms, the *Foča* trial and the decision signalled for the first time in history that an international criminal tribunal dealt exclusively with crimes of rape and enslavement. Second, it was the second case to find defendants guilty of rape as a crime against humanity (the *Akayesu* case at the ICTR in 1998 was the first). Third, the case was significant as it considered the 'mass rape' phenomenon in the war in Bosnia-Herzegovina and the integral role that sexual violence played in the policy of ethnic cleansing (see Maravilla 2000). According to a spokesperson for the court:

> This is a landmark indictment because it focuses exclusively on sexual assaults, without including any other charges … There is no precedent for this. It is of major legal significance because it illustrates the court's

strategy to focus on gender-related crimes and give them proper place in the prosecution of war crimes.

(quoted in Simons 1996)

Amnesty International gave a statement after the decision, remarking that the verdict 'is a significant step for women's human rights – sexual enslave-ment in armed conflict is now legally acknowledged as a crime against humanity and perpetrators can and must be held to account' (Amnesty International 2001). However, some commentators, such as Kelly Askin (2005b), have criticized the decision because it did not use the term 'sexual slavery': 'The judgment often failed to even mention the sexual nature of the enslavement, and when it did it usually treated the rapes as merely one of a number of indicators of the enslavement, instead of treating it as an inherent part of and the principal purpose for the enslavement'. Moreover, while this case was legally significant and across the world many people were celebrating the achievement, little is known about the impact of the trials on the women who testified, many of whom returned to lives completely torn apart by war.

## The International Criminal Tribunal for Rwanda

The ICTR was established by the United Nations Security Council in 1994 in Arusha, Tanzania, for the crimes committed in Rwanda during its 1994 gen-ocide. During the genocide, 800,000 Rwandan Tutsis and Hutu political moderates were slaughtered over 100 days (see Des Forges 1999; Gourevitch 1999; Melvern 2004; Prunier 1995). The ICTR Statute includes the same sorts of violations of international humanitarian law as the ICTY.[26] Like the former Yugoslavia, rape has become a durable memory of the post-conflict legacy of Rwanda's past, due to organized propaganda inciting rape, as well as the brutality, extent and public nature of the rapes:

> Throughout the Rwandan genocide, widespread sexual violence, directed predominantly against Tutsi women, occurred in every prefecture. Thousands of women were raped on the streets, at checkpoints, in culti-vated plots, in or near government buildings, hospitals, churches, and other places where they sought sanctuary. Women were held individually and in groups as sexual slaves for the purpose of rape. They were raped to death using sharp sticks or other objects. Their dead bodies were often left naked, bloody and spread-eagled in public view. The hate propaganda before and during the genocide fuelled the sexual violence by demonizing Tutsi women's sexuality.

(Nowrojee 2005: 4)

In his 1996 report, the United Nations Special Rapporteur on Rwanda, Rene Degni-Segui, called rape a 'weapon of war' in Rwanda, noting that it was 'the rule and its absence the exception' (quoted in de Brouwer 2005: 11).

He estimated that between 250,000 and 500,000 women and girls were raped during the 1994 genocide. The Organization of African Unity's International Panel of Eminent Personalities further concluded in 2000: 'we can be certain that almost all females who survived the genocide were direct victims of rape or other sexual violence, or were profoundly affected by it' (ibid.). The post-conflict, legal response to wartime rape and other forms of sexual violence at the ICTR was dealt with in both innovative and problematic ways. Critics, for example, have pointed to an array of issues, including: inappropriate inter-viewing methodology; the lack of political will to investigate rape as part of an integral prosecution strategy; the failure of the ICTR to secure convictions for rape; dropped charges; acquittals; as well as the lack of preparation, information, follow-up and post-trial protection for victims who come to tes-tify at this court to these crimes (Nowrojee 2005). Arguably, this forms part of the collective memory of the ICTR and wartime rape. As Binaifer Nowrojee (2005: 4) writes, 'squandered opportunities … have characterized sexual vio-lence prosecutions over the past decade at the International Criminal Tribunal for Rwanda'. While the ICTR created groundbreaking precedent in the *Akayesu* case by prosecuting rape as a crime of genocide for the first time in history (see below), the problems related to the court's treatment of rape crimes and victims of these crimes form part of a dubious legacy that is arguably indicative of a persistent and broader indifference to crimes against women during warfare. Nowrojee (2005: 23–4) writes that at the ICTR:

> rape victims have been harangued and harassed on the stand by defense counsel without intervention by the prosecution lawyers or the judges. Because many of the trials are joint trials with numerous defendants, rape victims are often subjected to hours, days and weeks on the stand, being cross-examined by each defense counsel, sometimes going over the same questions again and again. A prosecution lawyer noted that a rape victim who she led on the stand was asked 1,194 questions by the defense counsel.

Judges at the ICTR have reportedly been reluctant to rein in intrusive or hostile cross-examination of witnesses, leaving some victims 'feeling violated for a second time … [outraged] at the fact that they had to endure days of repeated, detailed questioning about the intimate details of the rapes they endured' (ibid.: 23). During the *Butare* trial,[27] three judges reportedly laughed out loud as a rape victim described how she was raped (The Monitor 2001). While the laughter was in response to the insensitive questions posed by the defence lawyer ('did you bathe in between the rapes?'; 'how was it introduced into our vagina?' and 'were you injured in the process of being raped by nine men?'), the witness never received an apology nor were the judges repri-manded for their behaviour. The witness spoke to human rights advocate Binaifer Nowrojee (2005: 24) about her experience of testifying before the ICTR, saying that when the judges laughed she felt 'angry and nervous'.

After testifying, she said her fiancé refused to marry her because she had 'told everyone that you were raped'.

### Genocidal rape: Akayesu

The 1998 ICTR *Akayesu* decision was groundbreaking in the history of international criminal justice.[28] For the first time in history, an individual was charged with the crime of genocide, and for the first time in history, the Trial Chamber found that rape constituted a crime against humanity and, more significantly, a crime of genocide. It declared that 'sexual assault formed an integral part of the process of destroying the Tutsi ethnic group and that the rape was systematic and had been perpetrated against Tutsi women only, manifesting the specific intent required for those acts to constitute genocide' (*Akayesu* Judgment, 1998: para. 733). No evidence of explicit orders to rape was found; however, the Trial Chamber was satisfied that military leaders had encouraged or ordered their men to rape Tutsi women and there was little effort to stop this from happening.[29]

Jean-Paul Akayesu, a former teacher and school inspector, married with five children, was charged with genocide, crimes against humanity and violations of the Geneva Conventions for his role as mayor of the Taba commune from April 1993 until June 1994. He was charged with individual criminal responsibility for planning, instigating, ordering, committing or otherwise aiding and abetting such crimes, due to his exclusive control of the communal police and the administration of justice in the Taba commune, in the prefecture of Gitarama, 11 miles from the capital Kigali. The indictment described that while displaced Tutsi civilians sought refuge at the *bureau communal*, murders and rapes were frequent on or near the premises: '[Women were] regularly taken by armed local militia and/or communal police and subjected to sexual violence, and/or beaten on or near the bureau communal premises. Many of these women were forced to endure multiple acts of sexual violence which were at times committed by more than one assailant' (*Akayesu* Indictment, 1996: para. 12A). The prosecution alleged that the killings, beatings and rapes were so widespread that the accused must have known about them, yet he did nothing to prevent them from occurring.

Initially, there were no sexual violence charges in the *Akayesu* indictment, despite the extensive documentation from human rights groups in the region. The ICTR's first deputy prosecutor reportedly said: 'It is a waste of time to investigate rape charges in Rwanda, because African women don't like to talk about rape. We haven't received any real complaints' (quoted in Goodwin 1997). According to Nowrojee (Human Rights Watch 1996), the problems first occurred with the UN investigation teams who sent out teams of two men with a Rwandan interpreter, and due to the stigma and shame of rape, women were reluctant to speak to these teams.

The failure to charge the accused initially with crimes of rape caused much outrage among feminist and human rights organizations,[30] and the indictment was amended later to include additional charges against the accused regarding allegations of sexual violence. This occurred after a prosecution witness, Witness J, a Tutsi woman, spontaneously mentioned during her testimony how her six-year-old daughter was raped by three Interahamwe (Hutu milita), as well as Witness H's testimony that she was raped in a sorghum field just outside the compound of the *bureau communal* and had seen other Tutsi women being raped. Beth Van Schaack (2009: 7) writes, 'If J had not offered the fact that her six-year-old daughter had been raped, the existence of sexual violence in Taba Commune may never have made it into the formal record'. She adds, however, that during these two testimonies, few details from the witnesses were solicited regarding these rapes – 'almost as if no one wanted to touch the material or failed to immediately recognize its significance'.

Based on the amended indictment, the trial was temporarily suspended to investigate the allegations of sexual violence. The trial recommenced on 23 October 1997. Five female witnesses testified to having either witnessed extreme acts of sexual violence, or having been raped themselves in or near the compound where the accused exercised authority. Witness JJ, for example, testified that after her home was destroyed by her Hutu neighbours, she fled and sought refuge in a nearby forest with her baby and her younger sister, before then going to the compound for protection. According to the judgment, Witness JJ testified that:

> the Interahamwe took young girls and women from their site of refuge near the bureau communal into a forest in the area and raped them. Witness JJ testified that this happened to her – that she was stripped of her clothing and raped in front of other people. At the request of the Prosecutor and with great embarrassment, she explicitly specified that the rapist, a young man armed with an axe and a long knife, penetrated her vagina with his penis. She stated that on this occasion she was raped twice. Subsequently, she told the Chamber, on a day when it was raining, she was taken by force from near the bureau communal into the cultural center within the compound of the bureau communal, in a group of approximately fifteen girls and women. In the cultural center, according to Witness JJ, they were raped. She was raped twice by one man. Then another man came to where she was lying and he also raped her. A third man then raped her, she said, at which point she described herself as feeling near dead ... Witness JJ testified that she could not count the total number of times she was raped. She said, 'each time you encountered attackers they would rape you', – in the forest, in the sorghum fields. Witness JJ related to the Chamber the experience of finding her sister before she died, having been raped and cut with a machete.
>
> (*Akayesu* Judgment, 1998: para. 421)

Witness JJ later fled the *bureau communal*, leaving her one-year-old child who was subsequently killed: 'Witness JJ spoke of the heavy sorrow the war had caused her. She testified to the humiliation she felt as a mother, by the public nudity and being raped in the presence of children by young men. She said that just thinking about it made the war come alive inside her' (*Akayesu* Judgment, 1998: para. 423) (see also Neuffer 2001). Her younger sister, Witness NN, also testified in this trial, describing how she too was raped. Again, according to the judgment: 'her mother begged the men, who were armed with bludgeons and machetes, to kill her daughters rather than rape them in front of her, and the man replied that the "principle was to make them suffer" and the girls were then raped ... She said her sister was raped ... at the same time, near her, so that they could each see what was happening to the other. Afterwards, she said she begged for death' (*Akayesu* Judgment, 1998: para. 430).

The trial heard from Witness OO, who was aged 15 years at the time she and her family sought refuge at the *bureau communal* in April 1994. She too experienced multiple rapes by the Interahamwe. Another rape victim, Witness KK, had also sought refuge with her family. She was a Hutu woman who was married to a Tutsi man, who was later killed by the Interahamwe. In addition to other witnesses, she testified to seeing women and girls 'taken away to the cultural center at the bureau communal by Interahamwes who said they were going to "sleep with" these women and girls ... She described the Interahamwes forcing a piece of wood into [a] woman's sexual organs while she was still breathing, before she died' (*Akayesu* Judgment, 1998: para. 429).

The defence in this cased raised discrepancies between the pre-trial statements made by the witnesses and their testimonies. The Chamber, however, found the discrepancies unfounded and immaterial, stating that any inconsistencies 'can be explained by the difficulties of recollecting precise details several years after the occurrence of the events, the trauma experienced by the witnesses to these events, the difficulties of translation, and the fact that several witnesses were illiterate and stated that they had not read their written statements' (*Akayesu* Judgment, 1998: para. 455).

There was no evidence that the accused had personally raped any of the women; however, the Trial Chamber concluded beyond reasonable doubt that the accused 'had reason to know or in fact knew that sexual violence was taking place on or near the premises of the bureau communal, and that women were being taken away from the bureau communal and sexually violated' (*Akayesu* Judgment, 1998: para. 452). They could find no evidence that the accused took any measures to prevent or punish acts of sexual violence. The Chamber found the accused guilty of rape as a form of genocide, because there was a specific intent to destroy, in whole or in part, a particular group. Jean-Paul Akayesu was subsequently sentenced to three life terms and 80 years' imprisonment, which he is currently serving in Mali.

Polish lawyer Raphael Lemkin coined the term 'genocide' in 1944 by combining the Greek word for race or tribe (*genos*) with the root of the Latin word for killing (*occidere*), and in 1948, the United Nations adopted the

Genocide Convention. Subsequently, the invocation of genocide as the most egregious of all crimes has resulted in calls for humanitarian intervention in genocidal conflict zones, such as Darfur, the Democratic Republic of Congo and other locations; prosecutions at the international level (as discussed here); and the reconceptualization of past historical atrocities as 'genocide' (e.g. the Stolen Generations in Australia). The study of genocide has culminated in extraordinary debates surrounding all of the above issues, for example, the literal interpretation of various parts of the Genocide Convention (e.g. the level of intention required); whether various conflicts or situations constitute forms of genocide; and whether colonialist and imperialist policies and practices should or could fall under the Convention (see e.g. Moses and Stone 2007).

Due to the general reluctance of academics, politicians and courts to classify certain crimes as genocide or 'genocidal', the decision rendered in the *Akayesu* case has had enormous significance for the development of international humanitarian law, as various courts have considered genocidal sexual violence and/or upheld the *Akayesu* findings (see de Brouwer 2005).[31] Wartime rape as a form of genocide has also incited much controversy and debate (see e.g. Engle 2005). Anne Marie de Brouwer (2005: 43) argues that reference to gender in the Genocide Convention as a group capable of being destroyed was 'blatantly absent' in 1948 when it was adopted, and much debate surrounds whether or not rape and other forms of sexual violence can constitute the crime of genocide. Copelon (1993), for example, was hesitant about distinguishing between different forms of rape due to the hierarchical effect that this creates (e.g. genocidal rape being conceived as much worse than other forms of rape during periods of armed conflict). Debate has also centred around whether or not forced impregnation should be the measuring stick for the definition of rape as a form of genocide (see e.g. Carpenter 2000; Goldstein 1993), while others have argued that the rapes perpetrated against Rwandan women were random acts of violence, rather than acts of genocide (Lyons 2001).

The stories told of rape, humiliation, sexual slavery, torture and mutilation at the Rwandan Tribunal help to implant a collective narrative of suffering, of women in war generally, and of the Tutsi women of Rwanda more specifically. The decision that rape constitutes a form of genocide represents an opportunity to reconceptualize wartime sexual violence as falling under the most egregious categories of international crimes. The *Akayesu* decision importantly established that genocidal rape was perpetrated because of both a woman's ethnicity *and* her gender, signalling not only that rape can achieve the whole or partial destruction of an entire group, but that these crimes cause considerable bodily and psychological harm to individual women: 'rape is considered to be one of the worst ways of inflicting bodily and mental harm upon an individual' (de Brouwer 2005: 45). This is a far cry from the treatment of gendered harms at the historic war crimes trials after the Second World War. As Catharine MacKinnon (2005: 940) has argued, 'Each time a rape law is created or applied or a rape case is tried, communities rethink what rape is'. Also, as mentioned in footnote 3 of Chapter 1, the Trial Chamber adopted a broad definition of rape as 'a physical invasion of a sexual nature, committed on a person under circumstances which are coercive'. This too signals a major reconceptualization of rape in law 'as what it is in life' (ibid.: 944). Askin (2000: 52) described the case as 'the most important decision rendered thus far in the history of women's jurisprudence'. She writes that:

> The *Akayesu* Judgment formally recognized that gender-related crimes are systematically used as instruments of war and terror, and the impact of the crime is extensive and devastating, resulting in harm inflicted far beyond the immediate victim, extending to families, whole communities, associated groups and the public at large. The significance of the law developed in this case is unparalleled.
>
> (Askin 2005a: 1012)

No doubt, the case has contributed substantively to the collective memory of wartime rape but its legacy remains uncertain, due to the inadequacies of subsequent trials, including dropped charges, acquittals on sexual violence charges, as well as 'other missed opportunities and debacles' (ibid.: 1008; see also MacKinnon 2008; Nowrojee 2005 and above discussion). Van Schaack (2009: 29) further concludes:

> Subsequent cases – at least before the ICTR – have not, by and large, built on the *Akayesu* precedent. If anything, the cause of gender justice seems to have been subject to backsliding. As the two ad hoc tribunals wind down under their Completion Strategies, the story of *Akayesu* is likely to become a mere introduction to further developments in gender justice achieved before the International Criminal Court. For now, *Akayesu* stands alone in recognizing rape as a form of genocide.

Although the legacy of the *Akayesu* case remains to be seen (particularly in the work of the International Criminal Court), there is no doubt that it has contributed substantively to the development of international law and much discussion has centred on this legacy (see e.g. MacKinnon 2008). However, it is important to point out that the legacy of these courts extends beyond the narrow confines of legal interpretation and application. As such, I believe that the cases discussed in this chapter have contributed to a major reconceptualization of wartime sexual violence beyond the legal realm. Specifically, the *Akayesu* trial and decision have significantly shaped the collective memory of wartime rape, and indeed have contributed to an entire political discourse surrounding the ever controversial subject matter of genocide, and of genocidal rape.

## Beyond the International Criminal Court

In July 2002, the International Criminal Court (ICC) was established as the world's first permanent war crimes court to try individuals for the most 'serious crimes of international concern' (see Bassiouni 2002; Cassese, Jones and Gaeta 2002; Sadat 2002; Schabas 2001). Adopted on 17 July 1998, the statute of this court reflects – in theory – a progressive shift towards a victim-focused forum of justice and is evidence of the increasing trend towards a more restorative approach within retributive models of international criminal justice.[32] Rape, sexual slavery, enforced prostitution, forced pregnancy, enforced sterilization and any other forms of sexual violence of comparable gravity are explicitly prohibited in the ICC Statute as a crime against humanity and a war crime in international and non-international armed conflict. Rape is not, however, explicitly enumerated as a crime of genocide.

On 23 June 2004, the Office of the Prosecutor announced the beginning of formal investigations regarding serious international human rights violations in the Democratic Republic of Congo (DRC) since 1 July 2002. The investigations included patterns of rape, sexual enslavement and other forms of sexual violence. Since 2004, the court has opened investigations into four situations: Northern Uganda (July 2004), Darfur (June 2005), the Central African Republic (March 2007) and the Republic of Kenya (November 2009). To date, the ICC has indicted 14 persons, 7 of whom remain at large, 2 deceased, 4 in custody and one appearing voluntarily before the court. Beginning on 26 January 2009, the trial of Congolese militia leader Thomas Lubanga Dyilo was the court's first trial.[33] The second trial began on 24 November 2009 of the Congolese militia leaders Germain Katanga and Mathieu Ngudjolo Chui. Among other things, the accused are charged with war crimes and crimes against humanity, which include crimes of rape and sexual slavery.[34] A warrant for the arrest of Sudan's President, Omar Hassan Ahmad Al Bashir, was issued by the ICC in March 2009, of which the charges include rape as a crime against humanity.

The implementation of the rules and evidence of procedure within the ICC Statute are illuminative of the victim-friendly shift that deviates from traditional retributive frameworks of criminal justice. The attention given to gender violence is likewise unprecedented in the history of international criminal justice. Governing the establishment of a Victims and Witness Unit and the appointment of a gender advisor, the court expressly provides gender-sensitive expertise, including the employment of staff with a background in trauma work, including trauma caused by sexual violence.[35] Article 68(1) provides that the Court takes appropriate measures:

> to protect the safety, physical and psychological well-being, dignity and privacy of victims and witnesses. In so doing, the Court shall have regard to all relevant factors ... *in particular, but not limited to, where the crime involves sexual or gender violence* or violence against children.

> The Prosecutor shall take such measures particularly during the investigation and prosecution of such crimes. These measures shall not be prejudicial to or inconsistent with the rights of the accused and a fair and impartial trial.
>
> (emphasis added)

One of the most progressive provisions relating to the rights of victims is participation in court proceedings. For the first time in history, victims are able to express their views and concerns and are entitled to legal representation. Furthermore, the court may award reparations, compensation, restitution and rehabilitation to victims and it has established the first victim trust fund in the history of international criminal justice. These formal procedural mechanisms are unparalleled and they reflect a greater appreciation of the importance of participation and process for victims of gross human rights violations. However, it is important to note that in practice we are yet to ascertain whether these various measures will indeed provide victims and witnesses of rape with more just and fair experiences. Moreover, it remains to be seen what contribution the ICC will have not only to the memory of Darfur, the Democratic Republic of Congo, Northern Uganda and the Central African Republic, but also to the memory to the prolific nature of wartime sexual violence in these various sites of armed conflict. It is simply too soon to determine what the ICC's legacy will be.

*[handwritten margin note: * trying to address gap between legal process + needs of victims.]*

In conclusion, post-conflict justice mechanisms aim to foster accountability for perpetrators, justice for victims, as well as peace and reconciliation for local, national and international communities. The rhetoric underlying judicial proceedings is thus inextricably linked to the liberation of a violent past characterized by trauma, pain and ultimately injustice. The prosecution of wartime sexual violence as a crime of genocide, torture, crimes against humanity and grave breaches of the Geneva Conventions represents a major advance within international humanitarian law. This represents acknowledgment of the gendered harms done to women through the prosecution and punishment of perpetrators. The process has, to some extent, been inclusive of victims who have historically been denied a voice and a platform upon which to seek justice for crimes of wartime sexual violence, and courts have demonstrated unsurpassed gender sensitivity that may be contrasted to rape trials in domestic jurisdictions. Many scholars and practitioners have thus welcomed these developments as importantly recognizing the illegality of systematic sexual violence as a legitimate political concern. The prosecution of rape at the international level has also been symbolically significant in providing a collective narrative of sexual violence, contributing to and validating a public memory of wartime violence against women. As Osiel (2000: 278) remarks, 'What the victims want is an authoritative narrative, an "official story", as the remedy for the wrongs they have endured'.

However, while the rhetoric surrounding the legacy and collective memory of wartime rape is a praiseworthy goal of international courts, the key question is whether these courts are able in practice to faithfully and adequately play a pivotal role in not only prosecuting war crimes against women, but also contributing to a historical consciousness about such crimes. It is important to note here that the legal trial is conducted in a specified time and place and it may not extend the narrative beyond the trial itself, so in a sense the story of wartime rape, as told through and by law, is always incomplete. While the trial does help to construct a narrative about sexual atrocities and this helps to break an enduring historical silence on this matter, the narrative is inherently fragmented, sterilized through the procedural and evidential limits of law.

My intention is not to undermine the momentous achievements in recognizing, prosecuting and validating women's experiences of wartime rape, but I want to underscore the importance of the continual critique of law in order to demonstrate both the potentials and limitations of processes and outcomes for women who have been raped during periods of armed conflict. Indeed, despite the laudable developments within this body of jurisprudence, legal testimony may contribute to the marginalization of victims and witnesses, as well as the subversion of sexual violence as collective memory. The following chapter will address this issue in more detail, and then in the final chapter, drawing on all trials discussed throughout this book, I examine the limits and potential of law in the construction of collective memory.

# 5   Trials and trauma
## The impossibility of bearing witness

> The impossibility of telling is not external to this story: it is the story's heart ... The function of the trial thus becomes precisely to articulate the impossibility of telling through the legal process and to convert this narrative impossibility into legal meaning.
>
> (Felman 2002: 159)

In July 1996, a 41-year-old Muslim woman from the Prijedor region in Bosnia-Herzegovina testified to having been raped before the historic International Criminal Tribunal for the Former Yugoslavia. She was the first sexual violence survivor in history to bear witness before an international war crimes tribunal. There is little doubt that the appearance of witnesses testifying to wartime rape is an important constituent of justice, but the trial process and outcome provide little guarantee that victims will get to tell their story, let alone that they will feel justice has been done. Holocaust survivor Primo Levi (1987: 15) famously described the inherent paradox of bearing witness; that not only was the need to tell one's story a 'violent impulse', but the telling of that story itself was impossible because of the inherent limitations of language for describing inexplicable horror. Elaine Scarry (1985: 3) too discusses the 'impossibility of bearing witness',[1] but writes that even though 'Physical pain has no voice ... when it at last finds a voice, it begins to tell a story'. A key question then is how does the legal trial convert this narrative impossibility into legal meaning (Felman 2002)?

Scarry (1985) argues that there are three inseparable and embedded themes told through the overarching story of human pain. The first refers to the difficulty of expressing suffering; the second is the political consequences of that difficulty; and the third is the creativity of pain's expression. What this chapter grapples with is the articulation of human suffering – of 'trauma' – through a variety of personal and political mechanisms as part of the story of trauma (Felman 2002), and the political consequences of that articulation (Scarry 1985). An examination of legal institutions in the transmission and preservation of memory has two dimensions: the first is the representations and articulations of witnesses at criminal trials, and the second is the way in which legal institutions interpret, transmit, distort or undermine these individualized memories. This chapter thus examines the coming together of public and private memories through law; as Susannah Radstone (2008: 33) states, 'where memory is concerned, the personal *is* political' (emphasis original).

This focus is part of an ongoing discourse on the relationship between trauma and memory (see e.g. Appelbaum, Uyehara and Elin 1997; Caruth 1996), and the growing conversation about the mediation of trauma through law (see e.g. Felman 2002; Sarat, Davidovitch and Alberstein 2007). My concern therefore is with the ways in which witnesses themselves experience an internal loss of language to describe their suffering, as well as the external, legal imposition of this impossibility. This recognizes 'the unprecedented and repeated use of the instruments of law to cope with the traumatic legacies and the collective injuries left by these events' (Felman 2002: 2) and the promise of justice (as well as the impossibility of justice) in the aftermath of mass atrocities.

## Trauma trajectories

The study of psychological trauma, psychiatrist Judith Herman (2001: 7) argues, 'has a curious history [of] ... episodic amnesia'. This is not through lack of interest, but rather due to an intense controversy:

> The study of psychological trauma has repeatedly led into realms of the unthinkable and foundered on fundamental questions of belief. To study psychological trauma is to come face to face both with human vulnerability in the natural world and with the capacity for evil in human nature. To study psychological trauma means bearing witness to horrible events.
>
> (ibid.)

In part, this controversy is due to the complexity and ensuing disagreements about the concept and origins of trauma in the first place. Herman (2001) claims that psychological trauma has been popular at various historical junctures. She argues that the first phase of public consciousness resulted from French neurologist Jean-Martin Charcot's study of hysteria in the late 1870s. Hysteria, a condition which has been studied and viewed as a predominantly female affliction,[2] was studied by Charcot as a psychical response to the effects of a physical trauma (see Micale 1995; Veith 1965). Victims of a railway accident, for instance, experience traumatic shock as an emotional response to physical injury, often years after the event, a period which Charcot called 'incubation'. Drawing on Charcot's conceptualization of hysteria as psychological trauma, French psychiatrist Pierre Janet and Austrian physician Sigmund Freud, in their own separate works, used the concepts of disassociation and repression to characterize the psychical or psychological effects of physical trauma. Freud, for example, saw trauma in terms of the conscious mind actively working to block unpleasant experiences, while the unconscious mind compulsively repeats trauma in dreams and nightmares.

Although many have argued that trauma defies definition (Figley 1985), based on psychoanalytic conceptions of psychological injury, Jean Laplanche and Jean-Bertrand Pontalis (1988: 465) define trauma as 'An event in the subject's life, defined by its intensity, by the subject's incapacity to respond adequately to it and by the upheaval and long-lasting effects that it brings about in the psychical organization'. This marks a significant deviation from the original meaning of trauma as a physical wound that can be healed through medical intervention and through the body's own system of regeneration and repair.

In order to unlock the emotional energy of the unconscious, Freud's choice of treatment – for what he ultimately considered to be sexual neurosis – was 'talk therapy'. This continues to have resonance today with the popular therapeutic conjecture that talking through traumatic experiences is the key to psychological restoration.[3] In 1896, Freud argued that women's experience of childhood sexual abuse was 'at the bottom of every case of hysteria' (quoted in Herman 2001: 13). This was a controversial finding due to the gravity of the revelation; namely that sexual oppression of women and children was an alarmingly widespread phenomenon. Freud thus 'crossed the outer limits of social credibility [which] brought him to a position of total ostracism within his profession' (ibid.: 18). In 1925, Freud retreated from his original hypothesis, declaring that his patients had not actually experienced sexual abuse in childhood rather, he argued, 'these scenes of seduction had never taken place ... they were only fantasies which my patients had made up' (quoted in ibid.: 14). Ultimately, Freud's retreat from hysteria led to a halt in the study of trauma, the disappearance of the disease of hysteria altogether, and (arguably) the reinforcement of the long-standing rape myth that women fantasize, embellish or make up stories of sexual assault.

The study of psychological trauma re-emerged some years later in response to the devastation of the First World War and the range of behaviours resulting from combat exposure, also known as 'combat stress reaction', 'war neurosis' or 'shell shock' (ibid.). Again, there was controversy surrounding the hypothesis that exposure to violence, death and suffering in war produced a psychological syndrome resembling hysteria in men. Shell shock was seen as an affront to the glory and heroism of battle, and patients were often declared cowards and 'moral invalids' (ibid.). Attention to combat neurosis was reignited during the Second World War, but again, it receded into oblivion at the war's end:

> Little attention was paid to the fate of these men once they returned to active duty, let alone after they returned home from the war ... With the end of the war, the familiar process of amnesia set in once again. There was little medical or public interest in the psychological condition of

returning soldiers. The lasting effects of war trauma were once again forgotten.

(ibid.: 26)

It was not until after the Vietnam War that attention to psychological trauma resurfaced again (see Lifton 1973). The attention to the experiences of Vietnam veterans of psychological trauma led to the invention of the term Post-Traumatic Stress Disorder (PTSD) (see Figley 1985; Lund, Foy, Sipprelle and Strachan 1984) and in 1980 the American Psychiatric Association (APA) formally created PTSD as a new category in its official manual, the Diagnostic and Statistical Manual of Mental Disorders. The basic elements of PTSD are: (a) experiencing an event that is outside the range of normal human experience that would be distressing to almost anyone; (b) recurrent and intrusive re-experiencing of the trauma (e.g. images, perceptions, nightmares); (c) avoidance and numbing (e.g. avoiding thoughts or feelings about the trauma, feelings of detachment from others); and (d) increased arousal (e.g. irritability, difficulty concentrating, hyper-vigilance, exaggerated startled responses) (DSM-IV) (American Psychiatric Association 2000). PTSD has since been widely used for treating and understanding trauma and modern-day psychiatric treatment for refugees and displaced persons has been contingent on this classification (see e.g. Ai, Peterson and Ubelhor 2002; Dahl, Mutapcic and Schei 1998; Favaro, Majorani, Colombo and Santonastaso 1999; Weine, Kulenovic, Pavkovic and Gibbons 1998). However, this too is not without controversy (see e.g. Bracken and Petty 1998 and discussion below).

The feminist movement marks the third dialectic of trauma. Attention to the psychological trauma of sexual abuse, rape and domestic violence revealed some striking similarities between women's experiences and the experiences of those who had survived the Vietnam War (Herman 2001). Ann Burgess and Lynda Holmstrom (1974), for example, coined the term 'rape trauma syndrome' to convey the long-lasting consequences resulting from rape, including nausea, insomnia, nightmares, as well as dissociative or numbing symptoms. Their study revealed that one in four female victims had not recovered from rape four to six years afterwards (see also Nadelson, Notman, Zackson and Gornick 1982; Sutherland and Scherl 1970).

While Herman (2001) identified three phases of trauma discourse over the past 100 years, a fourth phase can be identified. This is the study of trauma within the discursive framework of cultural or collective memory. Generally speaking, this body of literature views trauma as the central experience of the past (Felman 2002). This includes studies on 'traumatic' events such as the Holocaust (see e.g. Felman 2002; Hartman 1994; LaCapra 1994); mass disaster (see e.g. Erikson 1979, 1994; Marsella, Johnson, Watson and Gryczynski 2008); terrorist attacks (see e.g. Kaplan 2005; Tumarkin 2005); and general collections on all of the above (see e.g. Alexander, Eyerman, Giesen, Smelser and Sztompka 2004; Antze and Lambek 1996; Bal, Crewe and Spitzer 1999; Bracken and Petty 1998; Caruth 1995; 1996; Edkins 2003; Hodgkin and Radstone 2003; Kleber, Figley and Gersons 1995). These diverse works demonstrate an important development within the study of psychological trauma, moving human pain beyond the medical, psychiatric and psychological disciplines and into philosophical, literary, historical and political realms of understanding. Due to rapid social change and the subsequent crises of memory and identity (Antze and Lambek 1996), these trauma studies, while continuing to draw upon traditional, psychoanalytic notions of repression and disassociation (see e.g. Caruth 1996; Felman 2002), have emerged not only to capture the inseparability of the individual within the socially and historically constituted past, but also to give validity to the lived experiences of survivors themselves.

The notion of trauma has thus evolved as not simply a medical diagnosis, but also a way to make sense of a catastrophic past. This takes place through the narratives of survivors, their communities and subsequent generations, as well as historians, scholars and others. Like the preceding trauma research, generally speaking, contemporary studies of collective suffering, memory and trauma have attracted debate in three interconnected ways.

The first issue concerns the actual concept of trauma. Some have argued, for instance, that 'trauma' has become devoid of its original meaning and used in the vernacular to imply any injurious (psychological and/or physical) event or experience (Benyakar, Kutz, Dasberg and Stern 1989; see also Becker 1995). According to Steven Hayes, Kirk Strosahl and Kelly Wilson (2003: 251), a distinction should be made between psychological pain and psychological trauma: 'Psychological *pain* … hurts … but it does not in itself do damage. Psychological *trauma* is pain compounded by an unwillingness to experience the pain. It not only hurts, it damages' (emphasis added). There may also be an important distinction between trauma and PTSD. The latter is seen as a maladaptive way of dealing with suffering, characterized by chronic trauma: continual hyper-vigilance, anxiety, agitation, as well as a profoundly altered consciousness of dissociation and avoidance over a prolonged period of time (Herman 2001). A woman who has been raped, therefore, may experience psychological pain as a result of the attack, but may not be 'traumatized' (unable to respond to the pain in her conscious mind) or may not in fact be suffering from PTSD or chronic trauma.[4]

An interrelated concern is with overly medicalized and individualized understandings of trauma. Adopting a Foucauldian critique of the production of scientific knowledge, Antze and Lambek (1996) argue that the medical disciplines have narrowly individualized and physiologized trauma, appropriating traumatic experiences through intervention strategies such as hypnosis and psychotherapy. In the context of armed conflict, genocide and other forms of political violence, this therapeutic approach has led to concern about applying western psychiatric models – what Derek Summerfield (2002) refers to as a 'Western medicotherapeutic prism' – to explain, diagnose and treat psychological injury in non-western contexts. Indeed, a therapeutic approach to international criminal justice and within transitional justice studies in general has raised alarm about the articulation of increasingly ambitious goals of war crimes trials, truth commissions and other legal or non-legal mechanisms for dealing with violent pasts. This concern likewise applies to a predominantly individualistic approach to diagnosis and treatment and the neglect of collective and social dimensions of suffering (Becker 1995; Bracken 1998; Bracken, Giller and Summerfield 1995; Summerfield 2002).[5] The definitional and conceptual confusion surrounding trauma discourse continues to beleaguer humanities and social sciences research into human suffering, and, as I will demonstrate below, there are certain legal ramifications in using what may be considered overly medicalized or positivist/scientific (Leys 2000) understandings of trauma.

In contrast to the above issue, a second problem within contemporary studies of trauma is the tendency to conflate the collective with the individual dimensions of suffering (e.g. 'the traumatized nation'). This conflation has arisen within the transitional justice field – in research and in post-conflict justice institutional frameworks – as a way to understand how post-conflict societies come to terms with a violent past. For example, Neil Kritz (1996) argues that groups, nations and individuals have similar responses to trauma in the aftermath of massive human rights violations. This metaphor emerged during the early phase of transitional justice research (e.g. the late 1980s and early 1990s) in an attempt to go beyond thinking about trauma as simply an individual problem. But it is also arguably symptomatic of the confusion surrounding trauma as both a concept and a tool for developing post-conflict justice mechanisms. Such an approach can lead to overly idealistic or unrealistic post-conflict or reconciliation strategies in the aftermath of conflict. It has also meant that 'healing' has been used frequently in a metaphysical sense without clarification of its meaning for victims, perpetrators and their communities (Allan and Allan 2000; Lansing and King 1998).[6] What is interesting here is that the legal paradigm for dealing with mass atrocities committed in armed conflict (for example a war crimes trial) takes a predominantly individualized approach to justice, but, as I have argued thus far, this is really only in relation to the accused on trial, not the victims or witnesses whose individual narratives of suffering are absorbed within the narrow confines of legal procedure.

The third controversy in many ways reflects the previous two debates mentioned here, and moreover it mirrors a controversy also found in memory studies in general. This concerns the 'knowability', reliability and ownership of traumatic experience. I return to Herman's (2001) explanation for the interconnected fascination and controversy of trauma. Trauma forces a coming to terms with human vulnerability in terms of, on the one hand, psychological pain and, on the other, the capacity for human 'evil'. Trauma not only brings into focus the existential crisis of meaning, but its controversy also lies in its phenomenology: the absence of pure objective 'truth', as well as the lack of uniformity to the phenomenon of human pain. This is why trauma or pain cannot be fully communicated from one person to another because language immediately runs dry, as Virginia Woolf once said (quoted in Scarry 1985).

A psychoanalytic understanding of trauma as 'unclaimed' (Caruth 1996) or inaccessible raises some critical questions about the authenticity and subjectivity of memory. If trauma resists language, as many scholars claim, it also 'resists simple comprehension' (ibid.: 6). In other words, if communicating pain is impossible in the sense that language cannot adequately capture pain, victims cannot fully know their own experiences of trauma and others cannot understand or know this pain, what are the consequences of this crisis of representation? These questions form part of a heated debate about the nature of traumatic memory that is currently taking place in both scholarly discourse and medical practice. Ruth Leys (2000: 304), for example, argues that unspeakable, unrepresentable trauma is currently a 'modish idea', and that current perspectives on trauma are polarized between two competing positions: one being that trauma does not exist; and the other that it does (arguably this dualism is similar to the problem I mentioned earlier in the book: about the way in which scholars assert whether or not rape is the 'worst' thing that can happen to a woman during war). There are consequences of approaching trauma in either way in legal discourse. For example, if trauma cannot be claimed by the individual subject, this would put into question their reliability as a legal witness. On the other hand, if 'traumatic' experiences *can* be located and articulated by the survivor, this may beg the question about the inexplicability of events. I am not in any way suggesting that victims of mass atrocities are unreliable witnesses because they are too traumatized to have reliable memories, or not traumatized enough to have had grievous experiences; rather my point here is that there is a danger that the current discourse on trauma, from my understanding, fosters a dualism which in effect leaves little room for individual subjectivity and agency. As Herman (2001: 8) states, there has been a constant 'tendency to discredit the victim or to render her invisible … [and] [i]n spite of a vast literature documenting the phenomenon of psychological trauma, debate still centers on the basic question of whether these phenomena are credible and real'.

While some might say these three issues, respectively conceptual understanding, application and knowledge, are 'unfortunate side effects' of trauma research (Kansteiner 2004: 194), alternatively this might be thought of as part of the study of both trauma and memory: a fascination, popularity and controversy for what can only be the uncertainty, mystery and deep complexity of the human condition. The trauma debate reiterates the very point that Herman (2001) raises; that is, the study of psychological trauma has been, and will continue to be, embroiled in much controversy. An alternative way of interpreting the relationship between trauma and memory (and one I prefer to adopt) is that in cases of inexpressibility and/or incomprehensibility, this can be seen as an essential constituent of the traumatic narrative itself (Scarry 1985); or 'an integral part of the history' (Felman 2002: 159).

For the remainder of the chapter, I will discuss the conceptualization of trauma within law, particularly in terms of the relationship between law and sexual trauma. Therefore, my focus is not on the nature and debate of psychological trauma as a result of wartime rape, but rather I am more interested in examining the ways in which war crimes courts have adopted traditional conceptions of trauma – of dissociation and repression – to raise questions concerning victim reliability in the aftermath of armed conflict.

## Articulating trauma

There has been much scholarly discussion in recent times on the unrepresentability of human suffering. Giorgio Agamben (2002: 39), for example, argues that testimony is 'the disjunction between two impossibilities of bearing witness'. The first impossibility is that the language of testimony cannot come close to articulating the force of the experience. Human language is thus deficient for capturing the true nature of human pain and suffering (Scarry 1985). Drawing on Primo Levi's (1987) notion of the 'true witness' being the one who cannot speak, Agamben's second impossibility is that nonlanguage is the most accurate or authentic representation of human suffering. Shoshana Felman (2002), for instance, examines the dramatic fainting of a Holocaust witness during the Adolf Eichmann trial as the metaphoric collapse of language. But the impossibility of bearing witness is more than an internal contradiction within the individual. My point here is that there is an 'impossibility of bringing [pain] to the knowledge of others' (Lyotard 1988: 5).

In the previous chapter, I discussed in detail the *Foča* trial at the ICTY, where 16 women testified to being raped by three defendants accused of rape, torture and enslavement. Some witnesses had not spoken about their experiences of rape even the day before they testified. Some of the examples below demonstrate the unspeakability of wartime rape and the difficulties in articulating the experience within the legal realm:

Q:   These persons you mentioned, were they all soldiers?
WITNESS:   Yes.
Q:   And they were all in that house on that day when you were taken there for the first time?
WITNESS:   Yes.
Q:   You said that you had to give them pleasure. What do you mean by this?
WITNESS:   Well, I mean – I cannot express myself.

(*Foča* Transcript, 30 March 2000: 1415)

During this same trial, Witness 50, who was 16 years old at the time, had not spoken about her experiences until she had contact with the ICTY in 1995. She told the prosecutor that she had not told Tribunal investigators the details of her rape by Vukovič, which was the first time she had been violated: 'Those words could not leave my mouth' (*Foca* Transcript, 29 March 2000: 1246). She added:

> I never described what happened to me in detail to anyone. If I wanted to say what happened, I said the worst had happened, referring to rape, and from then onwards throughout my stay in this camp, I never talked to anyone about anything from that event onwards; I kept silent.
>
> (*Foča* Transcript, 29 March 2000: 1253)

In cross-examination, attention was given to the witness's failure to disclose the details about the first time she was raped. Her response was that because this was the first time she had been raped, it was the most painful experience and one that she was unwilling to relive. In another example, Witness 205 was cross-examined by the defence counsel about how many times she was raped. The defence claimed that there was a discrepancy in the number of times she was raped according to her initial statement to the Office of the Prosecutor and her testimony during the trial. The defence sought to raise this in order to demonstrate lack of credibility: 'The witness is saying 11 times, and I want to check her credibility … I believe that by cross-examining the witness in this way, we can see to what extent she is telling the truth' (*Foča* Transcript, 18 May 2000: 3545–6). This example points to the deeply embedded liberal ideal of rationality within legal discourse. Law places heavy emphasis on proof and evidence as 'truth', but yet the very nature of human memory lies beyond scientific objectivity.

It is commonly accepted that revealing the intimate details of sexual violation is extremely difficult for sexual violence survivors, particularly in front of strangers in a courtroom and particularly when cultural and social barriers to disclosure dictate what can and cannot be said in a public context. Due to its limited mandate and time constraints, a legal trial ultimately fails to interpret or represent wartime rape in its emotional and physical complexity (Lusby 1994). A criminal trial does not provide the witness with an opportunity to use her own language to talk about her experiences of rape (Mertus 2004). As Lucinda Finley (1989: 903) points out, 'One of the other languages that the law does not easily hear is that associated with the emotions, with expression of bursting human passion and aspirations'.

The prosecution of wartime rape, therefore, does not tell a larger story of trauma and sexual humiliation; nor does it tell a story about the causes and consequences of armed conflict, ethnic cleansing and massive human rights violations. The prosecution of rape at international war crimes trials thus has limited 'jurisprudential *speaking power*' (Felman 2002: 166, emphasis original). It does not grasp or translate the unspeakability of testimony, nor does it pave the way for speaking or disclosing trauma or pain. Furthermore, law gives the impression of having dealt with crimes of wartime rape. Agamben (2002: 19), for example, states that it is possible that both the Nuremberg and Eichmann trials are responsible for the 'conceptual confusion' of Auschwitz, making it impossible to think through because of the notion that law has overcome this human catastrophe. In a similar way, despite the 'necessity of the trials and despite their evident insufficiency' (ibid.), there might also exist a misconception that the problem of wartime rape has been overcome through the few criminal prosecutions that have taken place at the international level.

## Legal conceptions of trauma

Although the psychological condition of hysteria is no longer recognized as a medical disorder, once upon a time it was viewed as an exclusively female malady. Likewise, trauma is sometimes treated as a predominantly feminine phenomenon. For example, in a community survey of trauma exposure in Canada, Murray Stein, John Walker and David Forde (2000) sought to explore the gender differences associated with PTSD. They demonstrated that women have higher rates of PTSD than men and attribute this to the higher rates of sexual trauma exposure in women as a partial explanation for this difference. They also found that women were at an increased risk of PTSD following non-sexual assaultive violence. The study concluded that the reasons for differential susceptibility are unknown, but that it may be due to biological/genetic and/or sociocultural factors. Other studies have also found a higher rate of PTSD among women.[7] Whether or not there are gender differences in trauma presentation is not something I have expertise to consider; however, my example below demonstrates the legally constructed understandings of trauma that are not only gendered, but that contribute to the impossibility of bearing witness.

### *The impossibility of memory: Furundžija*

The *Furundžija* trial[8] was the first trial at the ICTY to deal exclusively with rape charges. Anto Furundžija, a Bosnian Croat paramilitary chief, was the local commander of a unit called the 'Jokers' that helped the Croatian Defence Council (HVO) ethnically cleanse the Lašva Valley area in central Bosnia-Herzegovina. Many Bosnian Muslims were killed or wounded, deported or detained in detention facilities where they were tortured, beaten and raped. Furundžija was indicted for individual criminal responsibility, including 'committing, planning, instigating, ordering or otherwise aiding and abetting in the planning, preparation or execution of any crimes referred to in Articles 2 and 3 of the Tribunal Statute' (*Furundžija* Indictment, 1998: para. 11).

The evidence of this trial was almost entirely based on the testimony of Witness A, who had been interrogated by Furundžija while she was being assaulted. According to the indictment, Furundžija and another soldier brought Witness A into the Jokers' Headquarters, a former restaurant known as 'The Bungalow', for questioning. While she was being interrogated by Furundžija, the other soldier rubbed his knife against the witness, threatening to put the knife inside her vagina if she did not tell the truth. According to the judgment, the witness was also 'maintained in a state of forced nudity' (*Furundžija* Judgment, 1998: para. 45). After this incident, she was taken to another room where the accused continued to interrogate her. She was then beaten and the soldier forced her to have oral and vaginal sexual intercourse with him in the presence of the accused and another victim. Despite his position of authority, Furundžija did nothing to prevent this from happening.

The defence did not dispute that Witness A had been raped on multiple occasions; rather they argued that her memory was flawed because she was suffering from PTSD. They also claimed that she was suggestible to the statements made about the defendant's culpability during her psychological treatment at a woman's therapy centre in Bosnia-Herzegovina, as well as the views of political activists and journalists at the time of the trial. As a result, they argued that Witness A had misidentified the accused, who they said was not present during the rapes (for a discussion of this trial, see Askin 1999; Campbell, K. 2002; Sparr and Bremner 2005). According to the defence in their opening statement:

> The evidence will show you that Witness A is wrong, not that she is a liar, but that she is wrong, that the circumstances of the crime and the difficulties of the identification process make it impossible to share her opinion as it relates to Mr. Furundzija beyond a reasonable doubt … Witness A will take the stand. She will be a sympathetic witness. Every one of us will wish we could undo her trauma and compensate her somehow for her ordeal. She will come before you and she will tell you a story, a story that she has been asked repeatedly over the last five years to develop, to revise and to repeat … We believe that the evidence will show that her reconstruction is inaccurate and unreliable.
>
> (*Furundžija* Transcript, 8 June 1998: 81–2)

At the end of the trial, the defence discovered that the prosecution had not disclosed evidence relating to counselling and therapy that Witness A had received. The defence subsequently filed a motion to strike the testimony of the witness and reopen the trial upon conviction. In July 1998, the Trial Chamber ordered that the trial be reopened based on Rule 68(A), which requires the Prosecutor to, 'as soon as practicable, disclose to the defence any material which in the actual knowledge of the Prosecutor may suggest the innocence or mitigate the guilt of the accused or affect the credibility of pro-secution evidence' (ICTY Rules of Procedure and Evidence). The witness was

*[handwritten marginalia: wow – attack witness's mental state + credibility to get her raped off. sick thats a new low]*

called to testify again and was cross-examined a second time. Her confidential client file was subpoenaed.

The evidence in question concerned a one-off therapy session Witness A had received from a women's therapy centre in Bosnia-Herzegovina. The file stated that it was possible to conclude that the client was exhibiting symptoms of PTSD because she 'could not sleep without therapy and was afraid to fall asleep, thought of herself as unimportant, had an uncontrolled recollection of events and allowed herself to cry, and suppressed thoughts of the rapes' (*Furundžija* Judgment, 1998: para. 94). The defence thus claimed that because Witness A was suffering from PTSD, her memory was contaminated as a result. They called expert witness Dr Charles Morgan, associate professor of psychiatry at Yale University School of Medicine and associate director of the PTSD Program at the National Center for PTSD. Dr Morgan claimed that high levels of stress can cause damage to an area of the brain called the hippocampus, resulting in impaired memory. He said that he personally would not consider the testimony from a PTSD sufferer to be scientifically reliable, adding, 'I would want independent corroborating evidence of some sort' (*Furundžija* Transcript, 12 November 1998: 1312). The defence also called Dr Jeffrey Younggren, a clinical forensic psychologist from California and a fellow of the American Psychological Association. Dr Younggren likewise testified that trauma can have a detrimental impact on memory ('the more trauma, the worse the memory') and that inadequate treatment can contaminate memory, leading to false beliefs.

Here the contested nature of trauma and memory has been played out in the judicial realm. This contestation concerns not only memory amnesia but also false memory creation. In fact, it is argued that this was the first time in legal history that psychiatric experts were called to testify about the controversial relationship between PTSD and the accuracy of recovered memory (Sparr and Bremner 2005). The defence claimed that the witness gave several varying accounts of her experience during the different phases of the trial. For example, in 1995 in her deposition, she said the defendant had 'short blond hair', while in 1998 during the trial itself, she said he had chestnut to black hair (ibid.). It is interesting to note that the defence did not call into question the testimony of the other (non-rape) witness, Witness D, at the trial based on the flawed memory argument (Coalition for Women's Human Rights in Conflict Situations 1998). The defence did not request that the personal records of Witness D be disclosed, even though he 'underwent medical treatment for about 20 days, because [of] mental problems' (*Furundžija* Transcript, 15 June 1998: 522). This suggests that the disclosure order was discriminatory against victims of rape specifically. It arguably perpetuates the myth that women who have been raped are unreliable and suggestible witnesses (see Bushby 1997; Campbell, K. 2002).

Law, by its nature, 'is solely directed toward judgment, independent of truth and justice' (Agamben 2002: 18). As such, it is the inanimate evidence – the parts devoid of humanity and of pain and suffering – that are the most valued parts of the trial. It is not the witness herself, as an autonomous individual, who testifies, rather the witness essentially *becomes or is equivalent to the evidence* and as such her evidence testifies to the truth or otherwise of the case. This happens also through the narrow script that has been manufactured for the witness even before she enters the courtroom (see Mertus 2004). The fixation on evidence can also be seen through the defence of non-corroboration. In this particular case, for example, the defence in their closing statement argued that, in addition to the trauma suffered by the witness, her evidence was unreliable because there was no corroboration. This is despite Rule 96 of the Tribunal's Rules of Procedure and Evidence, which provides that 'no corroboration of evidence given by victims is required'.[9]

The construction of trauma as the source of incapacitation is striking in this particular case. The problem with PTSD relates not only to the pathologizing of responses to events such as war and rape, but also to ownership and subjectivity. Witness A claimed that the woman's therapy organization who diagnosed her had in fact approached her and she had not sought assistance. More importantly, Witness A did not agree with the report or the diagnosis of PTSD. On the other hand, the defence witness, Dr Morgan, testified that Witness A's denial of both treatment and PTSD 'were consistent with findings in studies of PTSD' (*Furundžija* Judgment: para. 98). The prosecution conversely argued that the women's therapy organization had not established an ongoing therapeutic relationship with Witness A and that she merely had an 'informal talk' with them (*Furundžija* Judgment, 1998: para. 99). In her closing statement, Patricia Viseur-Sellers for the prosecution stated that the witness's evidence was credible and had remained consistent throughout the five years since her contact with the ICTY: 'I think Witness A has shown the proposition to be true that [for] many people who have been sexually assaulted and particularly violated, the problem is not remembering; the problem is forgetting' (*Furundžija* Transcript, 22 June 1998: 670).

Viseur-Sellers explained that the inaccuracy of a rape victim's testimony 'speaks more about the volumes of sexual violence that they endured as opposed to the question of credibility as to the acts' (Personal Interview, 14 October 2002). This resonates with Caruth's (1995: viii) understanding of traumatic memory:

> the concern with false memories also teaches us, I believe, another and equally important lesson: the difficulty that many people have in believing memories that seem to them to be false simply because they do not appear in easily recognizable forms, and the urgency of creating new ways of listening and recognizing the truth of memories.

At the end of the trial, the court declared that 'Witness A is mistaken in saying that she was not referred for treatment' and that 'it is likely that Witness A had PTSD' (*Furundžija* Judgment, 1998: para. 100–1). It did, however, emphasize

that persons suffering from PTSD are not necessarily unreliable witnesses. T[.]
sum up the range of perspectives on trauma here: the defence argued that
PTSD contaminated memory; the prosecution claimed that the witness had
not been given adequate diagnosis or treatment; the witness herself stated that
she was not suffering from PTSD, she had not sought treatment and her
memory was accurate; while the Trial Chamber, as the final word on the
matter, declared that the witness *did* undergo treatment and most likely had
PTSD, but she was nonetheless a reliable witness. As Allan Young (1995: 5)
argues, PTSD is a product of historical construction that has been 'glued
together by the practices, technologies, and narratives with which it is diagnosed, studied, treated and represented and by the various interests, institutions, and moral arguments that mobilized these efforts and resources'. My
point here is that despite the contested nature of memory, there are vested
interests in legal constructions of PTSD. This reveals the power of the law
(Smart 1989) to proclaim authority over trauma and the traumatic event,
and in doing so law effectively diminishes witness testimony and contributes
to the further entrenchment of social and legal constructions of rape myths.

It is interesting to compare the mediation of trauma in a different ICTY
rape trial. In the *Foča* trial, for example, the defence argued that the witnesses
were not credible because they had not displayed any signs of psychological
trauma. The defence argued that the strength the witnesses conveyed in the
witness box cast doubt on the validity of their testimonies. The defence called
a number of expert witnesses to demonstrate not only that there was insufficient medical evidence to corroborate the witnesses' testimonies of rape
(they also argued that the victims had not sufficiently resisted rape) but that
because the witnesses did not appear to be suffering from any traumatic
disorders, they could not have been raped. For example, Dusan Dunjic, a
specialist in forensic medicine in Belgrade, appeared as an expert witness for
the defence, telling the court: 'Half of the women who report themselves to be
rape victims weren't actually raped, and half of them either want to deceive a
young man or blackmail him' (*Foča* Transcript, 12 September 2000: 5438). In
this trial, the defence also called an expert witness, Dr Sanda Rašković-Ivič,
to demonstrate the psychological impact of rape. The defence counsel asked
Rašković-Ivič whether 'the absence of such psychosis in alleged victims of
rape mean that there are no grave consequences?' The witness replied: 'Yes. If
there are no psychoses, then there are no grave consequences' (*Foča* Transcript, 12 September 2000: 5459).[10]

In the legal context, wartime sexual violence witnesses are thus put in what
John Conley and William O'Barr (1998) call a 'double bind'. If the witness is
too emotional or too 'traumatized', her memory is corrupted and she cannot
be a reliable witness, but if she is calm and in control, she could not have been
violated and she is therefore calculating and lacking in credibility. While
the former treats the witness as merely evidence, lacking in both subjectivity and agency, the latter treats the witness as an agent of manipulation.
Neither judicial interpretation of trauma, as it is argued here, provides much

insight into the causes and consequences of wartime rape, nor the actual experiences of the victim. Indeed law, by its very purpose – its force of judgment (Agamben 2002) – is ill-suited to the revelation and articulation of traumatic experiences. Kirsten Campbell (2002: 334, 337) argues that the act of rape as a crime against humanity is understood as a trauma to the body and to the person under international humanitarian law. She states that the ICTY's understanding of trauma 'rests upon a conception of a trauma to the right to bodily and subjective integrity'. As such, she goes on to argue, through procedure, punishment and recognition, the Tribunal conceives of justice as the '*legal* resolution of trauma' (emphasis original) and the impossibility of representing trauma leads to the impossibility of justice for capturing or symbolizing trauma (see also Campbell 2003).

These examples also show the ways in which courts adopt medicalized and individualized understandings of trauma. The ideal that we must attend to psychological wounds through disclosure in legal testimony has become ingrained in post-conflict justice mechanisms. However, despite this, I have shown here that the articulation of trauma through the legal paradigm is not utilized to validate or give meaning to women's experiences of wartime sexual violence. Rather, trauma and memory are used as a way to undermine and undervalue women's testimonies. As Carol Smart (1989) has argued, law's power has been extended through the vehicle of the 'psy' professions. In the ICTY rape trials discussed here, the invocation of trauma through the discourse of psychiatry and the influence of Freudian notions of repression and disassociation serve to undermine the testimony of the witness. This is the legal meaning of trauma and it contributes to the external imposition of the impossibility of bearing witness. Not only do witnesses have difficulty finding words to express their experiences of rape, medico-legal understandings of human suffering (of trauma) make the retelling of the story impossible.

It is important to point out that I do not wish to question the impact of trauma *per se* as much evidence has been documented to illustrate the calamitous consequences for survivors suffering from trauma or traumatic related injury. I am convinced too that there is much benefit to talking about horrific experiences not only to begin the long, slow process of recovery, but also to seek justice and redemption. However, my argument is centred on the way in which law co-opts popular, conventional or positivist understandings of trauma. The consequences, as I have shown in this chapter, are that these interpretations have led to the disqualification of women's experiences and their attempts to testify to them (ibid.). As Mark Seltzer (1997: 11) has argued in his article on 'wound culture' and trauma, 'The psychoanalytic understanding [of trauma] points to the manner in which the interpretation, representation, or reduplication of the event (real or posited) is inseparable from the concept of trauma'. This points to both the crisis of representation and the impossibility of bearing witness because victims, their subjectivity and their representations, are inextricably bound to the traumatic experience and, as such, are inseparable from the original trauma and effectively 'the scene of the crime' (ibid.).

It is argued that the popular idea that trauma is a representational impossibility is 'just another grand narrative of Western philosophy' that essentially treats all victims of traumatic history as voiceless (Kansteiner 2004: 201). But victims are not voiceless. The powerful impulse to share traumatic experiences is a human phenomenon reflected in autobiographies, film, literature, art, memorials, museums and other commemoration sites. Essentially, speaking about unpleasant experiences is a form of testimony to human limits – in terms of the capacity for human evil, the transformation of the battered body into voice and the remarkableness of human survival and resilience. For example, one witness said during her testimony at the ICTY: 'I have taken the oath here ... to tell the truth before this Tribunal and in front of all the people here. And I wanted to tell the truth once and for all so that people know what happened. And did it have to happen to us? Did we have to be raped?' (*Foča* Transcript, 29 March 2000: 1207).

Although the inherent limitations of law – of language, process and outcome – may offer little in the way of justice and vindication for rape crimes, this does not mean that testimony is futile. Indeed, survivors of gross human rights violations may find some comfort in testifying before inter-national war crimes trials (see Stover 2005). Michael Jackson (2002) argues that storytelling is the capacity of self-narration to a wider audience that operates as a mediation between the personal and private realm. War crimes trials, truth commissions and other legal or quasi-legal mechanisms may therefore provide a platform for survivors to testify to a larger public about their experiences of gross human rights violations.

However, specifically for victims of rape crimes, there is not merely the internal impossibility of bearing witness, but the externally imposed obstacles that many victims face when they come to bear witness to these crimes. It is the nature of rape – the articulation of the experience and the mediation of this within the public context – that forces silence upon many victims in the aftermath of armed conflict. The silence that thus envelops wartime rape is both inside and outside of language (Felman 2002). Victims may struggle to find a language to express the pain or trauma of wartime rape. The examples discussed here demonstrate the political and perceptual consequences relating to the difficulty of expressing physical and psychological pain (Scarry 1985). My aim was to investigate the way in which language is used to communicate experiences of rape within the constraints of a legal trial, and the ways in which law negotiates or makes sense of these so-called 'unspeakable' experiences.

Although criminal trials for the expression of human pain or trauma may represent a fractured, incomplete and inadequate forum, the trial nonetheless 'enables pain to enter into a realm of shared discourse that is wider, more social, than that which characterizes the relatively intimate conversation of patient and physician' (ibid.: 9). This assists a collective understanding of the resilience of both survival and destruction, of both disclosure and silence and, most of all, the deep need for survivors to bear witness and to disclose their traumatic experiences. These paradoxes reflect the deeply contested nature of trauma and memory. They also contribute to the collective memory of rape and war crimes trials.

# 6    Wartime rape and the legacy of law

The spate of mass rapes that have occurred throughout the history of warfare have, by and large, been crimes that have shaped history. They have shaped history because even though silence and impunity have relegated women's experiences of wartime rape to the marginalized, forgotten abyss of history, rape has nonetheless occupied a central part of wartime collective memory, from the rape of the Sabine women in early Roman history, to the rape of women in the Democratic Republic of Congo today. In other words, wars are well remembered not only for pillage and murder, but also for the rape of women. An important distinction, however, is that wartime rape is often remembered not to honour the traumatic personal experiences of women, but rather to celebrate or exalt a masculinized war narrative of victory and defeat. The main argument of the book is that official narratives of both past and present forms of wartime sexual violence are compellingly political, despite the crime itself and the impact on victims being irrefutably private. In a similar way, these crimes are both highly visible and invisible. These striking paradoxes between visibility and invisibility, and the personal and political, are reflected both inside and outside legal mechanisms that are designed to deal with mass atrocities.

The establishment of international war crimes courts, from the Nuremberg and Tokyo tribunals to the international criminal tribunals for the Former Yugoslavia and Rwanda, as well as the International Criminal Court and other contemporary courts, is deeply embedded within a collective consciousness about the past, present and future. While there are many and varied interpretations of the existence and operation of these courts and there is no one collective memory of genocides, wars and other political conflicts, these courts do indeed shape narratives about egregious crimes. Such crimes ultimately test the limits of law and, at the same time, challenge idealized or otherwise conceptions of humanity. The 'selective memory' of these courts informs which atrocities will be remembered. As such, they exhibit a great deal of power in the representation of the past. Thus, when wartime sexual violence failed to capture the serious attention of international war crimes courts prior to the 1990s, this contributed to women's experiences of warfare being left off the historical record. The British Chief Prosecutor at

Nuremberg, Sir Hartley Shawcross, declared that international war crimes tribunals can 'provide a contemporary touchstone and an authoritative impartial record to which future historians may turn for truth and future politicians for warning' (quoted in Marrus 1999: 107). The contemporary ramifications of legal silence for the surviving comfort women, as well as other victims of sexual violence during the Second World War, remind us of the importance of international courts for the preservation of past memories.

Of course, the law is inherently flawed as a mechanism for delivering justice and serving pedagogical functions in the aftermath of gross violations of human rights. Law by its very nature is selective, narrow, distanced, adversarial, politicized, gendered, partial and unequal. Law often fails abysmally to offer vindication or comfort to victims, and almost always is unable to capture or grasp the extent and gravity of crimes that have shocked humanity. However, much faith is nonetheless invested in the retributive function of an international court as an authoritative, impartial, truth-recording mechanism in the aftermath of mass atrocities. Below, I will reflect on the legacy, the trauma and the 'violence' of law in addressing crimes of wartime sexual violence. This analysis is based on the following key questions: to what extent does the law do 'representational justice' (Douglas 2001: 113) to wartime rape? How does law as a space of ritual construct – directly and indirectly – collective memory of past events? And how is the past history of wartime rape through law made to matter?

## The legacy of law

While the legacy and contribution to collective memory through the establishment and operation of international courts remain to be seen and will invariably change over time, it is possible to make a number of provisional observations about the potentials and limitations of law for shaping and obscuring a collective narrative about wartime rape. Below, I use Joachim Savelsberg and Ryan King's (2007) seven key connections between law and collective memory to demonstrate this legacy.

First, law as a space of ritual plays an important role in the *construction of collective memory* (ibid.). The 1990s represent the era when, for first time in history, victims of rape appeared as witnesses before international war crimes courts. In Chapter 4, I discussed the 'counter-memory' as representing subjugated or disqualified knowledge (Foucault 1977); a shift from state-centric and masculinized versions of the past that have excluded the voices of those historically silenced. The testimonies of women who have been raped during wartime in a sense constitute a counter-memory. These testimonies importantly contribute to a collective narrative, not only about wartime rape in a specific context; they also help to establish a 'historical truth' about wartime rape in general. Our understanding of women's experiences during armed conflict, not simply as *victims* of sexual violence, but also as agents of both survival (surviving war) and retribution (seeking justice), is greatly enhanced through these institutional mechanisms. As Douglas (2001) remarks, bearing witness is 'an act of resistance'. Osiel (2000: 293) too states that 'criminal courts *have* often shaped collective memory of such national tragedies as administrative massacre' (emphasis original). For this reason, 'courts will continue to be drawn willy-nilly into the process of memory construction' (ibid.: 294). Kirsten Campbell (2002), for example, discusses the role of law as memory through rape trials, arguing that legal memory is constituted not only through the substantive law (e.g. rape being recognized under international humanitarian law) but also through prosecutorial and procedural practices that construct various narratives of memory, including gendered memory and the contestation over individual memory.

Second, law helps *create narratives that are distinct* from those produced in other institutional realms. Law tends to focus on the perpetrators rather than the historical, social and cultural forces of conflict (Savelsberg and King 2007). While this focus may be centred on establishing facts in order to ensure a guilty or not guilty verdict for the accused (and thereby declare individual criminal responsibility and accountability), courts do provide a site where different sides of the story are presented and contested. As Michael Schudson (1997) claims, contest and conflict are the hallmarks of collective memory. The defence and prosecution teams, and the testimonies of accused persons, witnesses and direct victims, contribute to a narrative that shapes how historical events are to be remembered. A degree of acquiescence to conflicting narratives should be accepted as fundamental to the construction of what we may think of as multiple 'truths' and indeed the notion of the contest is fundamental in many legal jurisdictions across the globe. For this reason, law produces a distinctive recounting of past events. Osiel (2000: 51) writes:

> Postmodernist accounts of narrative typically view the cacophony of alternative tales about the same large-scale event and the resulting conflict between them, as valuable in themselves. The proliferation of 'little meta narratives', each by performative utterance, ensures that no single 'grand meta narrative' will ever consolidate itself as *the* collective memory of an event.
>
> (emphasis original)

Of course, an adversarial contest is also a major limitation of retributive justice because witnesses are often subject to hostile cross-examination strategies and law fails to tell a story about the broader context in which atrocities occurred.

A third key connection between law and collective memory is that *the construction of collective memory through law is mediated by other institutions* (Savelsberg and King 2007). There is no doubt that the ICTY and ICTR trials, for example, have contributed to the collective memory of the horrors endured during not only the respective conflicts, but arguably armed conflict in general. This would be impossible without the media, feminist advocacy groups and NGOs. One example is the extensive media coverage of the three detention camps mentioned in the *Tadić* trial. One of the most iconic (and widely used) images from the Bosnian conflict is that of an emaciated prisoner named Fikret Alić standing behind barbed wire at the Trnopolje camp in 1992. Reminiscent of Nazi-style concentration camps, the image caused widespread international outrage and has very much become part of a collective memory of the conflict. The picture was also used as evidence at the ICTY.[1]

While this and other pictures of skeletal male inmates have predominated the imagery and memory of the Bosnian camps, the 1996 documentary film *Calling the Ghosts* (1996) chronicled the sexual violence endured by women at the Omarska camp and likewise contributes to the enduring memory of rape camps and the Bosnian conflict. The film follows childhood friends Nusreta Sivac and Jadranka Cigelj as they prepare to testify before the ICTY about being raped in the camps. This is a good example of how collective memory is mediated by other institutions in conjunction with, and outside of, law. The reception and aftermath of the film point to not only the *consolidation* of memory, but also the *contestation* of memory. Following the documentary, a television appearance and her testimony at the ICTY (albeit as a protected witness), Nusreta Sivac (who happened to be a judge prior to the conflict) was 'exposed to fear, provocation and threats on a daily basis' when she returned to Prijedor ten years after her detainment at Omarska (Katana 2002). Her story, and the story of the 35 other women detained at Omarska, has circulated widely across a variety of mnemonic forms and undoubtedly has helped to preserve the memory of rape and war. However, like the image of Fikret Alić, the film and its characters have been the subject of heated debate. Diana Johnstone's book *Fool's Crusade* (2002) is one example, pointing to Cigelj's political association with former Croatian President Franjo Tudjman's party and other Croatian agencies. Controversially, Johnstone calls Cigelj an unreliable witness and argues that the phenomenon of mass rape as a weapon of war was deliberately manufactured as wartime 'propaganda' against the Serbs.[2] It is interesting to note the relationship between collective memory and the law in this case, and in a variety of other trials at international courts, where external influences such as the media, NGOs and academia play a pivotal role in their mediation.

Fourth, law *indirectly shapes collective memory* because, like it or not, it disseminates information about the past (Savelsberg and King 2007). Crimes of the past must meet certain criteria in order to be classified as ones worthy of international prosecution. As such, international courts inescapably shape how the past will be remembered through their 'selective memory'. Of course, this has been shown to be problematic when courts fail to adequately prosecute certain crimes, such as the crimes of the Holocaust during the Nuremberg trial (Douglas 2001), as well as the vivisection of prisoners, biological warfare and the systematic sexual enslavement of comfort women at the Tokyo trial (Osiel 2000). Michael Marrus (1999) makes the same point about the Doctors' trial of Nazi physicians who were charged with the murder and torture of hundreds of thousands of concentration camp inmates in the name of medical science. He argues that the proceedings paid little attention to the historical context and failed to show why and how things happened, 'ultimately narrowing and distorting the history of medical crimes in the Third Reich'.[3] The point here is that international war crimes courts play a powerful role in shaping what is to be remembered, regardless of whether or not they do a good job of it.

Fifth, law itself can *constitute collective memory in and of itself* (Savelsberg and King 2007). For example, the very establishment of the ICTY in 1993 was in part premised on the extent and gravity of rape crimes against women during the conflicts in the former Yugoslavia. Thereafter, a number of formal developments reflective of gender sensitivity within this court and others have no doubt contributed to a foundational narrative about international courts. The prosecution of rape within these legal institutions thus forms part of the epic legacy of international law. International courts have created gender advisor positions and have established victim and witness support units to recommend protective measures and to provide counselling and support, especially in cases of rape and sexual assault. This has helped to establish these crimes as worthy of international prosecution and attention. The rules relating to the presentation of evidence, the adjudication of sexual offences, as well as the participation and representation of witnesses, are unique in their special consideration of the rights of victims. This signals that rape is not merely a crime against a nation or community, but a crime against the individual. Rape is explicitly listed as a serious violation of international humanitarian law in the statutes of the ICTY, ICTR and ICC, again pointing to the seriousness of such crimes. And finally, rape and enslavement have been successfully prosecuted as crimes of genocide, war crimes (e.g. torture) and crimes against humanity, again demonstrating a sense of the gravity and seriousness with which the international community is willing to pursue gender-related crimes. For these reasons, the rise of international criminal justice during the 1990s, and the attention given to wartime sexual violence, is itself a crucial part of collective memory both of wartime rape and of the courts themselves.

Sixth, *carrier groups are crucial contributors to the legal process and outcome* (Savelsberg and King 2007). Carrier groups, including predominantly feminist and human rights advocacy organizations, have played a key role in ensuring that gendered harms are treated as serious crimes by the international community (see Engle 2005; Halley 2008b; Quénivet 2005). Although disagreement over the desirability or otherwise of certain measures certainly existed, without the effective lobbying and advocacy of these disparate carrier groups, wartime sexual violence (its past, present and future) may have remained in the margins of subjugated, forgotten history. The role of carrier groups was most striking and influential during the 1990s, when comfort women began to speak about their experiences, plans were underway for the establishment of the international criminal tribunals for the former Yugoslavia and Rwanda, and negotiations were taking place over the Rome Statute and the eventual establishment of the International Criminal Court. Herman (2001: 9) argues that 'Advances in the field occur only when they are supported by a political movement powerful enough to legitimate an alliance between investigators and patients and to counteract the ordinary social processes of silencing and denial'. As such she argues that the feminist movement was the political impetus behind the legitimation of women's experiences of violence, suggesting that in order for public consciousness to embrace a serious issue, it requires a political context that challenges it. The same may be said for the issue of wartime rape.

The final, seventh key connection between collective memory and the law is that *historical analogies* (Savelsberg and King 2007) play a role in spurring the impetus for criminal prosecutions and for the selection of crimes that are prosecuted at war crimes trials. I argued earlier that the failure of the historical war crimes trials after the Second World War to adequately deal with crimes of sexual violence, and the ensuing silence surrounding this issue, helped pave the way for a wave of prosecutions for rape crimes in the 1990s. While legal silence helped to fuel denialism towards the stories of surviving comfort women and other women who have been raped throughout the history of warfare, silence and then the breaking of this silence, nonetheless ensured that wartime rape is no longer treated as an inevitable by-product of armed conflict (at least symbolically). There is no doubt then that the lessons of the past play an important role in contemporary post-conflict environments.

Based on the major developments within international humanitarian law since the establishment of the ICTY in 1993, it seems fair to conclude that the international community has not only made significant progress in recognizing sexual violence and the harm inflicted on women during armed conflict, but has sought to make the experience of seeking justice in the aftermath of conflict more victim-friendly.

Whether international courts are the best forum for the disclosure of these counter-memories; whether the trials obscure or clarify women's experiences of sexual violence and warfare; and whether witnesses are retraumatized or empowered by the experience of disclosure and cross-examination in this context, are important questions that must also be posed. While I have not attempted to answer all of these questions in this book, below I summarize some of the limitations and harms inherent within the system of international law in order to reveal the ways in which law thwarts our understandings of wartime rape as collective memory.

## The limitations of law

The ICTY is, or perhaps in time will be, remembered for its long overdue attention to rape crimes. Although the ICTR arguably has less credibility regarding its track record for rape prosecutions, the *Akayesu* trial and the enduring memory of mass rape during the Rwandan genocide have helped to implant a connection between law, memory, justice and wartime rape. We are yet to see how the International Criminal Court will evolve as a site or repository of collective memory and wartime sexual violence, but it is reasonable to conclude that international rape trials do bring a human dimension to suffering through the invaluable testimonies of witnesses, and such accounts do contribute to a valuable narrative of wartime sexual violence. ~~This establishes and clarifies an authentic historical record; however,~~ it would be wrong to accept this contribution to collective memory uncritically. Legal scholars have repeatedly pointed to the inherent limitations of law (see e.g. Sarat, Douglas and Umphrey 2005), particularly its combative, adversarial format and its impact on both defendants and witnesses. A focus on legal procedure and evidence, moreover, invariably impacts on the didactic legacy of past events. While the trial does help to construct a narrative about sexual atrocities and this helps to break an enduring historical silence on this matter, the narrative is inherently fragmented, sterilized through the procedural and evidential limits of law.

[handwritten margin note: law + courts do shape + create memory. Is this problem-atic in some way?]

First, international courts fixate on prosecuting defendants, but their stories, as well as those of witnesses, are not fully told through law, and witnesses and defendants play a relatively passive role in the prosecution of serious international crimes. Specifically, rape trials are often conducted in closed session and a great deal of what goes on 'behind the scenes' (before, during and after the trial) is not documented or disseminated by the court or by other institutional avenues. Moreover, <u>testimony does not belong to either perpetrators or victims; rather the story belongs to the court.</u> Within such short time frames, witnesses may not be permitted to tell the court their stories in their words. Prosecutors and defence lawyers tend to focus exclusively on confirming factual evidence, such as the order and timing of the offence, or the size and colour of the room. Julie Mertus (2004: 118) argues that witness testimonies are often curtailed into truncated question-and-answer-form, allowing victims little opportunity to express their suffering in their own terms, and focusing 'myopically on the actions of perpetrators'. Subsequently, the limitations of telling one's story at an international criminal trial are an impediment to the collective memory of wartime rape. As Paul Gewirtz (1996: 7–8) puts it, 'a witness's story usually furnishes discrete pieces in a mosaic whose overall shape emerges only as the trial progresses ... In short, a trial consists of fragmented narratives and narrative multiplicity'. Thus only a small fragment of the actual story is and can be told through the legal site of memory. This is compounded by the fact that very few victims will ever get to testify to rape before international criminal courts, and overall women have played a very limited role in the prosecution of war criminals.[4]

Second, while international humanitarian law individualizes guilt and accountability, often defendants are not accused of having personally committed rape, but their position of seniority or superiority means they are attributed individual criminal responsibility for the crimes committed under their command or leadership. While the individualization of crimes committed during armed conflict and the prosecution of high-level offenders for failing to prevent such crimes are important, the problem is that few perpetrators of wartime rape have been apprehended or will ever be brought to trial, whether before international or domestic war crimes courts. While it could be said that impunity for rape crimes continues to form the collective memory of wartime rape (as it has done in the past), it could also be argued not only that impunity represents a barrier to justice for victims, but that the existence and operation of international courts, and the prosecution of rape within these courts, obscures the enduring reality that few perpetrators of wartime rape will ever be prosecuted. Further, because the focus of international courts is on one or few perpetrators, war crimes courts fail to capture the collective frenzy of warfare and crimes of rape. As Ian Buruma argues, because a trial is fixated on individual crimes, 'history is reduced to criminal pathology and legal argument'. As such, the judicial process 'fails to grasp the most disturbing and fundamental issues raised by traumatic history' (quoted in Douglas 2001: 4). In other words, international criminal courts represent a limited space for the construction of a collective memory that contextualizes the broader historical, political, social and gendered framework to explain the very prevalence of rape throughout the history of warfare; its causes and its consequences.

Third, there is much debate about the impact and legacy of these trials in the post-conflict communities of, for example, the former Yugoslavia and Rwanda. The ICTY held a legacy conference in February 2010, defining 'legacy' as 'that which the Tribunal will hand down to successors and others', including, but not limited to, the findings, judgments, records and archives of the Tribunal, as well as its contribution to international law, the rule of law in the former Yugoslavia and the development of international criminal justice (see ICTY 2010). Archival access in these regions, as well as the translation of key documents into local language, remains an outstanding impediment to outreach efforts within these communities. While it is important to underscore the importance of civil disagreement about the past (and namely that the contestation of the past is healthy for the present and future (Osiel 2000)), a more protracted problem relates to reconciliation, peace and stability in post-conflict communities, which have diverse effects on how collective memories of past atrocities are formed and shaped, now and into the future.

The contribution that international courts such as the ICTY, ICTR, ICC and others make to the construction of historical consciousness is extremely difficult to assess at this point in time. The documentation and dissemination of the work of these courts invariably lie with the media, governments, NGOs, academics and others. This is no different to the unique formation (and ever evolving) conception of both the Nuremberg and Tokyo war crimes trials after the Second World War. This indicates the active role of memory preservation. The major obstacle for the memorialization of wartime rape is the shame and stigma, a timeless problem that continues to thwart both collective and individual memory of these atrocities, both inside and outside the law.

Finally, while the promise of justice is omnipresent in the aftermath of armed conflict, justice is elusive, subjective and even impossible. Justice is much broader than the prosecution of a few offenders; it involves not simply legal justice, but social and political justice, including both practical and symbolic forms of security, safety and stability. The limitations of justice are also the limitations of collective memory. The collective memory of international criminal courts is thus a potent reminder of both the promise and the impossibility of justice in the aftermath of mass atrocities.

## The violence of law

The aforementioned limitations of international war crimes courts contribute to and thwart both the deliverance of justice and the preservation of collective memory. In this final section, I will explore what is another limitation and legacy of the law. This is the 'violence' of law; the way in which law constitutes a narrative of violence in its creation of meaning and its re-enactment of violence. 'Law is not simply or even primarily, a gentle, hermeneutic apparatus; it always exists in a state of tension between a world of meaning which is pursued, and a world of violence in which "legal interpretation takes places in a field of pain and death"' (Sarat 2001: 5). I do not employ a conventional, literal definition of 'violence' as some scholars have done, for example the violence and legitimation of capital punishment through law (see e.g. Cover 1986), but rather violence is understood here in a metaphysical sense as the legitimation of power and authority through legal rules, values and procedures, and most of all, the way in which law is 'implicated in injustice' (Sarat 2001: 6).

The main argument of the book is that international rape trials are fundamentally political. Like the adversarial system in western liberal societies, international criminal courts for the prosecution of serious violations of international humanitarian law operate according to the ideology of liberalism; that is, law as separate and independent from politics, and law as fundamentally premised on the pivotal notions of justice, equality and individualism. Judith Shklar (1986: 111) states that,

> Politics is regarded not only as something apart from law, but as inferior to law. Law aims at justice, while politics looks only to expediency.

The former is neutral and objective, the latter the uncontrolled child of competing interests and ideologies.

Following the Second World War, the Nuremberg and Tokyo trials were famously declared 'political trials' by trial defendants, critics and academics alike (see e.g. Bass 2002; Shklar 1986). Although some major developments have occurred within contemporary war crimes courts to lessen charges of a political trial or victor's justice, some scholars have argued that, nonetheless, these trials are always inherently 'political'. Gerry Simpson (2007: 1), for example, argues that 'international law produces a form of displaced politics or conducts politics in a different key'. This, he says, is due to two factors. First, a war crimes trial is conducted against the political ideology of the accused and what she or he stands for (e.g. fascism, ethnic homogeneity, communism, etc.). Second, prosecutorial decisions dictate which crimes to focus on, and thus war crimes trials are both partial and selective.

As mentioned throughout the book, intergovernmental and nationalistic politics has determined the outcome and procedures of criminal prosecution. The silence of law in turn reflects the power and 'violence' of law. International courts wield enormous power in dictating which crimes make the historical record and which memories are disqualified and subjugated. This legal silence was most notable during the historical tribunals at both Nuremberg and Tokyo. Although prosecutions for rape crimes during the 1990s and beyond have served to challenge past silence and celebrate in a way of the counter-memory for rape victims, nonetheless there is a danger that wartime sexual violence will once again be relegated to the margins of history.

This is not to say that international courts should pursue each and every crime ever committed during periods of armed conflict. Obviously this would be completely unrealistic and financially and time-wise impossible. However, it is important to point out that for the international community to pursue sexually motivated crimes as serious international human rights violations, such crimes need to be connected to a political motivation and contextualized as a public violation in order to be tried as a crime against humanity, torture, genocide and a war crime. Preconditions of the jurisdiction may thus pose a number of barriers to justice for victims of sexual violence. For example, in the case of the ICC there are a number of situations where a case may be inadmissible. These include when the case is being investigated by the state with jurisdiction over the accused; when the state concludes there is no basis to prosecute; when the accused has already undergone a trial; and when the case is not sufficiently serious to proceed with prosecution (Askin and Koenig 1999). Kelly Askin and Dorean Koenig (1999) argue that this could deprive the ICC of the right to hear a case involving the most heinous of sexual crimes.

The politics of prosecution extend much more widely than prosecutorial decision-making. Askin and Koenig (1999: 29) state that 'discrimination, naivete, and reluctance' contribute to a discrepancy in the treatment of women and the crimes committed against them and that this continues to negatively affect women within international criminal jurisdictions. In other words, lack of political will has been shown to obstruct a serious reckoning with rape crimes, particularly at the ICTR. There is also a risk that this will impact on the nature of proceedings at the ICC and that sexual violence once again will be left off the agenda.

In addition to the above two factors, a third factor gives both historical and contemporary war crimes trials a distinctly political flavour; that is, these trials are highly gendered spaces that purport to support gender neutrality, equality and justice, but in reality replicate the same sorts of gendered biases found within the adversarial tradition of modern liberal democracies. And  yet, international law, like domestic law, is carefully disguised and obscured by the ideology of liberalism and the 'greatness of legalism' (Shklar 1986: 112). My point here is that the politics of war crimes trials is critical to understanding the relationship between law and collective memory, and politics can be a form of 'violence'.

International feminist scholars have shown the ways in which male-defined substantive, procedural and conceptual structures may serve to undermine, marginalize or obscure women's experiences of warfare (see e.g. Charlesworth, Chinkin and Wright 1991; Fellmeth 2000; Lusby 1994; Ray 1997). In domestic rape trials, feminist scholars have pointed to the ways in which the combative, adversarial, hierarchical format (Polan 1982) privileges male conceptions of consent, serving to thwart women's experiences of sexual violation. Catharine MacKinnon (1983: 644), for instance, argues that 'The law sees and treats women the way men see and treat women'.  Post-modernist feminists too have rejected the claims of objective, scientific truth that law has a particular stake in (see Smart 1989). Finley (1989: 888) writes:

> Law is, among other things, a language, a form of discourse, and a system through which meanings are reflected and constructed and cultural practices are organized. Law is a language of power, a particularly authoritative discourse. Law can pronounce definitely what something is or is not and how a situation or event is to be understood ... It reinforces certain world views and understandings of events ... Through its definitions and the way it talks about events, law has the power to silence alternative meanings – to suppress other stories.

Although there are a number of 'gender-friendly' developments within international law, cunning lawyers are able to effectively bypass rules relating to consent, captivity and cross-examination. As such, they are also able to deliberately construct an alternative narrative about the implicit authenticity of witness truth and memory. Subsequently, law can disqualify or obscure certain meanings and experiences (for example, the emotional and physical pain of rape). What perhaps is most worrying is that international courts have replicated and reproduced stock-standard cross-examination and prosecutorial strategies all too familiar within domestic rape trials. This reflects perpetual cultural values about female sexuality, and in the process may serve to disqualify women's experiences of wartime sexual violence (Smart 1989).

The violence of law through legal language and discourse supports Felman's (2002) hypothesis about what she calls the 'juridical unconscious'. She argues that there exists a paradox between, on the one hand, the attempt of law to articulate trauma and, on the other hand, the re-enactment of trauma:

> The juridical unconscious consists not only in the way in which the law repeats the trauma but also, more specifically, precisely in the way in which *what cannot be articulated in legal language* is, however, *played out on the legal stage* and is enacted and reenacted in the courtroom in two dramatic legal modes: (a) in compulsive structures of *legal* repetitions …
> and (b) in moments of explosion and of interruption of the legal framework.
>
> (ibid.: 182, emphasis original)

For victims of wartime rape, as I demonstrated in the previous chapter, due to the inherent limitations of language for capturing the 'unspeakable', testimonies are particularly vulnerable to speculation and distrust from outsiders, and in this context 'storytelling … may contribute to securing relations of power and the marginalisation of storytellers' (Colvin 2004: 12). The recent popularity within the study of traumatology has further contributed to this marginalization because trauma is used not to validate the experiences of women during warfare, but to undermine their authenticity, reliability and credibility as witnesses in post-conflict judicial realms.

In a similar way to peacetime but perhaps more so, rape in war frequently lacks the requisite evidentiary basis from which to secure a guilty-beyond-reasonable-doubt conviction. Victims thus may suffer from a damage 'accompanied by the loss of the means to prove the damage' (Lyotard 1988: 5). Victims of rape are also the victims of a representational wrong, a 'differend', which should be put into language but does not fit the laws of representation (ibid.). This adds fuel to the fire that defence lawyers aim to create. Like domestic rape trials, there is an inherent power imbalance between female witnesses and defence lawyers, reflected in the hostile and manipulative cross-examination strategies that have 'a poignancy in the rape context that is unmatched elsewhere' (Conley and O'Barr 1998: 32). Accordingly, the utilization of techniques designed to question credibility and raise evidence of prior sexual behaviour and/or complicity represents an affirmation of power and domination. Aggressive argument, legal complexities, cunning distortion and exploitation of words may be disempowering to women who testify before these courts. Nonetheless, it is important to

*[handwritten margin note: law's discourse fails to serve women in a way, law is violent to women.]*

point out that power is not monolithic or simply reflective of hierarchical ordering, and as such witnesses may also feel empowered by the opportunity to stand up and bear witness to sexual atrocities. Despite the possibilities for strength, agency and empowerment, international courts are no doubt powerful institutions that have the authority to declare how the past is to be remembered and whose memories are privileged.

International courts have had a mixed record in terms of contributing to collective memory and a historical consciousness about the past. On the one hand, a story of wartime sexual violence has been told that includes the authentic voices of women who suffered during the conflicts of the past three decades. The developments within international law should thus be applauded. However, on the other hand, the danger is that these developments may lead to complacency or even forgetting. As James Young (1999: 2) argues in his article on monuments and memory, a finished monument may put a 'cap on memory work' and bury, reduce and coarsen memory:

> It is as if once we assign monumental form to memory, we have to some degree divested ourselves of the obligation to remember. In the eyes of modern critics and artists, the traditional monument's essential stiffness and grandiose pretensions to permanence thus doom it to an archaic, premodern status. Even worse, by insisting that its meaning is as fixed as its place in the landscape, the monument seems oblivious to the essential mutability in all cultural artifacts, the ways the significance in all art evolves over time. In this way, monuments have long sought to provide a naturalizing locus for memory, in which a state's triumphs and martyrs, its ideals and founding myths, are cast as naturally true as the landscape in which they stand. These are the monument's sustaining illusions, the principles of its seeming longevity and power.

Like the stone and mortar of a monument, law too may provide a fixed sense of permanence, an illusion to monumental power and longevity, but be unable to make reference to the historical past beyond its own parameters.

Throughout the history of warfare, the rape of women has been both an issue of deep silence and paradoxically an issue that is highly visible in political, nationalistic discourse. Moreover, in post-conflict, post-justice realms, while rape has been used to highlight a nation's victimhood or heroism, the actual experiences of women have been repeatedly marginalized, in both historic and contemporary international war crimes courts. Rape thus remains an unspeakable crime, and despite the resistance and remarkable documentation of survivors, it also remains seen as an *inevitable* crime of war. Women's experiences continue to be systematically sidelined not only in official narratives of war, but also during war crimes trials and within other mnemonic forms. There has no doubt been a discernible shift in attitudes towards wartime rape, particularly since the 1990s, but due to the inherent limitations of law, as well as the gendered nature of these institutional mechanisms, international courts ultimately fail to adequately capture the extent, nature and emotional impact of these crimes; nor do they help to explain the social, political, historical and ultimately gendered context of war and its aftermath. War crimes trials arguably create conceptual confusion because, by and large, they do not articulate a context or cause of egregious crimes. We might thus conclude that it is simply beyond the scope of these courts to serve such complex justice goals.

Testimonies of wartime sexual violence contribute to the preservation of post-conflict collective memory and the recognition of rape as a serious human rights violation. While acknowledgment and justice are no doubt imperative to ending silence, the articulation of so-called 'unspeakable' events through law reveals the impossibility of bearing witness, and seeking justice, as well as the construction of coherent collective narratives of past atrocities. It is Agamben's (2002) contention that 'testimony is the disjunction between two impossibilities of bearing witness'. We might think of this as the impossibility of language for expressing physical and psychological pain, and the impossibility of 'non-language' or silence as an alternative to disclosure. Criminal trials contribute to these impossibilities through both the appropriation of trauma and the failure of law to accommodate traumatic experiences. In sum, this reminds us of the power of law – particularly international law – to influence collective memory and to authoritatively pronounce what and how history shall be remembered. The legacy of silence continues to pervade women's experiences of wartime rape. This is due not only to the social stigma and shame of rape, but also to the inherent limitations of law to address such crimes.

# Notes

## 1 Introduction: how the past is made to matter

1 Note that there is a body of psychological literature on memory and law; see e.g. Brown, Scheflin and Hammond (1998); Goodman and Helgeson (1985); Loftus and Doyle (1997); Wells (1993). For a discussion of the contribution of truth commissions to collective memory, see e.g. Gibson (2004, 2006); Wilson (2003).

2 Rape has been informally and formally outlawed as a punishable offence throughout the history of warfare. For example, Totila the Ostrogoth who captured Rome in 546 AD forbade his troops to rape Roman women (Brownmiller 1976). In 1385, Richard II of England decreed that his soldiers would be hanged for rape, and in 1419 Henry V made rape subject to capital punishment under military codes (Brownmiller 1976; Meron 1993b). In 1474, Sir Peter Von Hagenbach became the first man in international legal history to be prosecuted and convicted for rape, perjury and other crimes by an international military tribunal in Breisach, Germany (although some legal scholars have argued that this was not technically a war crimes trial as no state of war existed at the time of the offences – see e.g. McCormack 1997; Parks 1973). In the seventeenth century, Dutch jurist Hugo Grotius deemed it a crime to 'violate chastity' in war and considered this subject to punishment. Rape was also explicitly listed as a capital crime in Article 44 of the 1863 Lieber Code during the American Civil War, which became the basis for subsequent laws governing rape. The Lieber Code was adopted as international law at the International Peace Conference in Copenhagen in 1907 and became the basis for the Hague Conventions of 1907. The codification of rape in international treaties and conventions by and large defines it as a crime against dignity and honour. For example, Article 27 of the 1949 Geneva Convention states: 'Women shall be especially protected against any attack on their honour, in particular against rape, enforced prostitution, or any form of indecent assault', whereas Common Article 3 of the Geneva Conventions prohibits acts against non-combatants, including 'outrages upon personal dignity'. See Askin (1997) for a detailed discussion of this.

3 There are varying definitions of 'rape' and 'sexual violence' within both academic literature and legal practice. Legal definitions often define rape as forcible penile-vaginal penetration without consent, yet this fails to take into consideration other forms of sexual violence. Moreover, this conceptualization is both phallo-centric and gender-specific. For a discussion of definitions relating to wartime sexual violence, see Campbell (2007). Throughout the book, I do not differentiate between wartime rape and wartime sexual violence and, as such, I use the terms interchangeably. I therefore use the broad definition adopted in the 1998 *Akayesu* case at the International Criminal Tribunal for Rwanda (ICTR):

The Chamber defines rape as a physical invasion of a sexual nature, committed on a person under circumstances which are coercive. Sexual violence which includes rape, is considered to be any act of a sexual nature which is committed on a person under circumstances which are coercive. This act must be committed: (a) as part of a wide spread or systematic attack; (b) on a civilian population; (c) on certain catalogued discriminatory grounds, namely: national, ethnic, political, racial, or religious grounds.

4 According to former 'comfort woman' Jan Ruff O'Herne (1994: 136–7), 'The euphemism "comfort women" is an insult, and I felt it was a pity that the media were also continually using these words. We were never "comfort women". Comfort means something warm and soft, safe and friendly. It means tenderness. We were war-rape victims, enslaved and conscripted by the Japanese imperial forces'. The term 'comfort women' is used widely by victims, scholars and others to refer to the systematic sexual enslavement of women and girls during the Second World War. I will refer to this euphemism throughout the rest of the book; however, due to reasons of convenience and readability, I will not continue to use quotation marks around the term.

5 As part of international law, international war crimes law (also known as international humanitarian law (IHL)) refers to the collection of laws in treaties and state practices that govern the rules of armed conflict. IHL places limits on the conduct of war and protects civilians and persons who are no longer participating in hostilities. See Best (1980); Charlesworth and Chinkin (2000); May (2007); Ratner, Abrams and Bischoff (2009).

6 There have been a number of significant international rape trials at the ICTY and ICTR since their establishment in 1993 and 1994 respectively. Due to space limitations, I only discuss four trials in this chapter – three from the ICTY (*Tadič*, *Čelebiči* and *Foča*) and one from the ICTR (*Akayesu*). A brief reflection on the ICC is undertaken at the very end of the chapter. The selection of cases was based on the significance of these trials in terms of creating important legal precedents (e.g. the first international trial; the trials that established rape as a crime against humanity, a crime of torture and a crime of genocide). Because of their legal significance, it could be argued that these trials are more likely to contribute to the collective memory of wartime rape. I do not mean to imply that other trials where rape has been prosecuted are not equally, or more, significant. Also, within the scope of the book, it was not possible to examine hybrid or domestic war crimes courts. Increasingly, though, there is recognition that such trials also need to take into account their future legacy and impact on post-conflict communities. This appears to be a new and emerging area of focus within the theory and practice of international criminal justice.

7 I acknowledge there are ethical issues surrounding using the testimonies of rape victims in academic writing. In this book I have strived to present testimonies in an appropriate way by removing any material that could be construed as 'voyeuristic' and I have provided pseudonyms for witnesses. See Lindsey (2002) for a critical analysis of wartime rape testimony in academic writing.

8 Transitional justice refers to periods of political change where justice is sought within the ambit of legal and quasi-legal responses that deal with the wrongdoings of prior regimes (Teitel 2000). Transitional justice studies have examined various responses to human rights violations in diverse geographical locations, including victim reparations, lustration initiatives, truth and reconciliation commissions and international criminal tribunals (see e.g. Hayner 2001; Hesse and Post 1999; Minow 1998; Roht-Arriaza 1995; Rosenberg 1995; Teitel 2000).

9 Historical consciousness is often used interchangeably with 'collective memory' to refer to the collective understandings of the past (see Lukacs 1968; Seixas 2004).

**2 Traces of truth: collective memory and the law**

1 Note that Nietzsche (2003) did see a positive role of history; for example, three modes of history – monumental, antiquarian and critical history – may provide meaning to the great achievements of humanity; an appreciation of life and culture; and a counter-balance to the past and present. Foucault takes up Nietzsche's critique of history in his seminal works, including *The History of Madness in the Classical Age* (2006); and *Discipline and Punish: The Birth of the Prison* (1979). For a discussion of Nietzsche's view of history, see Posner (2000).

2 The desirability or otherwise of memorial cultures is not the focus of this chapter, but see, for example, Adam (2009); Irwin-Zarecka (2007); Levy and Sznaider (2006); Williams (2008); Young (1993).

3 Internet social networking sites, such as Facebook, for instance, enable online memorials to be set up as tributes to loved ones as well as victims and survivors of atrocities (e.g. the Facebook memorials for the Virginia shooting victims). There is even a collective memory site set up through Facebook: http://www.facebook.com/pages/collective-memory/252182880012.

4 In the transitional justice realm, forgetting is not an option and rather 'The question today is not *whether* something should be done after atrocity but *how* it should be done' (Nagy 2008: 276, emphasis original).

5 On the other hand, Brown (1995) argues that modernity is characterized by a rise in 'ressentiment' (overtones of bitterness) through a moralizing discourse fixated on victimization, injustice and vengeance.

6 For a discussion of the lineage of memory and an excellent review of the diversity of works on social memory, see Olick and Robbins (1998), who contend that although the contemporary usage of 'collective memory' may be attributed to Halbwachs (1992), memory has preoccupied philosophers and social thinkers for centuries. Due to space constraints and the object of this chapter, it is impossible to mention all of the significant works within contemporary memory studies.

7 Another commonly identified problem within collective memory studies is the persistence of the dichotomy between history and memory (see e.g. Hutton 1994; 2000; Le Goff 1992; Nora 1989). Halbwachs (1992) argued that history stood in stark contrast to memory: while history traced the past retrospectively, memory was the 'living past' expressed via recollection/commemoration in the present. Nora (1989), following from Halbwachs (1992), views history as detached and inorganic, problematic and incomplete, compared to collective memory, which he declares is active and aware. Huyssen (1995: 3) too implies a similar distinction: 'It is this tenuous fissure between past and present that constitutes memory, making it powerfully alive and distinct from the archive or any other mere system of storage and retrieval'. The notion of collective memory as alive or active embraces a 'presentist approach'. According to Le Goff (1992: xi–xii), for example, 'Memory is the raw material of history … it is the living source from which historians draw'. In a critique of the concept of collective memory, Gedi and Elam (1996) claim that collective memory has replaced both 'real' or factual history and 'real' or personal memory with what may be termed a 'fabricated narrative' of the past. Yet, it is important to note that both personal memory and history are in a sense also fabricated or constructed since recollection can never be a perfect mirror of the past. For example, I may recount a dream I had last night to a friend, but my expression of the dream will never accurately convey the dream's content – not only because of the inadequacy of language for conveying the experience of the dream, but also because my memory is simply an imperfect representation of that experience. (Incidentally, Halbwachs (1992) argued that dreams are distinct to all human memory because they lack organization, coherency and a social framework for their preservation and interpretation.) Likewise, a historian may dig through

archives to construct an 'accurate' portrayal of the past, but most historians now recognize that all history is interpretative, regardless of scrupulous methodological investigation or claims to authenticity and objectivity (Burke 1989). Collective memory then is inextricably dependent on both personal memory and historical documentation, but paradoxically independent of them both too. Zerubavel (1995: 5), for instance, sees an interrelationship between history and memory, rather than a rigid opposition, stating that collective memory 'continuously negotiates between available historical records and current social and political agendas'.

8  Assmann (1995) lists several characteristics of *cultural* forms of memory. These include: the concretization of group identity and unity through memory; the reconstruction of the past through a contemporary lens; the crystallization and transmission of shared memory; the formalization of memory; the creation of values and symbols which structure knowledge; and the reflexivity and cultivation of memory through text, images and rituals within a society.

9  Interestingly, *A Woman in Berlin* (2006) has been the subject of much debate surrounding its authenticity. See Beevor's introduction in the book and his defence of the author's integrity. See also Halley's (2008a) discussion of the book.

10  My book is focused on law as the institutional location in which to examine the formation of wartime rape as collective memory. But the relationship between collective memory and wartime rape in general has received little attention within the current literature, and as such, more research is needed into the multiple and diverse mnemonic forms (and their relationship with each other) for proliferating contemporary understandings of wartime sexual violence.

11  Other law and memory scholars, however, do use collective memory to refer to collective narratives of particular groups of people. For example, Osiel (2000: 18) writes: 'Collective memory consists of past reminiscences that link given groups of people for whom the remembered events are important, that is, the events remain significant to them later on. The memory is later invoked to help define what such people have in common and guide their collective action'.

12  I attended a conference on transcultural memory in London in February 2010 and despite the conference calling for papers on gender and memory from the outset, there was no panel set up on this topic. Aside from my own presentation, I did not come across any that specifically dealt with the connection between gender and memory.

13  For a discussion of gender, memory and the Holocaust, see Baumel (1998); Eschebach (2003); Jacobs (2008); Reading (2002); Ringelheim (1997, 1998); Zelizer (2000). Jacobs (2008), for example, in her fieldwork at the museum/memorial at Auschwitz-Birkenau, concludes that women are represented primarily through two visual frames: as endangered mothers or as victims of sexual subjugation.

14  See Power's (1998) review of Osiel's book.

15  Douglas (2001: 3) defines 'didactic legality' as a balancing act between recognizing legal norms and precedents and stretching the law to 'reintroduce order into a space evacuated of legal and moral sense'.

16  Adolf Eichmann, argued Arendt (1994), was commonplace, ordinary and incapable of independent thought; though neither demonic nor a 'monster'.

17  There are some outstanding questions that must be raised when we speak of the pedagogical role of law: to whom are these lessons directed? What is being taught and how would we know, empirically, if such lessons are in practice 'learnt'? Since collective memory must be understood as non-consensual, variable and constantly shifting, it is inherently difficult to ascertain exactly what narratives emerge or exist in the present to represent the past. As such, I am purposefully avoiding identifying collective narratives that may or may not be floating around at present.

To reiterate my use of the term 'collective memory' – I am more concerned to make my own interpretations of the narratives that are told and not told through legal mechanisms since law is inescapably a repository of memory, rather than ascertain how wartime rape is remembered among specific groups of people.

### 3 A history of silence: the Nuremberg and Tokyo trials

1 This is the estimate given by Beevor (2003).
2 There was no international war crimes trial following the First World War although recommendations were made for a 'special tribunal' in the Treaty of Versailles, but this was never set up (see McCormack 1997; McCormack and Simpson 1997).
3 The prohibition of rape in national and international jurisdictions throughout history will not be examined in this chapter since this has already been well documented elsewhere (see e.g. Askin 1997; Brownmiller 1976; Meron 1993a, 1993b; Khushalani 1982; Krill 1985; Niarchos 1995; Tompkins 1995).
4 See e.g. Black and Falk (1971); Falk (2000); Glueck (1944); Jackson (2003); Orentlicher (1998); Tutorow (1986).
5 Agreement for the Prosecution and Punishment of the Major War Criminals of the European Axis, 8 August, 1945, 59 Stat. 1544, 82 UNTS 279 (also referred to as the London Agreement, Charter of the International Military Tribunal, Nuremberg Charter or IMT Charter). Article 6(c) of the IMT Charter listing crimes against humanity was specifically intended to cover crimes not listed within the 'war crimes' category (Chinkin 1994).
6 Note that in the remainder of the chapter, proceedings from the Nuremberg trial (International Military Tribunal) will be cited as *IMT*; and proceedings from the Tokyo trial (International Military Tribunal for the Far East) will be cited as *IMTFE*. The volume and then page number will also be provided in the citation where available. My access to the original proceedings for the IMTFE was through the E.H. Northcroft Collection at the University of Canterbury in Christchurch, New Zealand. My access to the IMT proceedings was via the Yale Law School Avalon Project website: http://avalon.law.yale.edu/subject_menus/imt.asp.
7 Men were also subjected to various forms of sterilization before the war and also in the concentration camps.
8 In the 42-volume proceedings of the Nuremberg trial, the 732-page index does not include 'rape', 'prostitution' or 'women' among the headings or subheadings, while three and a half pages are devoted to 'looting' (Askin 1997). In the trial of lesser German war criminals (enacted under Article II of Law No. 10 of the Control Council for Germany), rape was listed explicitly as a crime against humanity. For example, according to Article II(1)(c): 'Atrocities and offences, including but not limited to murder, extermination, enslavement, deportation, imprisonment, torture, rape, or other inhumane acts committed against any civilian population, or persecutions on political, racial or religious grounds whether or not in violation of the domestic laws of the country where perpetrated' (*Punishment of Persons Guilty of War Crimes, Crimes Against Peace and Crimes Against Humanity, Control Council Law No. 10*, 20 December 1945 [hereinafter Control Council Law No. 10]). The Control Council Law No. 10 authorized 12 unilateral trials in the zones of occupation, held also at Nuremberg between 1946 and 1945, for which there were a total of 185 defendants (see Lippman 1993). The accused included: 'medical doctors responsible for illegal human experiments, jurists who distorted law to achieve Nazi goals, high-ranking military officers responsible for atrocities, Foreign Ministry officials who helped plan aggression and industrialists who seized foreign properties and worked concentration camp inmates to death' (Ferencz 2003: 35).

Despite the inclusion of rape and an abundance of evidence regarding sexual violence at these other trials, no gender-specific crimes against women were ever charged (Askin 1997).

9 The Japanese Emperor Hirohito and all the members of the imperial family were not prosecuted at the Tokyo trial. For a discussion of the trial, see generally Minear (1971); Röling and Rüter (1993).

10 Rape was tried as 'inhuman treatment', 'ill-treatment' and as 'failure to respect family honour and rights'. Defendants were charged with acts 'carried out in violation of recognized customs or conventions of war … [including] mass murder, rape … and other barbaric cruelties'. For commentary on the prosecution of rape crimes at the Tokyo trial, see Askin (1997); Brownmiller (1976).

11 These crimes fell under the general charge of 'conspiracy to commit conventional war crimes and crimes against humanity' (counts 54 and 55). Under Count 54 specifically, defendants were charged with 'having conspired to order, authorize or permit their subordinates to commit breaches of the laws or customs of war'. Alongside General Matsui, Hirota Koki, Japan's foreign minister until May 1938, was also tried for Nanking atrocities.

12 The Nuremberg Tribunal too has been criticized on this basis (see e.g. Blumenthal and McCormack 2008; Luban 1994; Scharf 1997; Taylor 1992). Criticisms of the Nuremberg trials include: the American domination of the prosecution team; the lack of accountability for Allied violations of international law; and the unfair legal procedures and rules for the defendants.

13 This idea is borrowed from Neier (1998), who argues that at the Nuremberg trial, rape was a victim of victor's justice.

14 The concept of the 'silent witness' may seem like an oxymoron here and as such this term needs further clarification. According to Agamben (2002: 17), there are two types of witnesses. The first is a person who testifies in law as a third party, whereas the second witness 'designates a person who has lived through something, who has experienced an event from beginning to end and can therefore bear witness to it'. I use 'witness' in the latter sense here to refer to women who were raped, who could have testified to their experiences, but who were (and are) silenced by official legal discourse.

15 According to Arendt (1994: 9), for criminal prosecutions it is the wrongdoer and the body politic that are the central focus: 'The wrongdoer is brought to justice because his act has disturbed and gravely endangered the community as a whole … It is the body politic itself that stands in need of being "repaired", and it is the general public order that has been thrown out of gear and must be restored … It is, in other words, the law, not the plaintiff, that must prevail'.

16 It is also worth noting the trial of General Tomoyuki Yamashita before an American military commission in Manila beginning in October 1945 (before the Tokyo trial had even begun). Yamashita was charged with 'command responsibility' for the commission of atrocities against Filipino civilians that included the rapes of hundreds of Filipino women. This concept of criminal liability became the basis of the indictments against Radovan Karadžič and Ratko Mladič at the International Criminal Tribunal for the Former Yugoslavia (ICTY). For a discussion of the Yamashita trial, see Lael (1982).

17 I too have gone through these exhibits, held at the University of Canterbury in Christchurch, New Zealand (and elsewhere).

18 Dolgopol (1995) argues that the perceived humiliation of having to publicly recount the details of sexual crimes meant that victims were not considered as witnesses at these trials.

19 Julius Streicher was the founder and publisher of the anti-Semitic weekly newspaper *Der Stürmer*, which became central to the Nazi propaganda machine.

20 Those who were charged with both crimes against peace and war crimes received the death penalty. In total, only five defendants were convicted of ordering or approving conventional war crimes.

21 Of course, this does not mean that sexism and patriarchy are not 'political'; indeed, the gendered nature of legal discourse is very political, but in a different way to the political factors discussed in the section here.

22 The two main Nanking witnesses, Hsu Chuan-ying and John Gillespie Magee, were both males. Note, Askin (1997) speculates whether the presence of three female assistant prosecution counsels at the Tokyo trial helped to secure charges of rape within the indictment.

23 Liebman and Michelson (1995) argue that in 1945 few Germans could have remained unaware of the mass rapes by Russian soldiers that were committed against German women due to the massive health and social problems that followed. In recent years, there has been much attention to these rapes; see e.g. Anonymous (2006); Beevor (2003); Grossman (1995); Halley (2008a).

24 On the basis of the Japanese government's investigation into the comfort women issue, the Chief Cabinet Secretary Kono Yohei issued a statement on 4 August 1993, stating: 'The then Japanese military was, directly or indirectly, involved in the establishment and management of the comfort stations and the transfer of comfort women ... The Government of Japan would like to take this opportunity once again to extend its sincere apologies and remorse to all those, irrespective of place of origin, who suffered immeasurable pain and incurable physical and psychological wounds as comfort women ... We hereby reiterate our firm determination never to repeat the same mistake by forever engraving such issues in our memories through the study and teaching of history' (Kono 1993).

25 For my own research into international trials and wartime rape, when searching for references to rape in the original trial transcripts of the Tokyo trials, I was struck that the 1980 index contained no reference to women or sexual crimes whatsoever since rape is mentioned relatively frequently throughout the trial (Wells 1983).

26 See also En-han (2002); Eykholt (2000); Fogel (2000); Higashinakano (2005); Li, Sabella and Liu (2002); Masaaki (2000); Wakabayashi (2007); Yoshida (2006); Young and Yin (1996).

## 4 Casualties of law: wartime rape and war crimes courts

1 I am not suggesting that types of property destruction (e.g. looting and pillaging) are not serious international crimes. Like rape crimes, cultural property destruction, for example, has also been neglected by international courts (see Petrovic 2008). Rather, my point is that the clichéd triad of 'rape, loot and pillage' is problematic given that women have in the past been viewed as part of the 'booty' or 'spoils' of war. While this may be the mindset of perpetrators, arguably it has infiltrated the way in which sexual violence has been dealt with during and after periods of armed conflict, as demonstrated earlier. We now have more appreciation and understanding that rape is not simply something that happens incidentally in war (e.g. as a manifestation of soldierly frustration) but that women's bodies are also often integral to the battlefield (e.g. as a weapon of war; or as part of a genocidal or ethnic cleansing campaign to destroy an entire group).

2 For a discussion of victims, see e.g. Elias (1986); Fletcher (1995); Henderson (1985); Karmen (2001); Minow (1993); Shapland, Willmore and Duff (1985). For a discussion of victims and witnesses at international courts, see e.g. Bassiouni (2006); de Brouwer (2007); Cohen (2009); Stover (2005); Trumbell (2007).

3 Despite the proliferation of the feminist movement specifically and the victims' movement more generally, attention to wartime sexual violence was ill-considered until the early 1990s. For example, the issue of rape was not raised in 1969

within the United Nations Commission on the Status of Women (Mertus 2000). In 1974, the United Nations General Assembly adopted the Declaration on the Protection of Women and Children in Emergency and Armed Conflict, yet there was no specific mention of rape within these provisions. Even as late as the mid-1980s, sexual violence during armed conflict remained largely unrecognized at the international level. For example, the 1985 Nairobi Forward-looking Strategies for the Advancement of Women, although referring directly to the situation of women and armed conflict, did not specifically link sexual violence to armed conflict. The research undertaken by Professor Yun Chung-Ok during the 1970s and 1980s regarding the sexual enslavement of Korean women during the Second World War prompted women's organizations in South Korea to conduct further investigation into this issue. The increasing role of legal institutions to address gross human rights violations during this period also gave impetus to the resolution of past violence, including sexual violence, in post-conflict arenas. In December 1991, three elderly South Korean women filed a claim in the Tokyo District Court against the Japanese for military sexual slavery (Helm 1992; Sanger 1992). Across Asia, elderly women who had suffered for years in silence, often in extreme poverty and with extensive physical and psychological problems, began to speak out against their victimization (Chinkin 2001). In December 2000, the Women's International War Crimes Tribunal on Japan's Military Sexual Slavery was set up as a civil society initiative to hear the suffering and pain endured by the former comfort women at the hands of the Japanese military fifty years earlier. The Tribunal was established to determine the criminal liability of leading military figures, political officials and the Japanese state, although it lacked binding legal authority. Significantly, the Tribunal declared the proceedings of the Tokyo Tribunal incomplete (Chinkin 2001). This, and a range of other activity, demonstrated a contrast to the past indifference towards wartime sexual violence that had come to define the entire discourse, at least until the early 1990s.

4 In November 1995, the Dayton Peace Agreement brought an end to the conflict, dividing the country into two separate entities: the Bosnian Serb Republic (Republika Srpska) and the Muslim-Croat Federation (Federacija Bosne i Hercegovine), together comprising a state called Bosnia and Herzegovina. Out of a population of over 4 million in 1991, the war resulted in the deaths of over 100,000 people and displaced a further 1.8 million people (Tabeau and Bijak 2005).

5 Ethnic cleansing refers to 'rendering an area ethnically homogeneous by using force or intimidation to remove individuals of given groups from the area' (United Nations 1994).

6 Reports of ethnic cleansing culminated in the United Nations sending Special Rapporteur Tadeusz Mazowiecki to investigate allegations of rape crimes in Croatia and Bosnia-Herzegovina. This was closely followed by the establishment of a United Nations Commission of Experts to investigate allegations of serious violations of international humanitarian law in the region (Bassiouni 2002). Among other things, the Commission found that patterns of rape in Bosnia-Herzegovina constituted a practice of ethnic cleansing, 'intended to humiliate, shame, degrade and terrify the entire ethnic group' (Mazowiecki 1993). Patterns of rape were strongly suggestive of a systematic policy, and the Commission stated that rape and sexual assault could clearly be viewed as grave breaches of the Geneva Conventions and other violations of international humanitarian law. This was a groundbreaking moment in history, instigating a succession of legal outcomes, including the subsequent prosecution of rape crimes within international courts. A medical team comprising medical and psychiatric experts was dispatched to Bosnia-Herzegovina and the Federal Republic of Yugoslavia (Serbia and Montenegro) to collect and analyze victim and witness testimonies. The United Nations

Commission on Human Rights (1994) subsequently published a report condemning 'the abhorrent practice of rape and abuse of women and children in the areas of armed conflict in the Former Yugoslavia, which, in the circumstances, constitutes a war crime' and urged all nations to 'exert every effort to bring to justice ... all those individuals directly or indirectly involved in those outrageous crimes'. In March 1993, Bosnia-Herzegovina filed an application against Serbia and Montenegro in the International Court of Justice (ICJ) based in part on allegations of mass and systematic rape. Subsequently, the UN Commission on Human Rights passed a resolution placing rape clearly within the framework of international humanitarian law and called for an international tribunal to prosecute these crimes.

7 Note that the Serbian government did not view the ICTY as a neutral body, particularly in light of the NATO bombings during the Kosovo conflict in 1999. The ICTY Statute gives the Tribunal the power to prosecute persons for serious violations of international humanitarian law, including conventional and customary international laws. These include four types of violations: grave breaches of the Four Geneva Conventions of 1949 (Article 2); violations of the laws or customs of war (Article 3); genocide (Article 4); and crimes against humanity (Article 5). As of 17 March 2010, the ICTY had indicted a total of 161 persons. At this time, 36 persons were in custody and 2 on provisional release. Of the 40 accused in 17 cases, 13 were before the Appeals Chamber, 25 on trial and 2 at large. Of the 86 concluded cases, 11 have been acquitted and 61 sentenced. Because the ICTY was established as an *ad hoc* court, it is estimated that it will finish its trials by mid-2011; however, the trial of Radovan Karadžič is expected to finish in late 2012, with appeals to be completed by 2014. With the exception of the *Karadžič* case, all appeals are scheduled to finish by mid-2013. See: http://www.icty.org/sections/TheCases/KeyFigures.

8 This was based on *Control Council Law No.10*, which explicitly included rape as a crime against humanity. Article 5 of the ICTY Statute provides that the Tribunal 'shall have power to prosecute persons responsible for the following crimes when committed in armed conflict, whether international or internal in character and directed against any civilian population: (a) murder; (b) extermination; (c) enslavement; (d) deportation; (e) imprisonment; (f) torture; (g) *rape*; (h) persecutions on political, racial and religious grounds; (i) other inhumane acts' (Statute of the International Criminal Tribunal for the Former Yugoslavia, emphasis added). The incorporation of rape as a crime against humanity is the only provision within the ICTY Statute that explicitly deals with rape. There is no mention of rape under the category of 'violations of the laws or customs of war' (Article 3) or genocide (Article 4), nor is rape or sexual assault listed under the category of 'grave breaches' of the Geneva Conventions (Article 2). The lack of specific inclusion of rape as a war crime, a grave breach, and as a tool of genocide and torture initially raised concern regarding how an international tribunal would conduct prosecutions for sexual violence and whether existing laws could provide a sufficient basis for prosecuting these crimes (Copelon 1993; Jarvis 1999). However, international courts have been able to prosecute sexual assault under each of these crimes, for instance as genocide and as a 'grave breach' of the four Geneva Conventions, including torture and 'inhuman treatment', although it is widely recognized that it should be explicitly named as a 'war crime' rather than being covered by the nondescript language of 'great suffering', 'serious injury', 'inhuman treatment', 'degrading practices' and 'outrages upon personal dignity' (Askin 1997).

9 For discussion of the legal ramifications of prosecuting rape crimes, see: Aydellot (1993); Blatt (1992); Coan (2000); Copelon (1993); Green, Copelon, Cotter, Stephens and Pratt (1994); Healey (1995); McDonald (2000); Viseur-Sellers (1996); Viseur-Sellers and Okuizumi (1997).

10 *Prosecutor v. Tadič*, Case No. IT-94-1. For a discussion of the trial, see Scharf (1997). See also: http://www.icty.org/case/tadic/4. For a specific commentary on rape and the *Tadič* trial, see Viseur-Sellers (2004). Note also that other trials dealing with crimes at Omarska, Trnopolje and Keraterm camps have taken place before the ICTY. These include the trial of the camp commandants, Miroslav Kvočka, Dragoljub Prcač, Milojica Kos and Mlađo Radič, and taxi driver Zoran Žigič, who were all found guilty of crimes against humanity. In other trials, Željko Mejakič, the *de facto* commander of the Omarska camp, Momčilo Gruban and Duško Kneževič were all found guilty of crimes against humanity (including sexual violence).

11 Tadič was accused of taking part in the beating of male prisoners and forcing two men to lick another prisoner's buttocks and genitals. These two prisoners were also forced to sexually mutilate this prisoner by biting off his testicles, after which he bled to death.

12 Judge Stephen nonetheless recommended that the name used in the Omarska prison camp for Witness F be disclosed to the accused.

13 Witnesses G, H and I were alleged victims of, or witnesses to, sexual mutilation. See Chinkin (1996).

14 This testimony was held in closed session and the trial transcripts are not publicly available. See *Prosecutor v. Miroslav Kvočka, Milojica Kos, Mlađo Radič, Zoran Žigič, Dragoljub Prcač*, Case No. IT-98-30/1 (http://www.icty.org/case/kvocka/4). For a discussion of this trial and its signficance for prosecuting low-level offenders and its attention the prosecution of gender-related crimes, see Askin (2003).

15 See *Tadič* Transcript, 13 August 1996, 14 August 1996 and 15 August 1996 (transcripts with testimony from Witness L regarding gang rape allegations).

16 Note, the witness's name was disclosed during the trial, but I have chosen to use her initials to protect her identity. She was not cross-examined by the defence.

17 *Prosecutor v. Zdravko Mucič, Hazim Delič, Esad Landžo*, Case No. IT-96-21-T. See: http://www.icty.org/case/mucic/4.

18 Mucič and Delalič were primarily charged as superiors with responsibility for the crimes committed by their subordinates, including those crimes committed by Landžo and Delič. Delič also was charged with various counts relating to his capacity as a superior with command responsibility.

19 This was requested by the witness. Subsequently the witness's name was used in the trial transcripts; however, I have only used her initials here.

20 *Prosecutor v. Dragoljub Kunarac, Radomir Kovač, Zoran Vukovič*, Case Nos. IT-96-23-T & IT-96-23/1-T. See: http://www.icty.org/case/kunarac/4. For a discussion of this trial, see Barkan (2002); Buss (2002); Hagen (2003); McHenry (2002); Mertus (2004).

21 After the war, only ten Muslims remained in Foča, whereas before the war, Muslims made up 52 per cent of the 40,513 persons living in the region. See *Foča* Judgment, 2001: para. 47.

22 Radovan Stankovič was arrested by the Stabilization Force in Bosnia and Herzegovina (SFOR) on 9 July 2002, transferred to the ICTY on 10 July 2002 and first appeared at the ICTY on 12 July 2002. His case was transferred to the State Court of Bosnia-Herzegovina in Sarajevo on 29 September 2005. He was tried and sentenced to 20 years' imprisonment. He escaped from prison in May 2007 and is still at large. Dragan Zelenovič was arrested in August 2005 and sentenced to 15 years' imprisonment in April 2007. Gojko Jankovič voluntarily surrendered in March 2005 and was sentenced to 34 years' imprisonment in February 2007.

23 Dragan Gagovič, chief of police in the Foča region and the first co-accused in the initial indictment, was killed by French troops in an arrest attempt on 9 January 1999. Janko Janjič blew himself up with a hand grenade during an arrest attempt by SFOR forces in Foča in October 2000.

24 Note that FWS (Foča Witness Statements) pseudonyms were used for the Foča trial discussed in this chapter.
25 In his testimony Kunarac told the prosecutor: 'I assert that absolutely never, not at a single point in time was I present anywhere where perhaps some of these women were sexually abused, if that is correct. I am not asserting that or something similar did not happen to them, but I am claiming that I did not know about it and that I was not present when they were possibly taken out or sexually abused in any way, nor did I have any knowledge of this ever' (*Foča* Transcript, 10 July 2000: 4674).
26 As of March 2010, the ICTR has completed 49 cases, has 24 cases in progress and 2 awaiting trial. In total, the Tribunal has acquitted 8 persons, convicted 40 accused, with 11 cases on appeal. There are currently 11 persons at large. Although the completion strategy is constantly shifting due to the enormity and complexity of trial proceedings, in December 2009 the UN Security Council extended the terms of office to all trial judges to 30 June 2010 and appeal judges to 31 December 2012. This suggests that all trials will be completed by mid-2010 and all appeals by the end of 2012 (Security Council 2009).
27 *Prosecutor v. Pauline Nyiramasuhuko, Arsène Shalom Ntahobali, Alphonse Nteziryayo, Sylvain Nsabimana, Elie Ndayambaje and Joseph Kanyabashi*, Case No. ICTR-98-42-T. The *Butare* case, beginning in 2001 and ending in 2009 (the longest and most costly trial in the history of international criminal justice) involved the prosecution of the former Minister of Women's and Family Affairs, Pauline Nyiramasuhuko and her son (who was the leader of a unit in the Hutu extremist militia Interahamwe in the Butare prefecture), among others. The 'Butare Six' have been accused of crimes against humanity, genocide and war crimes, which include the abduction and rape of Tutsi women as a form of genocide. The judgment is expected in September 2010.
28 *Prosecutor v. Jean Paul Akayesu*, Case No. ICTR-96-I (see: http://www.ictr.org). The crime of genocide is defined by Article 2 of the Genocide Convention as 'any of the following acts committed with the intent to destroy, in whole or in part, a national, ethnical, racial or religious group, as such (a) Killing members of the group; (b) Causing serious bodily or mental harm to members of the group; (c) Deliberately inflicting on the group conditions of life calculated to bring about its physical destruction in whole or in part; (d) Imposing measures intended to prevent births within the group; (e) Forcibly transferring children of the group to another group'. See Convention on the Prevention and Punishment of the Crime of Genocide, 9 Dec. 1948 (78 UNTS 277) [hereinafter Genocide Convention].
29 For a discussion of this case, see Askin (2005a); de Brouwer (2005); Franklin (2008); Haffajee (2008); Lyons (2001); MacKinnon (2005); Neuffer (2001); Nowrojee (2005); Oosterveld (2005a); Van Schaack (2009).
30 See, for example, *Amicus Brief Respecting Amendment of the Indictment and Supplementation of the Evidence to Ensure the Prosecution of Rape and Other Sexual Violence within the Competence of the Tribunal*, Coalition for Women's Human Rights in Conflict Situations: http://www.womensrightscoalition.org/site/.
31 The following cases at the ICTY and ICTR have considered rape as a form of genocide: *Kayishema and Ruzindana*; *Rutaganda*; *Bagilishema*; *Krstič*; *Musema*; *Gacumbitsi*; *Muhimana*; *Milosevič*; *Karadžič*; *Mladič*; *Krajisnik*; *Kovačevic*; *Stakič*; however, only in the *Akayesu* case has rape, thus far, been successfully prosecuted as a crime of genocide. According to Pilch (2009: 173): 'The gravity and specificity of the crime of genocide and the necessity to show intent to destroy in whole or in part a specific group of people to prove genocide, in addition to the extremely high standard of burden of proof, have made it difficult to link rape and genocide in the former Yugoslavia'.
32 For a discussion of gender and the International Criminal Court, see e.g. Askin and Koenig (1999); Bedont (1999); de Brouwer (2005); Halley (2008b); Oosterveld (2005b).

33 Lubanga has been accused of war crimes consisting of enlisting and conscripting children under the age of 15 years into the Patriotic Forces for the Liberation of Congo (FPLC) and using them in the hostilities.

34 For the Central African Republic situation, Jean-Pierre Bemba Gombo has been charged with rape as a crime against humanity and war crime for his role as the alleged President and Commander-in-Chief of the Movement for the Liberation of Congo (MLC). The trial has been postponed until July 2010.

35 According to Article 43(6): 'The Registrar shall set up a Victims and Witnesses Unit within the Registry. This Unit shall provide, in consultation with the Office of the Prosecutor, protective measures and security arrangements, counseling and other appropriate assistance for witnesses, victims who appear before the Court, and others who are at risk on account of testimony given by such witnesses. The Unit shall include staff with expertise in trauma, including trauma related to crimes of sexual violence'. According to Article 42(9): 'The Prosecutor shall appoint advisers with legal expertise on specific issues, including, but not limited to, sexual and gender violence and violence against children'.

## 5 Trials and trauma: the impossibility of bearing witness

1 The phrase 'the impossibility of bearing witness' is taken from Agamben (2002).

2 Micale (1990: 363) states that 'In Plato's Timaeus and certain Hippocratic texts, we find graphic descriptions of the uterus as a restless animal, raging through the female body due to unnatural prolonged continence and giving rise to a bizarre series of symptoms, including a sensation of suffocation, heat palpitations, and loss of voice'. Charcot, though, studied both male and female hysteria. See also Libbrecht and Quackelbeen (1995).

3 The South African Truth and Reconciliation Commission privileged, for example, the curative powers of disclosure, exemplified by its slogan 'revealing is healing' (see Hamber 1998).

4 The term 'traumatic' may be a more appropriate label for experiences; this denotes the *potential* of gross human rights violations to induce psychological trauma given the intensity of the violent act.

5 Atlani and Rousseau (2000) have argued that although mental health interventions for refugee women who have suffered sexual violence may be inappropriate, the PTSD classification nonetheless may be beneficial for victims of rape because it may give them 'breathing space' to make sense of their suffering within a therapy context if and when the collective taboo becomes too overwhelming. Agger and Jensen (1990: 118) also make the point that the non-applicability of western therapeutic models 'should not lead us into the trap of cultural relativism, which emphasizes the untranslatable differences between human cultures'. The discourse on war trauma has subsequently led to development of the concept of 'psychosocial trauma'. This is understood as suffering that is both individually and socially constructed. See Agger (2001); Baró (1989); Weston (2001).

6 Osiel (2000: 173) likewise states that individual memory works differently from collective memory, arguing that we should be cautious in accepting a direct parallel between individual and collective memory: 'we should be reluctant to accept any such easy isomorphism, such direct parallelism between the workings of individual memory (over personal trauma) and collective memory (of national trauma)'.

7 See e.g. Breslau, Davis, Andreski and Peterson (1991); Breslau, Kessler, Chilcoat, Schultz, Davis and Andreski (1998).

8 *Prosecutor v. Anto Furundžija*, Case No.IT-95-17/1 (see: http://www.icty.org/cases/party/684/4).

9 This trial also raised serious issues about whether the defence could have access to the confidential counselling and treatment records for survivors of sexual violence

(see Askin 1999; Campbell, K. 2002). The case established a precedent that the confidentiality of the therapist–client relationship was not privileged. The Coalition for Women's Rights in Conflict Situations submitted an amicus brief to the Trial Chamber during the trial, requesting that it reconsider its disclosure order. The Coalition submitted that it is discriminatory that the confidential records of sexual violence survivors be disclosed to the defence during the trial and that such requests are frequently based on prejudicial rape myths (Coalition for Women's Human Rights in Conflict Situations 1998).
10 The prosecution conversely argued that the witnesses who testified in this trial displayed remarkable strength and that they had been carefully selected for that very purpose. The prosecution also argued that there is a diversity of psychological responses among women who have been raped and that many women are able to disguise their trauma.

## 6 Wartime rape and the legacy of law

1 Interestingly, the photograph sparked debate, with a libel case between Independent Television News (ITN) (who had filmed the inmates) and *Living Marxist* magazine, which published an article entitled: 'The Picture that Fooled the World', claiming that Alić was so emaciated because of 'a childhood bout of tuberculosis'. See Campbell, D. (2002); Connolly (2002).
2 According to Johnstone: 'The accusation that the Serbs initiated a deliberate policy of mass rape has never been substantiated. But the belief that this happened is widespread and persistent' (quoted in Proyect 2003). See also Kalnich (2000).
3 Marrus (1999: 118) argues that the principal reason the trial is remembered today is the 'ghastly medical experiments' that were conducted by the doctors in the concentration camps, and that this has distorted the historical record since less attention was given to the 400,000 victims of forcible sterilization and more than 100,000 victims of the euthanasia campaign.
4 According to the ICTY's Victims and Witnesses Section (VWS), between 1996 and 2006 about 18 per cent of all witnesses were female. The majority of witnesses have been between 41 and 81 years of age, and only 4 per cent aged between 21 and 30 years (Lobwein 2006).

# References

Abramovich, D. (2009) 'Hollywood Should Stop Exploiting the Holocaust', *The Age*, 2 November 2009. Online. Available http://www.theage.com.au/opinion/society-and-culture/hollywood-should-stop-exploiting-the-holocaust-20091102-ht5a.html (accessed 23 May 2010).

Adam, H. (2009) 'Divided Memories: how emerging democracies deal with the crimes of previous regimes', in S. Karstedt (ed.) *Legal Institutions and Collective Memories*, Oxford and Portland, Ore.: Hart Publishing.

Adatci, M. and Tachi, S. (1920) 'Commission on the Responsibility of the Authors of the War and on Enforcement Penalties: report presented to the Preliminary Peace Conference', *American Journal of International Law*, 14(1): 95–154.

Afsharipour, A. (1999) 'Empowering Ourselves: the role of women's NGOs in the enforcement of the Women's Convention', *Columbia Law Review*, 99(1): 129–72.

Agamben, G. (2002) *Remnants of Auschwitz: the witness and the archive*, trans. D. Heller-Roazen, New York: Zone Books.

Agger, I. (2001) 'Psychosocial Assistance During Ethnopolitical Warfare in the Former Yugoslavia', in D. Chirot and M.E.P. Seligman (eds) *Ethno-Political Warfare: causes, consequences and possible solutions*, Washington, D.C.: American Psychological Association.

Agger, I. and Jensen, S.B. (1990) 'Testimony as Ritual and Evidence in Psychotherapy for Political Refugees', *Journal of Traumatic Stress*, 3(1): 115–30.

Ai, A., Peterson, C. and Ubelhor, D. (2002) 'War-related Trauma and Symptoms of Posttraumatic Stress Disorder among Adult Kosovar Refugees', *Journal of Traumatic Stress*, 15: 157–60.

Alexander, J.C. (2002) 'On the Social Construction of Moral Universals: the "Holocaust" from war crime to trauma drama', *European Journal of Social Theory*, 5: 5–85.

Alexander, J.C., Eyerman, R., Giesen, B., Smelser, N.J. and Sztompka, P. (eds) (2004) *Cultural Trauma and Collective Identity*, Berkeley: University of California Press.

Allan, A. and Allan, M.M. (2000) 'The South African Truth and Reconciliation Commission as a Therapeutic Tool', *Behavioral Sciences and the Law*, 18: 459–77.

Allan, S. (2004) *Reporting War: journalism in wartime*, New York: Routledge.

Alvarez, J.E. (1998) 'Rush to Closure: lessons of the Tadič judgment', *Michigan Law Review*, 96(7): 2031–112.

American Psychiatric Association (2000) *Diagnostic and Statistical Manual of Mental Disorders: DSM-IV-TR*, Washington, D.C.: American Psychiatric Association.

Amnesty International (2001) 'Bosnia-Herzegovina: Foca verdict – rape and sexual enslavement are crimes against humanity', 22 February 2001. Online. Available http://asiapacific.amnesty.org/library/Index/ENGEUR630042001?open&of=ENG-373 (accessed 23 May 2010).

Anonymous (2006) *A Woman in Berlin*, trans. P. Boehm, London: Virago.

Antze, P. and Lambek, M. (eds) (1996) *Tense Past: cultural essays in trauma and memory*, New York: Routledge.

Anzia, L. (2007) 'Trafficking is a Long Standing Crime: US troop use of Japan's trafficked women 1945', 29 September 2007. Online. Available http://womennewsnetwork.net/2007/09/29/trafficking-a-long-standing-crime-us-troop-use-of-japans-trafficked-women-1945/ (accessed 23 May 2010).

Appelbaum, P.S., Uyehara, L.A. and Elin, M.R. (eds) (1997) *Trauma and Memory: clinical and legal controversies*, New York: Oxford University Press.

Arendt, H. (1994) *Eichmann in Jerusalem: a report on the banality of evil*, New York: Penguin Books.

Askin, K.D. (1997) *War Crimes Against Women: prosecution in international war crimes tribunals*, The Hague: Martinus Nijhoff.

—— (1999) 'Sexual Violence in Decisions and Indictments of the Yugoslav and Rwandan Tribunals: current status', *American Journal of International Law*, 93(1): 97–123.

—— (2000) 'Women's Issues in International Criminal Law: recent developments and the potential contribution of the ICC', in D. Shelton (ed.) *International Crimes, Peace, and Human Rights: the role of the International Criminal Court*, Ardsley, N.Y.: Transnational Publishers.

—— (2003) 'Omarska Camp, Bosnia: broken promises of "never again"', *Human Rights Magazine*. Online. Available http://www.abanet.org/irr/hr/winter03/omarska-campbosnia.html (accessed 23 May 2010).

—— (2005a) 'Gender Jurisprudence in the ICTR: positive developments', *Journal of International Criminal Justice*, 3(4): 1007–18.

—— (2005b) 'Foca's Monumental Jurisprudence', *Institute for War and Peace Reporting*, Tribunal Update No. 266, 18–23 June 2001. Online. Available http://www.iwpr.net/report-news/analysis-focas-monumental-jurisprudence (accessed 23 May 2010).

Askin, K.D. and Koenig, D.M. (eds) (1999) *Women and International Human Rights Law*, Ardsley, N.Y.: Transnational.

Assmann, J. (1995) 'Collective Memory and Cultural Identity', *New German Critique*, trans. J. Czaplicka, 65: 125–33.

Atlani, L. and Rousseau, C. (2000) 'The Politics of Culture in Humanitarian Aid to Women Refugees Who Have Experienced Sexual Violence', *Transcultural Psychiatry*, 37(3): 435–49.

Aydellot, D. (1993) 'Mass Rape During War: prosecuting Bosnian rapists under international law', *Emory International Law Review*, 7(2): 585–633.

Baer, E.R. and Goldenberg, M. (2003) *Experience and Expression: women, the Nazis, and the Holocaust*, Detroit, Mich.: Wayne State University Press.

Bal, M., Crewe, J. and Spitzer, L. (1999) *Acts of Memory: cultural recall in the present*, Hanover, N.H.: University Press of New England.

Barkan, J. (2002) 'As Old as War Itself: rape in Foca', *Dissent*, 49(1): 60–6.

Baró, I.M. (1989) 'Political Violence and War as Causes of Psychosocial Trauma in El Salvador', *International Journal of Mental Health*, 18(1): 3–20.

Bass, G.J. (2002) *Stay the Hand of Vengeance: the politics of war crimes tribunals*, Princeton, N.J./Oxford: Princeton University Press.

Bassiouni, M.C. (1999) *Crimes Against Humanity in International Criminal Law*, 2nd edn, The Hague: Kluwer Law International.

—— (ed.) (2002) *Post-Conflict Justice*, Ardsley, N.Y.: Transnational Publishers.

—— (2006) 'International Recognition of Victims' Rights', *Human Rights Law Review*, 6(2): 203–79.

Baumel, J.T. (1998) *Double Jeopardy. gender and the Holocaust*, London: Valentine Mitchell.

BBC News, 'Bosnian Serbs Reject Rape Plaque', 1 October 2004. Online. Available http://news.bbc.co.uk/2/hi/europe/3706554.stm (accessed 23 May 2010).

Beck, B. (2002) 'Rape: the military trials of sexual crimes committed by soldiers in the Wehrmacht, 1939–44', in K. Hagemann and S. Schiller-Springorum (eds) *Home Front: the military, war and gender in twentieth-century Germany*, London: Berg.

Becker, D. (1995) 'The Deficiency of the Concept of Posttraumatic Stress Disorder When Dealing with Victims of Human Rights Violations', in R. Kleber, C. Figley and B. Gersons (eds) *Beyond Trauma: cultural and societal dimensions*, New York: Plenum.

Bedont, B. (1999) 'Gender-Specific Provisions in the Statute of the ICC', in F. Lattanzi and W.A. Schabas (eds) *Essays on the Rome Statute of the ICC*, Naples: Editoriale Scientifica.

Beevor, A. (2003) *Berlin: the downfall*, London: Penguin.

Benedict, S. and Georges, J.M. (2006) 'Nurses and the Sterilization Experiments of Auschwitz: a postmodernist perspective', *Nursing Inquiry*, 13(4): 277–88.

Benyakar, M., Kutz, I., Dasberg, H. and Stern, M. (1989) 'The Collapse of a Structure: a structural approach to trauma', *Journal of Traumatic Stress*, 2: 431–49.

Berliner, D.C. (2005) 'The Abuses of Memory: reflections on the memory boom in anthropology', *Anthropology Quarterly*, 78(1): 197–211.

Best, G. (1980) *Humanity in Warfare: the modern history of the international law of armed conflict*, London: Weidenfeld and Nicolson.

Black, C.E. and Falk, R.A. (eds) (1971) *The Future of the International Legal Order*, Princeton, N.J.: Princeton University Press.

Blatt, D. (1992) 'Recognizing Rape as a Method of Torture', *New York University Review of Law and Social Change*, 19: 821–65.

Bloxham, D. (2001) *Genocide on Trial, War Crimes Trials and the Formation of Holocaust History and Memory*, Oxford: Oxford University Press.

Blumenthal, D.A. and McCormack, T.H. (2008) *The Legacy of Nuremberg: civilising influence or institutionalised vengeance?*, Leiden: Martinus Nijhoff.

Bock, G. (1983) 'Racism and Sexism in Nazi Germany: motherhood, compulsory sterilization, and the state', *Signs: journal of women in culture and society*, 8(3): 400–21.

Bodnar, J. (1992) *Remaking America: public memory, commemoration, and patriotism in the twentieth century*, Princeton, N.J.: Princeton University Press.

Bourke, J. (2008) *Rape: a history from 1860 to the present day*, London: Virago.

Bracken, P.J. (1998) 'Hidden Agendas: deconstructing Post Traumatic Stress Disorder', in P.J. Bracken and C. Petty (eds) *Rethinking the Trauma of War*, New York: Free Association Press.

Bracken, P.J. and Petty, C. (eds) (1998) *Rethinking the Trauma of War*, New York: Free Association Press.

Bracken, P.J., Giller, J.E. and Summerfield, D. (1995) 'Psychological Responses to War and Atrocity: the limitation of current concepts', *Social Sciences and Medicine*, 40: 1073–82.

Braithwaite, J. (2006) 'Rape, Shame and Pride', *Journal of Scandinavian Studies in Criminology and Crime Prevention*, 7: 2–16.

Breslau, N., Davis, G.C., Andreski, P. and Peterson, E.L. (1991) 'Traumatic Events and Posttraumatic Stress Disorder in an Urban Population of Young Adults', *Archives of General Psychiatry*, 48(3): 216–22.

Breslau, N., Kessler, R.C., Chilcoat, H.D., Schultz, L.R., Davis, G.C. and Andreski, P. (1998) 'Trauma and Posttraumatic Stress Disorder in the Community', *Archives of General Psychiatry*, 55(7): 626–32.

Brook, T. (2001) 'The Tokyo Judgment and the Rape of Nanking', *Journal of Asian Studies*, 60: 673–700.

Brooks, P. and Gewirtz, P. (eds) (1996) *Law's Stories: narrative and rhetoric in the law*, New Haven, Conn.: Yale University Press.

Brown, D., Scheflin, A.W. and Hammond, D.C. (1998) *Memory, Trauma Treatment and the Law*, New York/London: W.W. Norton & Company.

Brown, W. (1995) *States of Injury: power and freedom in late modernity*, Princeton, N.J.: Princeton University Press.

Brownmiller, S. (1976) *Against Our Will: men, women and rape*, London: Penguin Books.

Burds, J. (2009) 'Sexual Violence in Europe in World War II, 1939–45', *Politics and Society*, 37(1): 35–73.

Burgess, A.W. and Holmstrom, L.L. (1974) 'Rape Trauma Syndrome', *American Journal of Psychiatry*, 131: 981–6.

Burke, P. (1989) 'History as Social Memory', in T. Butler (ed.) *History, Culture and the Mind*, New York: Blackwell.

Bushby, K. (1997) 'Discriminatory Uses of Personal Records in Sexual Violence Cases', *Canadian Journal of Women and the Law*, 9: 148–78.

Buss, D. (2002) 'Prosecuting Mass Rape: Prosecutor v. Dragoljub Kunarac, Radomir Kovac and Zoran Vukovic', *Feminist Legal Studies*, 10(1): 91–9.

Campbell, D. (2002) 'Atrocity, Memory, Photography: imaging the concentration camps of Bosnia: the case of ITN versus *Living Marxism*, part 1', *Journal of Human Rights*, 1(1): 1–33.

Campbell, K. (2002) 'Legal Memories: sexual assault, memory, and international humanitarian law', *Signs: journal of women in culture and society*, 28: 149–78.

—— (2003) 'Rape as a "Crime against Humanity": trauma, law and justice in the ICTY', *Journal of Human Rights*, 2(4): 507–15.

—— (2007) 'The Gender of Transitional Justice: law, sexual violence and the International Criminal Tribunal for the Former Yugoslavia', *International Journal of Transitional Justice*, 1(3): 411–31.

Carpenter, R.C. (2000) 'Surfacing Children: limitations of genocidal rape discourse', *Human Rights Quarterly*, 22(2): 428–77.

Caruth, C. (ed.) (1995) *Trauma: explorations in memory*, Baltimore, Md.: Johns Hopkins University Press.

—— (1996) *Unclaimed Experience: trauma, narrative, and history*, Baltimore, Md.: Johns Hopkins University Press.

Cassese, A., Jones, J.R. and Gaeta, P. (eds) (2002) *The Rome Statute of the International Criminal Court: a commentary*, Oxford/New York: Oxford University Press.

Center for Research and Documentation on Japan's War Responsibility (2007), 'Latest Research on Japan's Military Sexual Slavery', Press Conference, Foreign Correspondents' Club of Japan, 17 April 2007. Online. Available http://space.geocities.jp/japanwarres/center/hodo/hodo38.pdf (accessed 23 May 2010).

Chang, I. (1997) *The Rape of Nanking: the forgotten holocaust of World War II*, New York: Basic Books.

Charlesworth, H. and Chinkin, C. (2000) *The Boundaries of International Law: a feminist analysis*, Manchester: Manchester University Press.

Charlesworth, H., Chinkin, C. and Wright, S. (1991) 'Feminist Approaches to International Law', *American Journal of International Law*, 85(4): 613–45.

Chinkin, C. (1994) 'Rape and Sexual Abuse of Women in International Law', *European Journal of International Law*, 5: 326–41.

—— (1996), 'Amicus Curiae Brief on Protective Measures for Victims and Witnesses (ICTY)', *International Criminal Law Forum*, 7(1): 179–212.

—— (2001) 'Women's International Tribunal of Japanese Military Sexual Slavery', *American Journal of International Law*, 95: 335–41.

Coalition for Women's Human Rights in Conflict Situations (1998) 'Amicus Curiae Brief Respecting the Decision and Order of the Tribunal of 16 July 1998 Requesting that the Tribunal Reconsider Its Decision Having Regard to the Rights of Witness 'A' to Equality, Privacy and Security of the Person and to Representation by Counsel'. Online. Available http://www.womensrightscoalition.org/site/advocacy-Dossiers/former Yugoslavia/Furundzija/amicusbrief.php (accessed 23 May 2010).

Coan, C.B. (2000) 'Rethinking the Spoils of War: prosecuting rape as a war crime in the International Criminal Tribunal for the Former Yugoslavia', *North Carolina Journal of International Law and Commercial Regulation*, 26(1): 183–237.

Cohen, M. (2009) 'Victims' Participation Rights within the International Criminal Court: a critical overview', *Denver Journal of International Law and Policy*, 37(3): 351–78.

Colvin, C.J. (2004) 'Ambivalent Narrations: pursuing the political through traumatic storytelling', *Political and Legal Anthropology Review*, 27: 72–89.

Confino, A. (1997) 'Collective Memory and Cultural History: problems of method', *American Historical Review*, 102: 1386–403.

Conley, J.M. and O'Barr, W.M. (1998) *Just Words: law, language and power*, Chicago: University of Chicago Press.

Connerton, P. (2003) *How Societies Remember*, Cambridge: Cambridge University Press.

Connolly, K. (2002) 'He was the Face of Bosnia's Civil War: what happened next?', *Guardian*, 4 August 2002. Online. Available http://www.guardian.co.uk/world/2002/aug/04/warcrimes.balkans (accessed 23 May 2010).

Copelon, R. (1993) 'Surfacing Gender: reconceptualizing crimes against women in Bosnia-Herzegovina', in A. Stiglmayer (ed.) *Mass Rape: the war against women in Bosnia-Herzegovina*, Lincoln, Nebr.: University of Nebraska Press.

Cover, R.M. (1986) 'Violence and the Word', *Yale Law Journal*, 95(8): 1601–29.

Dahl, S., Mutapcic, A. and Schei, B. (1998) 'Traumatic Events and Predictive Factors for Posttraumatic Symptoms in Displaced Bosnian Women in a War Zone', *Journal of Traumatic Stress*, 11: 137–45.

Damousi, J. and Lake, M. (eds) (1995) *Gender and War: Australians at war in the twentieth century*, New York/Melbourne: Cambridge University Press.

de Brouwer, A.L.M. (2005) *Supranational Criminal Prosecution of Sexual Violence: the ICC and the practice of the ICTY and the ICTR*, Antwerp-Oxford: Insentia.

——(2007) 'Reparation to Victims of Sexual Violence: possibilities at the International Criminal Court and the Trust Fund for Victims and Their Families', *Leiden Journal of International Law*, 20(1): 207–37.

Des Forges, A.L. (1999) *'Leave None to Tell the Story': genocide in Rwanda*, New York: Human Rights Watch.

Dolgopol, U. (1995) 'Women's Voices, Women's Pain', *Human Rights Quarterly*, 17: 127–54.

Donnelly, J. (2003) *Universal Human Rights in Theory and Practice*, 2nd edn, Ithaca, New York/London: Cornell University Press.

Douglas, L. (2001) *The Memory of Judgment: making law and history in the trials of the Holocaust*, New Haven, Conn.: Yale University Press.

—— (2006) 'The Didactic Trial: filtering history and memory into the courtroom', *European Review*, 14: 513–22.

Durkheim, E. (1982) *The Rules of Sociological Method and Selected Texts on Sociology and Its Methods*, trans. W.D. Halls, New York: Free Press.

—— (1984) *The Division of Labour in Society*, trans. W.D. Halls, Basingstoke: Macmillan.

Edkins, J. (2003) *Trauma and the Memory of Politics*, Cambridge: Cambridge University Press.

Elias, R. (1986) *The Politics of Victimisation: victims, victimology and human rights*, New York: Oxford University Press.

Engle, K. (2005) 'Feminism and its (Dis)Contents: criminalizing wartime rape in Bosnia and Herzegovina', *American Journal of International Law*, 99: 778–816.

En-Han, L. (2002) 'The Nanking Massacre Reassessed: a study of the Sino-Japanese controversy over the factual number of massacred victims', in F.F. Li, R. Sabella and D. Liu (eds) *Nanking 1937: memory and healing*, Armonk, N.Y.: M.E. Sharpe, Inc.

Erikson, K.T. (1979) *Everything in Its Path*, London: Allen and Unwin.

—— (1994) *A New Species of Trouble: explorations in disaster, trauma, and community*, New York/London: W.W. Norton & Co.

Eschebach, I. (2003) 'Engendered Oblivion: commemorating Jewish inmates at the Ravensbrück memorial', in J.T. Baumel and T. Cohen (eds) *Gender, Place and Memory in the Modern Jewish Experience*, London: Valentine Mitchell.

Eykholt, M. (2000) 'Aggression, Victimization, and Chinese Historiography of the Nanjing Massacre', in J.A. Fogel (ed.) *The Nanjing Massacre in History and Historiography*, Berkeley/Los Angeles: University of California Press.

Falk, R.A. (2000) *Human Rights Horizons: the pursuit of justice in a globalizing world*, New York: Routledge.

Favaro, A., Majorani, M., Colombo, G. and Santonastaso, P. (1999) 'Traumatic Experiences, Posttraumatic Stress Disorder and Dissociative Symptoms in a Group of Refugees from the Former Yugoslavia', *Journal of Nervous and Mental Disease*, 187: 306–8.

Fellmeth, A.X. (2000) 'Feminism and International Law: theory, methodology and substantive reform', *Human Rights Quarterly*, 22(3): 658–733.

Felman, S. (2002) *The Juridical Unconscious: trials and traumas in the twentieth century*, Cambridge, Mass.: Harvard University Press.

Fentress, J. and Wickham, C. (1992) *Social Memory*, Oxford: Blackwell.

Ferencz, B.B. (1998) 'International Criminal Courts: the legacy of Nuremberg', *Pace International Law Review*, 10: 203–35.

—— (2003) 'From Nuremberg to Rome: a personal account', in M. Lattimer and P. Sands (eds) *Justice for Crimes Against Humanity*, Oxford: Hart Publishing.

Figley, C.R. (ed.) (1985) *Trauma and Its Wake*, New York: Brunner/Mazel.

Finkelstein, N. (2000) *The Holocaust Industry: reflections on the exploitation of Jewish suffering*, New York: Verso.

Finley, L.M. (1989) 'Breaking Women's Silence in Law: the dilemma of the gendered nature of legal reasoning', *Notre Dame Law Review*, 64: 886–910.

Fitzgerald, K. (1997) 'Problems of Prosecution and Adjudication of Rape and Other Sexual Assaults Under International Law', *European Journal of International Law*, 8 (4): 638–63.

Fletcher, G.P. (1995) *With Justice for Some: victims' rights in criminal trials*, Reading, Mass.: Addison-Wesley.

Fletcher, L.E. and Weinstein, H.M. (2002) 'Violence and Social Repair: rethinking the contribution of justice to reconciliation', *Human Rights Quarterly*, 24: 573–639.

Fogel, J.A. (ed.) (2000) *The Nanjing Massacre in History and Historiography*, Berkeley/Los Angeles: University of California Press.

Fogelson, S. (1989) 'Nuremberg Legacy: an unfulfilled promise', *Southern California Law Review*, 63: 833–905.

Foucault, M. (1977) *Language, Counter-Memory, Practice: selected essays and interviews*, trans. D.F. Bouchard and S. Simon, Oxford: Blackwell.

—— (1979) *Discipline and Punish: the birth of the prison*, trans. A. Sheridan, London: Tavistock.

—— (2006) *History of Madness*, trans. J. Murphy and J. Khalfa, London/New York: Routledge.

Fournet, C. (2007) *The Crime of Destruction and the Law of Genocide: their impact on collective memory*, Aldershot, UK: Ashgate.

Franklin, D.J. (2008) 'Failed Rape Prosecutions at the International Criminal Tribunal for Rwanda', *Georgetown Journal of Gender and the Law*, 9: 181–214.

Friedlander, S. (1992) *Probing the Limits of Representation: Nazism and the 'Final Solution'*, Cambridge, Mass.: Harvard University Press.

Funkenstein, A. (1989) 'Collective Memory and Historical Consciousness', *History & Memory*, 1: 5–27.

Gardam, J.G. and Jarvis, M.J. (2001) *Women, Armed Conflict and International Law*, The Hague: Kluwer Law International.

Garfinkel, H. (1956) 'Conditions of Successful Degradation Ceremonies', *American Journal of Sociology*, 61: 420–4.

Gedi, N. and Elam, Y. (1996) 'Collective Memory: what is it?', *History and Memory*, 8: 30–50.

Gewirtz, P. (1996) 'Narrative and Rhetoric in the Law', in P. Brooks and P. Gewirtz (eds) *Law's Stories: narrative and rhetoric in the law*, New Haven, Conn.: Yale University Press.

Gibson, J.L. (2004) 'Does Truth Lead to Reconciliation? Testing the causal assumptions of the South African truth and reconciliation process', *American Journal of Political Science*, 48: 201–17.

—— (2006) 'The Contributions of Truth to Reconciliation: lessons from South Africa', *Journal of Conflict Resolution*, 50(3): 409–32.

Glueck, S. (1944) *War Criminals: their prosecution and punishment*, New York: Knopf.

Goldhagen, D. (1996) *Hitler's Willing Executioners: ordinary Germans and the Holocaust*, New York: Knopf.

Goldstein, A.T. (1993) *Recognizing Enforced Impregnation as a War Crime under International Law*, New York: The Center for Reproductive Law and Policy.

Goodman, G.S. and Helgeson, V.S. (1985) 'Child Sexual Assault: children's memory and the law', *University of Miami Law Review*, 40: 181–208.

Goodwin, J. (1997) 'Rwanda: justice denied', *On the Issues*. Online. Available http://www.ontheissuesmagazine.com/1997fall/f97rwanda.php (accessed 23 May 2010).

Gourevitch, P. (1999) *We Wish to Inform You that Tomorrow We Will Be Killed with Our Families: stories from Rwanda*, New York: Farrar, Straus, and Giroux.

Green, J., Copelon, R., Cotter, P., Stephens, B. and Pratt, K. (1994) 'Affecting the Rules for the Prosecution of Rape and Other Gender-Based Violence before the International Criminal Tribunal for the Former Yugoslavia', *Hastings Women's Law Journal*, 5(2): 171–241.

Gross, J.T. (2001) *Neighbors: the destruction of the Jewish community in Jedwabne, Poland*, Princeton, N.J.: Princeton University Press.

Grossman, A. (1995) 'A Question of Silence: the rape of German women by occupation soldiers', *October*, 72: 42–63.

Haffajee, R.L. (2008) 'Prosecuting Crimes of Rape and Sexual Violence at the ICTR: the application of joint criminal enterprise theory', *Harvard Journal of Law and Gender*, 29: 201–21.

Hagen, J. (2003) 'The Foca Rape Case', *Justice in the Balkans: prosecuting war crimes in the Hague Tribunal*, Chicago/London: University of Chicago Press.

Halbwachs, M. (1992) *On Collective Memory*, trans. L.A. Coser, Chicago: University of Chicago Press.

Halley, J. (2008a) 'Rape in Berlin: reconsidering the criminalisation of rape in the international law of armed conflict', *Melbourne Journal of International Law*, 9(1): 78–124.

—— (2008b) 'Rape at Rome: feminist interventions in the criminalization of sex-related violence in positive international criminal law', *Michigan Journal of International Law*, 30(1): 1–123.

Halley, J., Kotiswaran, P., Shamir, H. and Thomas, C. (2006) 'From the International to the Local in Feminist Legal Responses to Rape, Prostitution/Sex Work, and Sex Trafficking: four studies in contemporary governance feminism', *Harvard Journal of Law and Gender*, 29: 335–423.

Hamber, B. (1998) 'Remembering to Forget: issues to consider when establishing structures for dealing with the past', in B. Hamber (ed.) *Past Imperfect: dealing with the past in Northern Ireland and societies in transition*, Derry/Londonderry: University of Ulster Press.

Hartman, G.H. (1994) *Holocaust Remembrance: the shapes of memory*, Cambridge: Blackwell.

Hayashi, H. (2008) 'Disputes in Japan over the Japanese Military "Comfort Women" System and Its Perception in History', *Annals of the American Academy of Political and Social Science*, 617: 123–32.

Hayes, S., Strosahl, K. and Wilson, K. (2003) *Acceptance and Commitment Therapy: an experiential approach to behaviour change*, New York: Guilford Press.

Hayner, P.B. (2001) *Unspeakable Truths: confronting state terror and atrocity*, New York: Routledge.

Healey, S. (1995) 'Prosecuting Rape Under the Statute of the War Crimes Tribunal for the Former Yugoslavia', *Brooklyn Journal of International Law*, 21(2): 327–83.

Helm, L. (1992) 'Human Rights: Koreans won't let Japan bury "comfort" issue', *Los Angeles Times*, 8 August 1992, A3.

Henderson, L. (1985) 'The Wrongs of Victims' Rights', *Stanford Law Review*, 37(4): 937–56.

Henry, N. (2009) 'Witness to Rape: the limits and potential of international war crimes trials for victims of wartime sexual violence', *International Journal of Transitional Justice*, 3: 114–34.

Herman, J.L. (2001) *Trauma and Recovery: the aftermath of violence from domestic abuse to political terror*, London: Pandora.

Hersh, S.M. (2004) 'Torture at Abu Ghraib: American soldiers brutalized Iraqis. How far up does the responsibility go?' *New Yorker*, 30 April.

Hesse, C. and Post, R. (1999) *Human Rights in Political Transitions: Gettysburg to Bosnia*, New York: Zone Books.

Hicks, G. (1995) *The Comfort Women*, Sydney: Allen and Unwin.

Higashinakano, S. (2005) *The Nanking Massacre: fact versus fiction: a historian's quest for the truth*, Tokyo: Sekei Shuppan, Inc.

Hilberg, R. (1961) *The Destruction of the European Jews*, London: W.H. Allen.

Hirsh, M. and Smith, V. (2002) 'Feminism and Cultural Memory: an introduction', *Signs: journal of women in culture and society*, 28(1): 1–19.

Hodgkin, K. and Radstone, S. (eds) (2003) *Contested Pasts: the politics of memory*, London: Routledge.

Hovannisian, R. (1998) *Remembrance and Denial: the case of the Armenian genocide*, Detroit, Mich.: Wayne State University Press.

Howe, A. (1983) 'Anzac Mythology and the Feminist Challenge', *Melbourne Journal of Politics*, 15: 17–23.

Human Rights Watch (1996) *Shattered Lives: sexual violence during the Rwandan genocide and its aftermath*, New York: Human Rights Watch.

Hutton, P.H. (1994) 'Sigmund Freud and Maurice Halbwachs: the problem of memory in historical psychology', *The History Teacher*, 27: 145–58.

—— (2000) 'Recent Scholarship on Memory and History', *The History Teacher*, 33: 533–48.

Huyssen, A. (1995) *Twilight Memories: marking time in a culture of amnesia*, New York/London: Routledge.

Ignatieff, M. (1996) 'Articles of faith', *Index on Censorship*, 5: 110–22.

—— (2000) *The Rights Revolution*, Toronto: House of Anansi Press.

Institute for War and Peace Reporting (IWPR) (1997) 'False Witness "L" Goes Back to Sarajevo', *Institute for War and Peace Reporting*, Tribunal Update No. 31, 2–7 June 1997. Online. Available http://www.iwpr.net/report-news/false-witness-quotlquot-goes-back-sarajevo (accessed 23 May 2010).

—— (2000) 'Foca Rape Trial: prosecution witnesses recalled to rebut "girlfriend" claims', *Institute of War and Peace Reporting*, Tribunal Update No. 196, 23–30 October 2000. Online. Available http://www.iwpr.net/bs/node/4916 (accessed 23 May 2010).

International Criminal Tribunal for the Former Yugoslavia (2010) *Report of the President on the Conference Assessing the Legacy of the ICTY*. Online. Available http://www.icty.org/x/file/Press/Events/100427_legacyconference_pdt_report.pdf (accessed 23 May 2010).

Irwin-Zarecka, I. (2009) *Frames of Remembrance: the dynamics of collective memory*, New Brunswick, N.J.: Transaction Publishers.

Jackson, M. (2002) *The Politics of Storytelling: violence, transgression and inter-subjectivity*, Copenhagen: Museum Tusculanum Press.

Jackson, R.H. (2003) *The Global Covenant: human conduct in a world of states*, Oxford/New York: Oxford University Press.

Jacobs, J. (2008) 'Gender and Collective Memory: women and representation at Auschwitz', *Memory Studies*, 1: 211–25.

Jarvis, M. (1999) 'Prosecuting Rape Under International Law: implications for Australian jurisdictions', *Women Against Violence: an Australian feminist journal*, 6: 4–11.

Johnstone, D. (2002) *Fools' Crusade: Yugoslavia, NATO and Western delusions*, New York: Monthly Review Press.

Judah, T. (2009) *The Serbs: history, myth, and the destruction of Yugoslavia*, 3rd edn, New Haven, Conn.: Yale University Press.

Kalnich, L.J. (2000) 'Beyond Horror: sensationalism and the hermeneutics of war', *Journal of the North American Society for Serbian Studies*, 14(2): 143–58.

Kammen, M. (1995) 'Review of *Frames of Remembrance: the dynamics of collective memory*, by I.Irwin-Zarecka', *Historical Theory*, 34: 245–61.

Kansteiner, W. (2002) 'Finding Meaning in Memory: a methodological critique of collective memory studies', *History and Theory*, 41: 179–97.

—— (2004) 'Genealogy of a Category Mistake: a critical intellectual history of the cultural trauma metaphor', *Rethinking History*, 2: 193–221.

Kaplan, R.D. (2005) *Balkan Ghosts: a journey through history*, New York: Picador.

Kapur, R. (2002) 'The Tragedy of Victimization Rhetoric: resurrecting the "native" subject in international/post-colonial feminist legal politics', *Harvard Human Rights Journal*, 15: 1–37.

Karmen, A. (2001) *Crime Victims: an introduction to victimology*, Belmont, Calif.: Wadsworth/Thomson Learning.

Karstedt, S. (ed.) (2009) *Legal Institutions and Collective Memories*, Oxford/Portland, Ore.: Hart Publishing.

Kaszubinski, M. (2002) 'The International Criminal Tribunal for the Former Yugo-slavia', in M.C. Bassiouni (ed.) *Post-Conflict Justice*, Ardsley, N.Y.: Transnational Publishers.

Katana, G. (2002) 'Safeguarding Justice', *Institute for War and Peace Reporting*, Balkan Crisis Report, No. 275, 24 July 2002.

Khushalani, Y. (1982) *Dignity and Honour of Women as Basic and Fundamental Human Rights*, The Hague/Boston: Martinus Nijhoff.

Kirchheimer, O. (1961) *Political Justice: the use of legal procedures for political ends*, Princeton, N.J.: Princeton University Press.

Kleber, R., Figley, C. and Gersons, B. (1995) *Beyond Trauma: cultural and societal dynamics*, New York: Plenum.

Klein, K.L. (2000) 'On the Emergence of Memory in Historical Discourse', *Representations*, 69: 127–50.

Knightley, P. (2000) *The First Casualty*, 2nd edn, London: Prion Books.

Koch, G. (1995) 'Blood, Sperm and Tears', *October*, 72: 27–41.

Kono, Y. (1993) 'Statement by the Chief Cabinet Secretary Yohei Kono on the Result of the Study on the Issue of "Comfort Women"', 4 August 1993. Online. Available http://www.mofa.go.jp/policy/women/fund/state9308.html (accessed 23 May 2010).

Kreisler, H. (2001) 'Interview with Brenda Hollis', 18 April 2001. Online. Available http://globetrotter.berkeley.edu/people/Hollis/hollis-con6.html (accessed 23 May 2010).

Krill, F. (1985) 'The Protection of Women in International Humanitarian Law', *International Review of the Red Cross*, 249: 337–63.

Kritz, N.J. (1996) 'Coming to Terms with Atrocities: a review of accountability mechanisms for mass violations of human rights', *Law and Contemporary Problems: accountability for international crimes and serious violations of fundamental human rights*, 59: 127–52.

LaCapra, D. (1994) *History, Theory, Trauma: representing the Holocaust*, Ithaca, N.Y.: Cornell University Press.

—— (1998) *History and Memory after Auschwitz*, Ithaca, N.Y.: Cornell University Press.

Lael, R.L. (1982) *The Yamashita Precedent, War Crimes and Command Responsibility*, Wilmington, Del.: Scholarly Resources, Inc.

Lake, M. (2009) 'Fight Free of ANZAC, Lest We Forget Other Stories', *The Age*, 23 April 2009. Online. Available http://www.theage.com.au/opinion/fight-free-of-anzac-lest-we-forget-other-stories-20090422-afb5.html (accessed 23 May 2010).

Lansing, P. and King, J.C. (1998) 'South Africa's Truth and Reconciliation Commission: the conflict between individual justice and national healing in the post-Apartheid age', *Arizona Journal of International and Comparative Law*, 15: 753–89.

Laplanche, J. and Pontalis, J.B. (1988) *The Language of Psychoanalysis*, trans. D. Nicholson-Smith, London: Karnac.

Le Goff, J. (1992) *History and Memory*, trans. S. Rendall and E. Claman, New York: Columbia University Press.

Levi, P. (1987) *If This Is a Man/The Truce*, trans. S. Woolf, London: Abacus.

Levinger, E. (1995) 'Women and War Memorials in Israel', *Woman's Art Journal*, 16: 40–6.

Levy, D. and Sznaider, N. (2006) *The Holocaust and Memory in the Global Age*, trans. A. Oksiloff, Philadelphia, Pa.: Temple University Press.

Leys, R. (2000) *Trauma: a genealogy*, Chicago/London: Chicago University Press.

Li, F., Sabella, R. and Liu, D. (eds) (2002) *Nanking 1937: memory and healing*, Armonk, N.Y.: M.E. Sharpe.

Libbrecht, K. and Quackelbeen, J. (1995) 'On the Early History of Male Hysteria and Psychic Trauma', *Journal of the History of the Behavioural Sciences*, 31(4): 370–84.

Liebman, S. and Michelson, A. (1995) 'After the Fall: women in the house of the hangman', *October*, 72: 5–14.

Lifton, R.J. (1973) *Home from the War: Vietnam veterans: neither victims nor executioners*, New York: Simon and Schuster.

Lindsey, R. (2002) 'From Atrocity to Data: historiographies of rape in former Yugoslavia and the gendering of genocide', *Patterns of Prejudice*, 36(4): 59–78.

Link, P. (2002) 'Foreword', in F.F. Li, R. Sabella and D. Liu (eds) *Nanking 1937: memory and healing*, Armonk, N.Y.: M.E. Sharpe, Inc.

Lippman, M. (1993) 'The Other Nuremberg: American prosecutions of Nazi war criminals in occupied Germany', *Indiana International and Comparative Law Review*, 3(1): 1–100.

Lipstadt, D.E. (1993) *Denying the Holocaust: the growing assault on truth and memory*, New York: Free Press/Macmillan.

Lobwein, W. (2006) 'Experiences of the Victims and Witnesses Section at the ICTY', in U. Ewald and K. Turkovič (eds) *Large-scale Victimisation as a Potential Source of Terrorist Activities: importance of regaining security in post-conflict societies*, NATO Security through Science Series, E: Human and Societal Dynamics.

Loftus, E.F. and Doyle, J.M. (1997) *Eyewitness Testimony: civil and criminal*, Charlottesville, Va.: Lexis.

Luban, D. (1994) *Legal Modernism: a critique and defence of modern legal theory*, Ann Arbor: University of Michigan Press.

Lukacs, J. (1968) *Historical Consciousness: the remembered past*, New York: Harper & Row.

Lukes, S. and Scull, A. (eds) (1983) *Durkheim and the Law*, Oxford: Robertson.

Lund, M., Foy, D.W., Sipprelle, C. and Strachan, A. (1984) 'The Combat Exposure Scale: a systematic assessment of trauma in the Vietnam War', *Journal of Clinical Psychology*, 40: 1323–8.

Lusby, K. (1994) 'Hearing the Invisible Women of Political Rape', *University of Toledo Law Review*, 25: 911–54.

Lyons, M.A. (2001) 'Hearing the Cry without Answering the Call: rape, genocide, and the Rwandan Tribunal', *Syracuse Journal of International Law and Commerce*, 28: 99–124.

Lyotard, J.F. (1988) *The Differend: phrases in dispute*, trans. G. Van Den Abbeele, Minneapolis: University of Minnesota Press.

McCormack, T.H. (1997) 'Elective Reason to Atrocity: war crimes and the development of international criminal law', *Albany Law Review*, 60: 681–732.

McCormack, T.H. and Simpson, G.J. (eds) (1997) *The Law of War Crimes, national and international approaches*, The Hague: Kluwer Law International.

McDonald, G.K. (2000) 'Crimes of Sexual Violence: the experience of the International Criminal Tribunal', *Columbia Journal of Transnational Law*, 39: 1–17.

McDougall, G.J. (1998) *Systematic Rape, Sexual Slavery and Slavery-Like Practices during Armed Conflict: final report submitted by Ms. Gay J. McDougall*, Special Rapporteur, U.N. ESCOR, Commission on Human Rights, Sub-Commission on Prevention of Discrimination and Protection of Minorities, 50th Sess., Agenda Item 6, U.N. Doc. E/CN.4/Sub.2/1998/13.

McHenry, J. (2002) 'Justice for Foca: the International Criminal Tribunal for Yugoslavia's prosecution of rape and enslavement as crimes against humanity', *Tulsa Journal of Comparative and International Law*, 10(1): 183–222.

Mackie, V. (2000) 'Sexual Violence, Silence, and Human Rights Discourse: the emergence of the military prostitution issue', in A. Hilsdon, M. Macintyre, V. Mackie and M. Stivens (eds) *Human Rights and Gender Politics: Asia Pacific perspectives*, London: Routledge.

MacKinnon, C.A. (1983) 'Feminism, Marxism, Method and the State: toward feminist jurisprudence', *Signs: journal of women in culture and society*, 8(4): 635–8.

—— (2005) 'Defining Rape Internationally: a comment on *Akayesu*', *Columbia Journal of Transnational Law*, 44: 940–58.

—— (2008) 'The ICTR's Legacy on Sexual Violence', *New England Journal of International and Comparative Law*, 14(2): 101–10.

Maravilla, C.S. (2000) 'Rape as a War Crime: the implications of the International Criminal Tribunal for the Former Yugoslavia's decision in *Prosecutor v. Kunarac, Kovac & Vukovic* on international humanitarian law', *Florida Journal of International Law*, 13: 332–41.

Markovits, I. (2001) 'Selective Memory: how the law affects what we remember and forget about the past – the case of East Germany', *Law and Society Review*, 35: 513–63.

Marrus, M.R. (1999) 'The Nuremberg Doctors' Trial in Historical Context', *Bulletin of the History of Medicine*, 73(1): 106–23.

—— (2002) 'History and the Holocaust in the Court-room', in R. Smelser (ed.) *Lessons and Legacies V: the Holocaust and justice*, Evanston, Ill.: Northwestern University Press.

Marsella, A., Johnson, J., Watson, P. and Gryczynski, J. (2008) *Ethnocultural Perspectives on Disaster and Trauma: foundations, issues, and applications*, New York: Springer.

Masaaki, T. (2000) *What Really Happened in Nanking*, Tokyo: Sekai Shuppan, Inc.

Matoesian, G.M. (1993) *Reproducing Rape Domination through Talk in the Court-room*, Cambridge: Polity.

May, L. (2007) *War Crimes and Just War*, New York: Cambridge University Press.

Mazowiecki, T. (1993) *Report on the Situation of Human Rights in the Territory of the Former Yugoslavia*, Submitted by Mr. Tadeusz Mazowiecki, Special Rapporteur of the Commission on Human Rights, pursuant to Commission Resolution 1992/S-1/1 of 14 August 1992, E/CN.4/1993/50.

Melvern, L. (2004) *Conspiracy to Murder: the Rwandan genocide*, London/New York: Verso.

Meron, T. (1993a) 'Rape as a Crime under International Humanitarian Law', *American Journal of International Law*, 87: 424–6.

—— (1993b) *Henry's Wars and Shakespeare's Laws: perspectives on the law of war in the later Middle Ages*, Oxford: Oxford University Press.

Mertus, J. (2000) 'Truth in a Box: the limits of justice through judicial mechanisms', in I. Amadiume and A.N. Abdullahi (eds) *The Politics of Memory: truth, healing and social justice*, New York: Zed Books.

—— (2004) 'Shouting from the Bottom of the Well: the impact of international trials for wartime rape on women's agency', *International Feminist Journal of Politics*, 6: 110–28.

Micale, M.S. (1990) 'Charcot and the Idea of Hysteria in the Male: gender, mental science, and medical diagnosis in late nineteenth-century France', *Medical History*, 34: 363–411.

—— (1995) *Approaching Hysteria: disease and its interpretation*, Princeton, N.J.: Princeton University Press.

Minear, R.H. (1971) *Victors' Justice: the Tokyo War Crimes Trial*, Princeton, N.J.: Princeton University Press.

Minow, M. (1993) 'Surviving Victim Talk', *University of California Los Angeles Law Review*, 40: 1411–45.

—— (1998) *Between Vengeance and Forgiveness: facing history after genocide and mass violence*, Boston: Beacon Press.

Minow, M., Ryan, M. and Sarat, A. (eds) (2004) *Narrative, Violence, and the Law: the essays of Robert Cover (law, meaning, and violence)*, Ann Arbor: University of Michigan Press.

The Monitor, 'UN Judges Laugh at Rape Victim.' Online. Available http://www.globalpolicy.org/intljustice/tribunals/2001/0512rwa.htm (accessed 23 May 2010).

Morris, V. and Scharf, M.P. (1995) *An Insider's Guide to the International Criminal Tribunal for the Former Yugoslavia: a documentary history and analysis*, Irvington-on-Hudson, N.Y.: Transnational Publishers.

Morrison, J.G. (2000) *Ravensbrück: everyday life in a women's concentration camp, 1939–45*, Princeton, N.J.: Wiener.

Moses, A.D. (2005) 'Conceptual Blockages and Definitional Dilemmas in the "Racial Century": genocides of indigenous peoples and the Holocaust', in S. Gigliotti and B. Lang (eds) *The Holocaust: a reader*, Malden, Mass.: Blackwell.

Moses, A.D. and Stone, D. (eds) (2007) *Colonialism and Genocide*, London/New York: Routledge.

Moshman, D. (2001) 'Conceptual Constraints on Thinking about Genocide', *Journal of Genocide Research*, 3: 431–50.

Nadelson, C.C., Notman, M.T., Zackson, H. and Gornick, J.C. (1982) 'A Follow-up Study of Rape Victims', *American Journal of Psychiatry*, 139: 1266–70.

Nagy, R. (2008) 'Transitional Justice as Global Project: critical reflections', *Third World Quarterly*, 29: 275–89.

Neier, A. (1998) *War Crimes: brutality, genocide, terror, and the struggle for justice*, New York: Times Books.

Neuffer, E. (2001) *The Key to My Neighbor's House: seeking justice in Bosnia and Rwanda*, London: Bloomsbury.

Niarchos, C.N. (1995) 'Women, War, and Rape: challenges facing the International Tribunal for the Former Yugoslavia', *Human Rights Quarterly*, 17: 649–90.

Nietzsche, F.W. (1980) *On the Advantage and Disadvantage of History for Life*, trans. P. Preuss, Indianapolis, Ind.: Hackett Publishing Co.

—— (2003) *Untimely Meditations*, trans. R.J. Hollingdale, Cambridge: Cambridge University Press.

Nikolič-Ristanovič, V. (ed.) (2000) *Women, Violence and War: wartime victimization of refugees in the Balkans*, Budapest: Central European University Press.

Nino, C.S. (1996) *Radical Evil on Trial*, New Haven, Conn./London: Yale University Press.

Nishiyama, G. (2007) 'Japan Ruling MPs call Nanjing Massacre Fabrication', *Reuters*, 19 June 2007. Online. Available http://www.alertnet.org/thenews/newsdesk/T214128.htm (accessed 23 May 2010).

Nora, P. (1989) 'Between History and Memory: les lieux de mémoire', *Representations*, 26: 7–24.

Novick, P. (2000) *The Holocaust and Collective Memory*, London: Bloomsbury.

Nowrojee, B. (2005) *Your Justice Is too Slow: will the ICTR fail Rwanda's rape victims?*, United Nations Research Institute for Social Development (UNRISD) Occasional Paper No. 10, November.

Ofer, D. and Weitzman, L. (eds) (1998) *Women in the Holocaust*, New Haven, Conn.: Yale University Press.

Olick, J.K. (1999) 'Genre Memories and Memory Genres: a dialogical analysis of May 8, 1945 commemorations in the Federal Republic of Germany', *American Sociology Review*, 64: 381–402.

—— (2007) *The Politics of Regret: on collective memory and historical responsibility*, New York: Routledge.

Olick, J.K. and Robbins, J. (1998) 'Social Memory Studies: from "collective memory" to the historical sociology of mnemonic practices', *Annual Review of Sociology*, 24: 105–40.

Oosterveld, V. (2005a) 'Gender-Sensitive Justice and the International Criminal Tribunal for Rwanda: lessons learned for the International Criminal Court', *New England Journal of International and Comparative Law*, 12(1): 119–33.

—— (2005b) 'The Definition of "Gender" in the Rome Statute of the International Criminal Court: a step forward or back for international criminal justice?', *Harvard Human Rights Journal*, 18: 55–84.

Orentlicher, D.F. (1998) 'Settling Accounts: the duty to prosecute human rights violations of a prior regime', *Yale Law Journal*, 100: 1537–2615.

—— (2007) ' "Settling Accounts" Revisited: reconciling global norms with local agency', *International Journal of Transitional Justice*, 1: 10–22.

Osiel, M. (2000) *Mass Atrocity, Collective Memory, and the Law*, New Brunswick, N.J.: Transaction Publishers.

Parks, W.H. (1973) 'Command Responsibility for War Crimes', *Military Law Review*, 67: 11–15.

Patterson, D.M. (1990) 'Law's Pragmatism: law as practice and narrative', *Virginia Law Review*, 76: 937–96.

Perks, R. and Thomson, A. (2006) *The Oral History Reader*, 2nd edn, London/ New York: Routledge.

Petrovic, J. (2008) *The Old Bridge of Mostar and Increasing Respect for Cultural Property in Armed Conflict*, SJD Thesis, Melbourne Law School, University of Melbourne.

Piccigallo, P.R. (1979) *The Japanese on Trial: Allied war crimes operations in the east, 1945–1951*, Austin: University of Texas Press.

Pilch, F.T. (2009) 'Rape as Genocide', in S. Totten (ed.) *Plight and Fate of Women During and After Genocide*, New Brunswick, N.J.: Transaction Publishers.

Polan, D. (1982) 'Toward a Theory of Law and Patriarchy', in D. Kairys (ed.) *The Politics of Law: a progressive critique*, New York: Pantheon Books.

Posner, R.A. (2000) 'Past Dependency, Pragmatism and Critique of History in Adjudication and Legal Scholarship', *University of Chicago Law Review*, 67: 573–606.

Power, S. (1998) 'The Stages of Justice', *The New Republic*, 218: 32–8.

Proyect, L. (2003) 'Diana Johnstone's *Fools' Crusade*: a book review by Louis Proyect', 26 May. Online. Available http://www.swans.com/library/art9/lproy04.html (accessed 23 May 2010).

Prunier, G. (1995) *The Rwanda Crisis: history of a genocide*, New York: Columbia University Press.

Pupavac, V. (2004) 'International Therapeutic Peace and Justice in Bosnia', *Socio-Legal Studies*, 13: 377–85.

Quénivet, N.N.R. (2005) *Sexual Offenses in Armed Conflict and International Law*, Ardsley, N.Y.: Transnational Publishers.

Radstone, S. (2008) 'Memory Studies: for and against', *Memory Studies*, 1: 31–9.

Ratner, S.R., Abrams, J.S. and Bischoff, J.L. (2009) *Accountability for Human Rights Atrocities in International Law: beyond the Nuremberg legacy*, Oxford/New York: Oxford University Press.

Rawls, J. (1971) *A Theory of Justice*, London: Oxford University Press.

Ray, A.E. (1997) 'The Shame of It: gender-based terrorism in the Former Yugoslavia and the failure of international human rights law to comprehend the injuries', *American University Law Review*, 46(3): 793–840.

Reading, A. (2002) *The Social Inheritance of the Holocaust: gender, culture and memory*, New York: Palgrave Macmillan.

Ricœur, P. (2004) *Memory, History, Forgetting*, trans. K. Blamey and D. Pellauer, Chicago: Chicago University Press.

Ringelheim, J.M. (1985) 'Women and the Holocaust: a reconsideration of research', *Signs: journal of women in culture and society*, 10: 741–61.

—— (1997) 'Genocide and Gender: a split memory', in R. Lentin (ed.) *Gender and Catastrophe*, London: Zed Books.

—— (1998) 'The Split between Gender and the Holocaust', in D. Ofer and L. Weitzman (eds) *Women and the Holocaust*, New Haven, Conn.: Yale University Press.

Rittner, C. and Roth, J. (1993) *Different Voices: women and the Holocaust*, New York: Paragon House.

Roberts, A. (2008) 'Stalin's Army of Rapists: the brutal war crime that Russia and Germany tried to ignore', *Daily Mail*, 24 October. Online. Available http://www.dailymail.co.uk/news/article-1080493/Stalins-army-rapists-The-brutal-war-crime-Russia-Germany-tried-ignore.html (accessed 23 May 2010).

Roht-Arriaza, N. (ed.) (1995) *Impunity and Human Rights in International Law and Practice*, New York: Oxford University Press.

Röling, B.V.A. and Rüter, C.F. (1993) *The Tokyo Judgment: the International Military Tribunal for the Far East (IMTFE) 29 April 1946–12 November 1948*, Cambridge: Polity Press.

Rosenbaum, A.S. (1998) (ed.) *Is the Holocaust Unique? Perspectives on comparative genocide*, Boulder, Colo.: Westview.

Rosenberg, T. (1995) *The Haunted Landscape: facing Europe's ghosts after Communism*, New York: Random House.

Rothberg, M. (2006) 'Between Auschwitz and Algeria: multidirectional memory and the counterpublic witness', *Critical Inquiry*, 33: 158–84.

Ruff-O'Herne, J. (2004) *50 Years of Silence*, Sydney: Editions Tom Thompson.

Sadat, L.N. (2002) *The International Criminal Court and the Transformation of International Law: justice for the new millennium*, Ardsley, N.Y.: Transnational Publishers.

Sander, H. (1995) 'Remembering/Forgetting', *October*, 72: 15–25.

Sanger, D.E. (1992) 'Japan Admits It Set up Army Brothels', *New York Times*, 7 July A8.

Sarat, A. (ed.) (2001) *Law, Violence, and the Possibility of Justice*, Princeton, N.J./Oxford: Princeton University Press.

Sarat, A., Davidovitch, N. and Alberstein, M. (eds) (2007) *Trauma and Memory: reading, healing, and making law*, Stanford, Calif.: Stanford University Press.

Sarat, A., Douglas, L. and Umphrey, M.M. (eds) (2005) *The Limits of Law*, Stanford, Calif.: Stanford University Press.

Savelsberg, J.J. and King, R.D. (2007) 'Law and Collective Memory', *Annual Review of Law and Social Science*, 3: 189–211.

Scarry, E. (1985) *The Body in Pain: the making and unmaking of the world*, New York: Oxford University Press.

Schabas, W.A. (2001) *An Introduction to the International Criminal Court*, Cambridge: Cambridge University Press.

Scharf, M. (1997) *Balkan Justice: the story behind the first international war crimes trial since Nuremberg*, Durham, N.C.: North Carolina Academic Press.

Schellstede, S.C. (ed.) (2000) *Comfort Women Speak: testimony by sex slaves of the Japanese military*, New York: Holmes and Meier.

Schick, F.B. (1947) 'War Criminals and the Law of the United Nations', *University of Toronto Law Journal*, 7(1): 27–67.

Schudson, M. (1997) 'Dynamics of Distortion in Collective Memory', in D.L. Schacter (ed.) *Memory, Distortion: how minds, brains, and societies reconstruct the past*, Cambridge, Mass.: Harvard University Press.

Schwartz, B. (1996) 'Introduction: the expanding past', *Qualitative Sociology*, 9: 275–82.

Security Council (2009) 'Security Council Allows Judge of International Criminal Tribunal for Rwanda Extra Time beyond Term Limit to Complete Case', 16 December 2009. Online. Available http://www.un.org/News/Press/docs/2009/sc9819.doc.htm (accessed 23 May 2010).

Sedgwick, J.B. (2008) 'Memory on Trial: constructing and contesting the "Rape of Nanking" at the International Military Tribunal for the Far East', *Modern Asian Studies*, 43(5): 1229–54.

Seixas, P. (ed.) (2004) *Theorizing Historical Consciousness*, Toronto: University of Toronto Press.

Seltzer, M. (1997) 'Wound Culture: trauma in the pathological public sphere', *October*, 80: 3–26.

Shapland, J., Willmore, J. and Duff, P. (1985) *Victims in the Criminal Justice System*, Aldershot, UK: Gower.

Shirer, W.L. (1960) *The Rise and Fall of the Third Reich*, London: Secker and Warburg.

Shklar, J.N. (1986) *Legalism*, Cambridge, Mass.: Harvard University Press.

Silber, L. and Little, A. (1997), *Yugoslavia: death of a nation*, New York: Penguin Books.

Simons, M. (1996) 'For the First Time, Court Defines Rape as a War Crime', *New York Times*, 28 June.

Simpson, G. (2007) *Law, War and Crime: war crimes trials and the reinvention of international law*, Cambridge: Polity.

—— (2008) 'Writing the Tokyo War Crimes Trial', paper presented at Melbourne Law School Conference on the 60th Anniversary of the Judgment in the Tokyo War Crimes Trial: lessons for the future of international law, Melbourne, November 2008.

Smart, C. (1989) *Feminism and the Power of the Law*, London: Routledge.

Snyder, D.R. (2007) *Sex Crimes under the Wehrmacht*, Lincoln, Nebr.: University of Nebraska Press.

Sontag, S. (2003) *Regarding the Pain of Others*, New York: Farrar, Straus, and Giroux.

Sparr, L.F. and Bremner, J.D. (2005) 'Post-traumatic Stress Disorder and Memory: prescient medicolegal testimony at the international war crimes tribunal?', *Journal of the American Academy of Psychiatry and the Law*, 33: 71–8.

Spiegel Online International (2007) 'Nazi Sex Slaves: new exhibition documents forced prostitution in concentration camps'. Online. Available http://www.spiegel.de/international/0,1518,459704,00.html (accessed 23 May 2010).

Stein, M.B., Walker, J.R. and Forde, D.R. (2000) 'Gender Differences in Susceptibility to Posttraumatic Stress Disorder', *Behaviour Research and Therapy*, 38(6): 619–28.

Stover, E. (2005) *The Witnesses: war crimes and the promise of justice in the Hague*, Philadelphia, Pa.: University of Pennsylvania Press.

Strang, H. (2001) 'The Crime Victim Movement as a Force in Civil Society', in H. Strang and J. Braithwaite (eds) *Restorative Justice and Civil Society*, Cambridge/Melbourne: Cambridge University Press.

—— (2002) *Repair or Revenge: victims and restorative justice*, Oxford/New York: Oxford University Press.

Sturken, M. (1997) *Tangled Memories: the Vietnam War, the AIDS epidemic, and the politics of remembering*, Berkeley: University of California Press.

Summerfield, D. (1995) 'Addressing Human Response to War and Atrocity: major challenges in research and practices and the limitations of western psychiatric models', in R.J. Kleber, C.R. Figley and B.P.R. Gersons (eds) *Beyond Trauma: cultural and societal dimensions*, New York: Plenum.

—— (2002) 'Effects of War: moral knowledge, revenge, reconciliation and medicalised concepts of "recovery" ', *British Medical Journal*, 325(7372): 1105–7.

Sutherland, S. and Scherl, D.J. (1970) 'Patterns of Response among Victims of Rape', *American Journal of Orthopsychiatry*, 40: 503–11.

Szobar, P. (2002) 'Telling Sexual Stories in the Nazi Courts of Law: race defilement in Germany, 1933 to 1945', *Journal of the History of Sexuality*, 11: 131–63.

Tabeau, E. and Bijak, J. (2005) 'War-Related Deaths in the 1992–95 Armed Conflicts in Bosnia and Herzegovina: a critique of previous estimates and recent results', *European Journal of Population*, 21: 187–215.

Tanaka, Y. (1995) *Rape and War: the Japanese experience*, Melbourne: Japanese Studies Centre.

Taylor, T. (1955) 'The Nuremberg Trials', *Columbia Law Review*, 55(4): 488–525.

—— (1992) *The Anatomy of the Nuremberg Trials: a personal memoir*, New York: Knopf.

Teitel, Ruth G. (2000) *Transitional Justice*, New York: Oxford University Press.

Terdiman, R. (1993) *Present Past: modernity and the memory crisis*, Ithaca, N.Y.: Cornell University Press.

Tonkin, E. (1992) *Narrating Our Pasts: the social construction of oral history*, Cambridge/New York: Cambridge University Press.

Tompkins, T.L. (1995) 'Prosecuting Rape as a War Crime Speaking the Unspeakable', *Notre Dame Law Review*, 70: 845–90.

Trumbell, C.P. (2007) 'The Victims of Victim Participation in International Criminal Proceedings', *Michigan Journal of International Law*, 29: 777–826.

Tumarkin, M. (2005) *Traumascapes: the power and fate of places transformed by tragedy*, Melbourne: Melbourne University Press.

Tutorow, N.E. (ed.) (1986) *War Crimes, War Criminals and War Crime Trials: an annotated bibliography and source book*, New York: Greenwood Press.

United Nations (1994) *Final Report of the Commission of Experts Established Pursuant to Security Council Resolution 780 (1992)*, U.N. SCOR, Annex, U.N.Doc S/1994/674.

van der Kolk, B.A. and van der Hart, O. (1995) 'The Intrusive Past: the flexibility of memory and the engraving of trauma', in C. Caruth (ed.) *Trauma: explorations in memory*, Baltimore, Md.: Johns Hopkins University Press.

Van Schaack, B. (2009) 'Obstacles on the Road to Gender Justice: the International Criminal Tribunal for Rwanda as object lesson', *American University Journal of Gender, Social Policy and the Law*, 17: 361–408.

Veith, I. (1965) *Hysteria: the history of a disease*, Chicago: Chicago University Press.

Viseur-Sellers, P. (1996) 'Arriving at Rwanda: extension of sexual assault prosecution under the statutes of the ad hoc international criminal tribunals', *American Society of International Law Proceedings*, 90: 605–11.

——(2004) 'Individual(s') Liability for Collective Sexual Violence', in K. Knop (ed.) *Gender and Human Rights*, Oxford: Oxford University Press.

Viseur-Sellers, P. and Okuizumi, K. (1997) 'International Prosecutions of Sexual Assaults', *Transnational Law and Contemporary Problems*, 7(1): 45–80.

Wakabayashi, B.T. (ed.) (2007) *The Nanking Atrocity, 1937–8*, Oxford: Berghahn Books.

Wald, P. (2002) 'Dealing with Witnesses in War Crimes Trials: lessons from the Yugoslav Tribunal', *Yale Human Rights and Development Law Journal*, 5: 217–39.

Weaver, G.M. (2010) *Ideologies of Forgetting: rape in the Vietnam War*, Albany, N.Y.: State University of New York Press.

Weine, S.M., Kulenovic, A.D., Pavkovic, I. and Gibbons, R. (1998) 'Testimony Psychotherapy in Bosnian Refugees: a pilot study', *American Journal of Psychiatry*, 155: 1720–6.

Wells, G. (1993) 'What Do We Know about Eyewitness Identification?', *American Psychologist*, 48: 553–71.

Wells, K. (1983) *Index to the Records of the International Military Tribunal for the Far East (Japanese War Trials), 3 May 1946–4 November 1948*, Christchurch, New Zealand: University of Canterbury.

Weston, M.C. (2001) *A Psychosocial Model of Healing from the Traumas of Ethnic Cleansing: the case of Bosnia*, Stockholm: Kvinna till Kvinna.

Williams, P.H. (2008) *Memorial Museums: the global rush to commemorate atrocities*, Oxford/New York: Berg.

Wilson, R.A. (2003) 'Anthropological Studies of National Reconciliation Processes', *Anthropology Theory*, 3: 367–87.

Winter, J. (2000) 'The Generation of Memory: reflections on the "memory boom" in contemporary historical studies', *Bulletin of the German Historical Institute*, 27: 69–92.

Yerushalmi, Y.H. (1982) *Zakhor: Jewish history and Jewish memory*, Seattle: University of Washington Press.

Yoshida, T. (2006) *The Making of the 'Rape of Nanking'*, Oxford: Oxford University Press.

Young, A. (1995) *The Harmony of Illusions: inventing Post-Traumatic Stress Disorder*, Princeton, N.J.: Princeton University Press.

Young, J.E. (1993) *The Texture of Memory: Holocaust memorials and meaning*, New Haven, Conn.: Yale University Press.

—— (1999) 'Memory and Counter-Memory: the end of the monument in Germany', *Harvard Design Magazine*, 9: 1–10.

Young, S. and Yin, J. (1996) *The Rape of Nanking: an undeniable history in photographs*, Chicago: Triumph Books.

Zelizer, B. (2000) 'Gender and Atrocity: women in Holocaust photography', in B. Zelizer (ed.) *Visual Culture and the Holocaust*, New Brunswick, N.J.: Rutgers University Press.

Zerubavel, E. (2004) *Time Maps: collective memory and the shape of the past*, Chicago: Chicago University Press.

Zerubavel, Y. (1995) *Recovered Roots: collective memory and the making of Israeli national tradition*, Chicago: Chicago University Press.

# Index

Abe, S. 55; Japan's involvement in brothels 54, 55, 137n.24
Abu Ghraib prison: torture of prisoners 4
Agamben, G. 107, 109, 130, 136n.14, 142n.1
Agger, I.: and Jensen, S. 142n.5
Akayesu, J.P. 92
*Akayesu* trial 89; 92–6, 131–2n.3: Interahamwe assault 94; judgment 93; rape as crime of genocide 91; rape as destroying Tutsi ethnicity 92; sentencing 94; significance 95; UN investigation 92; Witness J 93; Witness JJ 93–4; Witness NN 94; Witness OO 94
Alič, F. 120, 143n.1
Allied rapes 26, 39–41, 50, 58–9
Alvarez, J. 71
American Psychiatric Association (APA) 103; Diagnostic and Statistical Manual of Mental Disorders 103; PTSD 103
Amnesty International 90
Antze, P.: and Lambek, M. 104
Arbour, L. 54, 79
Arendt, H. 23–6, 48, 134n.16, 136n.15; Eichmann trial as failure 24
Askin, K. 39, 40–1, 51, 80, 90, 96, 137n.22; on *Akayesu* judgment 96; on *Foča* judgment 80, 90; and Koenig, D. 126–7
Assmann, J. 16, 134n.8; oral history and cultural memory distinction 16
Atlani, L.: and Rousseau, C. 142n.5
Auschwitz 17, 32–3, 34, 109, 134n.13
Australia New Zealand Army Corps (ANZAC) 20; anti-ANZAC day protests 20
Al Bashir, O.H.A. 97; arrest 97

Bass, G.J. 40
Batavia trials 45
Beevor, A. 58, 134n.9, 135n.1
Ben-Gurion, D. 23
Benito, O. 78
Bosnia-Herzegovina: conflict as international 80; ethnic cleansing 64; mass rape phenomenon 89; population after war 138n.4; rape as ethnic cleansing 3, 72; social stigma for women 71
Bosnian Serb Army: Herzegovina Corps 88
Brackman, A. 49
Brook, T. 56
Brown, W. 133n.5
Brownmiller, S. 20–1, 30, 38–9, 43–4, 49, 51–2, 55, 58, 59
Burgess, A.: and Holmstrom, L. 103
Buruma, I. 124
*Butare* trial 141n.27: court humiliation 91

*Calling the Ghosts* (Jacobson and Jelincic film) 120; Cigelj, J. 120; Sivac, N. 120
Campbell, K. 114, 119, 131n.3
Caruth, C. understanding of traumatic memory 112
*Čelebići* trial 72–80: rape as crime of torture 74–6; judgment 80; victim memory recall 76; witness transcript 73–8; Witness G.C. 73–7; Witness M.A. 77–9
Center for Research and Documentation on Japan's War Responsibility 45
Central African Republic: ICC investigation 97, 142n.34
Charcot, J. 101; hysteria 101, 142n.2